JUSTICE UNDER FIRE

By Joseph W. Bishop, Jr.

OBITER DICTA
JUSTICE UNDER FIRE

Justice Under Fire

A STUDY OF MILITARY LAW

by

JOSEPH W. BISHOP, JR.

Charterhouse · New York

Justice Under Fire

Portions of chapter 7 appeared in different
form in the December, 1972, issue of *Commentary*.

LIBRARY OF CONGRESS CATALOG CARD NUMBER: 73-91121
MANUFACTURED IN THE UNITED STATES OF AMERICA
ISBN 0-88327-034-x
Designed by Jacques Chazaud

*To Charles Fairman, Myres S. McDougal,
Eugene V. Rostow, and Frederick Bernays
Wiener: Four lawyer-scholars from whose
publications and conversations I have
learned much over the years.*

Acknowledgments

I owe thanks to many people who helped in one way or another in the writing of this book. In particular I am grateful to Lieutenant Colonel Hugh E. Henson, Jr., on whose doctoral dissertation, *A Serviceman's First Amendment Rights*, I drew heavily in Chapter 4; to Richard Kluger and Carol Rinzler, whose editorial suggestions did much to make the book more comprehensible and readable; to the Editors of *Commentary*, for permission to reprint in Chapter 7 parts of an article which originally appeared in that magazine, and to the American Enterprise Institute, whose grant aided in the expansion and documentation of that article; to Lawrence Hollar, a recent graduate of the Yale Law School, who checked the citations, straightened out occasional errors, and shrewdly questioned a few of my conclusions; and to Susan Lucibelli, who typed hundreds of pages of illegible manuscript.

Contents

Introduction

*M*Y PURPOSE IN WRITING
this book is to give to general readers, and to the many
lawyers who lack familiarity with military law, a concise
account of that law—its origins, its procedures, its
peculiarities, and its defects and virtues—for, contrary
to popular impression, it does have virtues as well as
vices. This is not an exhaustive legal treatise, although
there is room for one. The classic work on the subject
is Colonel William Winthrop's *Military Law and Precedents,* the second and last edition of which appeared in
1896. To bring Winthrop up to date would be a labor
of years, which could be accomplished only by someone having Winthrop's uncommon combination of
scholarship and intimate familiarity with the history
and the day-to-day operations of the Office of The

Judge Advocate General. Indeed, the corpus of military law is now so vast that it is doubtful if Colonel Winthrop himself could do today what he did in 1886. A comprehensive treatise on military law, describing all the significant statutes, administrative regulations and rulings, and decisions of the military and civilian courts, to say nothing of the swelling flood of law review articles, probably could be produced only by a well-staffed enterprise such as those that publish and keep current standard legal tomes, often running to a dozen or so volumes weighing several pounds apiece, on bankruptcy or procedure in the federal courts. These are eminently useful works, but not even lawyers read them in their entirety or use them to gain an overall view of their subject. My hope is that this book will at least prove rather more readable.*

If there is a lack of scholarly treatises on military law, there is none of popular polemics on the subject. Practically all of these tracts start from the premise that the purpose of a court-martial is to terrorize and brutalize poor privates into numb subservience to the arrogant martinets (so reminiscent of Erich von Stroheim's version of a Prussian Junker) who form the officer corps of the United States Army, Navy, and Air Force. This is done by ignoring the most elementary constitutional rights of the accused and by ensuring that the members of the court, the prosecutor, and the defense

---

*The Public Law Education Institute has recently launched a loose-leaf publication entitled *Justice and the Military*, whose purpose is to provide and keep current a detailed survey of military justice. It does not deal with other aspects of military law.

counsel will be servile creatures of the military commander, anxious to carry out faithfully their orders that the accused be convicted, without regard to the law or the evidence, and subjected to sadistic punishment. Robert Sherrill's *Military Justice is to Justice as Military Music is to Music,* of which I wrote an unkind, but not unfair, review,* is by no means the most ignorant and biased of these effusions.

There is some truth at the bottom of these broadsides, but not very much. Nevertheless, they have had good reviews (except from me and one or two other cantankerous critics, whose point of view was distorted by actual knowledge of the subject), and even better sales. I doubt that books of equal badness on any other legal topic would have found so ready a market. Why this peculiar receptiveness to worthless works on military law?

The answer, I think, lies in the fact that nothing about military life has ever been popular among Americans, particularly those with sufficient intellectual pretensions to write, or even read, books. Such citizens may turn soldier, not too reluctantly, when they agree with the aims of a particular war, as in 1861–1865 and again eighty years later. But they rarely develop understanding, much less sympathy, for the needs and peculiarities of a military organization. To be in uniform, and subject to the orders of insensitive Philistines, is itself not the least of the horrors of war. When the literati and pseudo-literati write

---

* *Commentary,* June, 1971.

about their experiences, as frequently they do, the Army or Navy is at best comically stupid, as in *Mr. Roberts* or *The Caine Mutiny;* more often it is brutal and cruel, as in *Company K* or *The Naked and the Dead.* There is no such thing as an important American writer who glorifies the armed services as Kipling sometimes did, and hardly any (perhaps Ambrose Bierce in *Tales of Soldiers and Civilians*), who views war and armies with the objectivity and detachment of Stendhal or Tolstoy or Solzhenitsyn. Thus, it is hardly surprising that non-scholarly books on military justice, by which military discipline is enforced, take an exceedingly dim view of it, and that those books, mostly by people whose view of the court-martial system is based on emotion and intuition, rather than experience or research, find a ready market. The authors of these exposés like to talk of "so-called military justice" and "kangaroo courts," although courts-martial have, of course, as solid a base in the Constitution and statutes as any of our other courts.

But military law, like other fields of law, raises serious problems that are more likely to be solved intelligently if politicians and voters have a better knowledge of the facts than they are likely to get from such sources as *The New York Review of Books.* The remedy for indigestion caused by baloney is not, of course, more baloney of a different flavor. I have no intention of portraying military law as a system of justice that ought to serve as a model for civilians. It is a variety of law that has developed to meet the particular requirements of a particular part of our polity. I intend to describe and discuss its constitutional basis, its procedures and peculiarities, its jurisdiction, and its relation to the rest of our polity with as much objectivity and fairness as I can muster and to suggest some ways in which it could further approximate civilian norms without compromising military efficiency.

The history of military law and, particularly, military justice in the United States is one of long periods of quiescence, interrupted by cyclical bouts of intense public interest and reform, occasioned by war and the conscription of great numbers of civilians. Thus the military code was heavily amended and in some ways reformed in the middle of the Civil War and shortly after World Wars I and II. It was again amended in 1968, in the middle of the Vietnam War, and in the immediate aftermath of that war, Congress and the courts are still much concerned with its problems. But, if history is a guide, and with the draft at an end, the interest of the public and politicians will now abate. Thus it may be that the picture drawn in this book will remain a fairly good likeness for several years to come.

The main emphasis of the book is on military justice proper, the court-martial system by which the armed services enforce discipline among their own members. But I shall also speak of other, less well-known, contexts in which military tribunals may exercise criminal jurisdiction, notably martial rule in domestic emergencies, and the international law of war, violators of which are usually tried by military courts. I shall hold the citations and footnotes down to the minimum necessary to substantiate my statements, give readers who want to go deeper into a problem some helpful references, and make this book more reliable, if perhaps less lively, than all the recent revelations of the juridical atrocities perpetrated by the Pentagon.

JUSTICE UNDER FIRE

CHAPTER ONE

The Historical Background of American Military Law: The Constitution

I START FROM THE PREMISE that the United States will have, for as long as I can see into the future, several million men and women in its Army, Navy, Coast Guard, and Air Force.[1] Universal disarmament would, among its other inestimable benefits, make this book unnecessary, or at most of purely historical interest. But I do not think it will happen in my time, or yours. Only a Utopian, so far out of contact with reality as to be certifiably insane, can believe that the United States, Soviet Russia, and China—to say nothing of Israel, Egypt, or North and South Korea—will all become sane enough to agree and live up to the agreement to throw away their arms and disband their armies. The purer-souled pacifists, of course, urge the United States[2] to begin the process

1

by unilateral disarmament, which would at once relieve us of the enormous problems raised by the existence of an enormous military establishment and set a praiseworthy example to other governments. I cannot say that this theory is wrong: I can say that it lacks experimental verification, for no nation has ever of its own free will done, or even considered doing, such a thing. It is true that Germany and Japan, as a result of their total defeat in World War II, existed and throve mightily without armed forces for several years—largely because they counted on the United States (or, in the case of East Germany, Russia) to shield them from attack. Today, of course, Japan and both Germanies have military establishments.

The depressing truth is that at no time since mankind began to write its history on stones, clay tablets, and papyrus has any organized community voluntarily renounced its means of defense or aggression. There is some evidence that a few stone-age tribes, such as the Arawak Indians of the Caribbean, may have been innocent of the art of war. But we cannot be sure, for those Arawaks who were not eaten by the fierce Caribs were exterminated by the fiercer Spaniards, and little is known of their culture. (Still more depressing is the empirical suspicion that there may be a correlation between high creativity and pugnacity. The Hellenes of the Great Age fought, like Kilkenny cats, against Persians and—with equal enthusiasm and much more often—against each other. Elizabethan Englishmen excelled equally in poetry and piracy. These are by no means isolated examples.

As old as armies and navies is the idea of a special discipline and a special body of law applicable to the armed forces, usually taking the form of a curtailment or abolition of such rights as the soldier would have had as a citizen. That we do not know much about pre-Roman military law suggests that in antiquity law played no great role in the context of war: *"Silent leges inter arma,"* Cicero said. We do know that the foundation of Roman military law was complete subjection of the soldier to the will of the commander, whether that soldier was a citizen fulfilling his obligation to take the field when the state needed him or (from the time of Marius) a professional, having no other occupation. The greatest scholar of Roman law describes thus the discipline of the legions of the Republic: "The general was at liberty to behead any man serving in his camp, and to scourge with rods the staff officer as well as the common soldier; nor were such punishments inflicted merely on account of common crimes, but also when an officer had allowed himself to deviate from the orders which he had received, or when a division had allowed itself to be surprised or had fled from the field of battle."[3] The basic principle was not altered under the emperors, although capital punishment could not normally be inflicted without the authority of the legate or commanding general, and senior officers sometimes had a right of appeal to Caesar.[4]

Medieval military law, though its origins lay in the laws and customs of the German tribes, shared with Roman law the axiom that the king or other war commander could exercise unlimited powers of discipline

over his troops. Richard Coeur de Lion's Ordinance of
1190 deterred quarreling and brawling among his cru-
saders by decreeing, "with the common consent of fit
and proper men," that offenders should be subjected
to a series of penalties ranging from fines and ig-
nominious expulsion from the army (punishments
that were used by the Romans and are still found in
military codes) to tarring and feathering, loss of a
hand, and burial alive. The Statute of Westminster of
1279[5] refers to the royal power to punish soldiers
according to the law and customs of the realm. Richard II promulgated considerably more comprehensive
Articles of War in 1385, which punished a variety of
military offenses, such as disobedience of orders, pillage, and theft of "victuals . . . brought for the refresh-
ment of the army" with penalties that progressed from
amputation of the left ear for minor transgressions to
hanging, drawing and beheading for such major
offenses as touching "the body of our Lord, or the
vessel in which it is contained."[6]

These crude beginnings were improved upon in the
sixteenth and seventeenth centuries by elaborate and
far less barbarous military codes. They were still
founded on the ancient customs of the Franks, Goths,
and Burgundians, but they also showed the influence
of Roman treatises. Among them were the Articles of
War of the Free Netherlands of 1590 and Gustavus
Adolphus's Articles of War of 1621, a recognizable
ancestor of the British Articles of War and the American Uniform Code of Military Justice. Unlike the royal
ordinances of the Middle Ages, the codes of the six-

teenth and seventeenth centuries provided the rudi-
ments of what would become a regular judicial process
for the ascertainment of guilt and the assessment of
punishment through tribunals denominated as courts
or councils of war, or courts-martial.[7] They inaugurated the history of modern military justice, which is
not a debasement and corruption of the ordinary
criminal process in the interest of military discipline,
but a very gradual and still partial homologization of
civilian criminal justice by a penal system with totally
different purposes and origins.

Military discipline presented greater difficulties to
English kings than to continental monarchs. England,
being an island power with an ample supply of ships
and sailors who could readily be converted into a navy,
had never had a peacetime standing army (and was not
to have one until Oliver Cromwell's time). When it got
such an army, when Cromwell's power rested on the
redcoats, and again when James II raised a standing
army (whose mission, in the opinion of his subjects,
was to return the nation to the Catholic Church), the
ordinary Englishman of high or low degree did not
enjoy the experience.

The Crown's prerogatives undoubtedly included
power to discipline the Royal Navy and its land forces,
abroad or in time of war. But "the common law of
England knew nothing of courts-martial and made no
distinction, in time of peace, between a soldier and any
other subject. . . . A soldier, therefore, by knocking
down his colonel, incurred only the ordinary penalties
of assault and battery, and, by refusing to obey orders,

by sleeping on guard, or by deserting his colors, incurred no legal penalty at all."[8]

The Articles of Gustavus Adolphus of 1621 were translated into English in 1639, just in time for the civil war. They served as a model for both royalists and rebels. The former promulgated Articles of War in 1639, and the Parliament enacted generally similar articles in 1642.[9] The enforcement of these articles by courts-martial presented no serious constitutional or legal problems. Matters were different after the Stuart restoration in 1660, for England was at peace, and there was no longer any parliamentary or other legal sanction for courts-martial. One of the major causes of the "Glorious Revolution" of 1688, which put William of Orange on the throne hastily vacated by James II, was James's maintenance of a standing army, and his promulgation of Articles of War to discipline it, both done without the authority of Parliament.

Like James, William needed both a standing army (for the main goal of his policy was to bring England into the coalition against Louis XIV) and power to secure its discipline at home as well as abroad. At the very inception of his reign, in 1688, he was faced with mutiny of a regiment still loyal to James. Unlike James, he knew better than to act without the authority of the Parliament on which, indeed, his right to the throne depended. In 1689 Parliament passed the original Mutiny Act, which dealt with both problems: establishment of a standing, regular army, and provision for its discipline. Thus begins the modern history of Anglo-American military law.

The Mutiny Act is in every way an extraordinarily interesting piece of legislation. It plainly mirrors the conflicting fears which afflicted Parliament in 1689 and still bedevil the Congress of the United States nearly three centuries later. Englishmen had disagreeable memories of Cromwell's Major Generals and more recent and more disagreeable memories of the way in which Kirk's Lambs, and others of James's regular regiments, had suppressed Monmouth's rebellion in 1685. The Act starts with an emphatic declaration that "the raising or keeping a standing Army within this Kingdome in time of peace unlesse it be with consent of Parlyament is against Law."[10] But,

> it is judged necessary by their Majestyes and this present Parlyament That dureing this time of Danger severall of the Forces which are now on foote should be continued and others raised for the Safety of the Kingdome for the Common Defence of the Protestant Religion and for the reducing of Ireland.

The preamble continues:

> And whereas noe Man may be forejudged of Life or Limbe, or subjected to any kinde of punishment by Martiall Law, or in any other manner than by the Judgement of his Peeres, and according to the Knowne and Established Laws of this Realme. Yet, neverthelesse, it being requisite for retaineing such Forces as are or shall be raised dureing this Exigence of Affaires in their Duty an exact Discipline be observed. And that Soldiers who shall Mutiny or stirr up Sedition, or shall desert Their Majestyes Service be brought to a more Exemplary and speedy Punishment than the usuall Forms of Law will allow . . .

However exigent the needs of the military situation may have been, the Act gave courts-martial very limited jurisdiction. It applied only to soldiers, and indeed only to the regulars, since the militia were exempted. The only offenses triable were the cardinal military sins—mutiny, sedition, and desertion.[11] On the other hand, the procedural protections that the act accorded were somewhat primitive, even for that age. The court-martial could not be convened by an officer below the rank of colonel or have fewer than thirteen members, none below the rank of captain. The court had the authority to put witnesses under oath, although it was not explicitly required to do so. In capital cases the court had to be sworn, and the votes of nine of the thirteen were necessary to impose the death sentence. The Mutiny Act did confer on the accused one protection which is not found in the American Uniform Code, and which, one would hope, is not needed: "Noe Proceedings, Tryall or Sentence of Death shall be had or given against any Offender, but betweene the hours of eight in the morning and one in the afternoone"—a reflection, probably sufficiently warranted, on the drinking habits of the holders of King's commission.

Parliament kept the King and his army on a very short leash: the authority granted by the Act of 1689 was to endure only for seven months. It was re-enacted annually for more than two hundred and fifty years. In 1718 Parliament gave the Crown authority (also required to be re-enacted annually) to issue Articles of War, operative within and without the realm, in peace and war.[12]

The tendency to regard the armed forces as a necessary evil, to be carefully watched and regulated, is still very strong among us. Although it is an article of faith of many pious liberals that the United States is afflicted with pathological militarism, we have in fact never exalted the military or regarded its interests as paramount in the sense that this has, at times, been true of Germany or Japan or France or Russia. Nor have we ever regarded the armed services as our ultimate political arbiter. They do not so regard themselves; in this country there has never been any serious danger of a military coup. In the midst of war there was never any doubt that Lincoln, Wilson, and Franklin Roosevelt (of whom only the first had even a slight tincture of combat experience) were the masters of their generals. The man on horseback has been conspicuously absent from our politics. Several times we have elected great generals to the presidency, but only because they had become popular heroes. Washington and Jackson could be called strong executives; Grant and Eisenhower were passive to the point of lethargy.

This is the history and tradition that have shaped the development of military law in the United States. The fear of excessive military power, the disposition to keep it strictly subject to civilian authority (particularly that of the legislature), can fairly be termed a peculiarity of Anglo-American law. This problem was among the greatest, perhaps the greatest, with which the framers of the Constitution had to wrestle. Any study of the military law of the United States must begin with the Constitution.

"There is no law for the government of the citizens, the armies, or the navy of the United States," said Chief Justice Salmon P. Chase, "which is not contained in or derived from the Constitution."[13] His statement is as true today as it was in 1867. The enormous structure of American military power, and the authority to control and use it at home and abroad, rests on a few laconic, and sometimes Delphic, sentences in that remarkable document. They are so few and so brief that they can conveniently be quoted in full.

"The Congress shall have Power . . . to provide for the common Defence and general Welfare of the United States; . . . To declare War, grant Letters of Marque and Reprisal, and make Rules concerning Captures on Land and Water; To raise and support Armies, but no Appropriation of Money to that Use shall be for a longer Term than two years; To provide and maintain a Navy; To make Rules for the Government and Regulation of the land and naval Forces; To provide for calling forth the Militia to execute the Laws of the Union, suppress Insurrections and repel Invasions; To provide for organizing, arming, and disciplining the Militia, and for governing such Part of them as may be employed in the Service of the United States, reserving to the States respectively, the Appointment of the Officers, and the Authority of training the Militia according to the discipline prescribed by Congress; . . . And To make all Laws which shall be necessary and proper for carrying into Execution the foregoing Powers, and all other Powers vested by this

Constitution in the Government of the United States, or in any Department or Officer thereof.[14]

"No State shall, without the Consent of Congress; . . . keep Troops, or Ships of War in time of Peace, . . . or engage in War, unless actually invaded, or in such imminent Danger as will not admit of delay.[15]

"The President shall be Commander in Chief of the Army and Navy of the United States, and of the Militia of the several States when called into the actual Service of the United States.[16] He shall have Power, by and with the Advice and Consent of the Senate, . . . to appoint . . . Officers of the United States," including officers of the armed services.[17] "He shall take Care that the Laws be faithfully executed,"[18]—a responsibility whose fulfillment may sometimes require the use of troops, as in Little Rock in 1957.

The Bill of Rights, which was added to the Constitution in 1791, also touches on certain military problems in an indirect and fragmentary way. The Second Amendment recites that "A well regulated Militia, being necessary to the security of a free State, the right of the people to keep and bear Arms, shall not be infringed." The Third Amendment provides that "No Soldier shall, in time of peace be quartered in any house, without the consent of the Owner, nor in time of war, but in a manner to be prescribed by law." The Fifth excepts from its requirement of grand jury indictment in cases of capital, or otherwise infamous, crime, "cases arising in the land or naval forces, or in the Militia, when in actual service in time of War or public danger." (None of these Amendments has much significance today. The Second does no more than furnish occasional rhetorical embellishment to the arguments of the anti-gun-control lobby; the Third deals with a problem that has not arisen in modern times; the Fifth's exemption of the armed services from the grand jury requirement has from time to time played a somewhat confusing part in arguments about the application of the rest of the Constitution to courts-martial.)

As few and terse as are the provisions of the Constitution dealing explicitly with the defense and the armed forces of the United States, they did settle some questions that loomed very large in the minds of the men of 1787. As part of the great decision that the United States should be one nation instead of an alliance or confederation of sovereign and independent states, the war power was vested exclusively in the federal government.[19] The greatest controversy centered around the nature of the armed forces, particularly the land forces, with which the United States would prepare for and carry on war. The question was whether, as in the Revolution, Congress could wage war only by calling upon the States to contribute their militias, or whether Congress should itself have power to raise and maintain armies, which meant power to keep a standing army available for foreign service. The bitter dispute and deep division over this issue at the Constitutional Convention[20] is reflected in *The Federalist.* The opponents of a standing army, who included Jefferson[21] and George Mason,[22] drew arguments from ancient and recent history. Madison fairly summed up their thesis:[23]

[T]he liberties of Rome proved the final victim to her military triumphs, and . . . the liberties of Europe, as far as they ever existed, have, with few exceptions, been the price of her military establishments. A standing force, therefore, is a dangerous, at the same time that it may be a necessary provision. On the smallest scale it has its inconveniences. On an extensive scale its consequences may be fatal. On any scale, it is an object of landable circumspection and precaution.

Madison himself did not, however, draw the conclusion that a standing army was so great a danger that the Constitution ought to prohibit it or drastically restrict its size:[24] "If a federal constitution could chain the ambition, or set bounds to the exertions of all other nations, then indeed might it prudently chain the discretion of its own government, and set bounds to the exertions for its own safety."[25]

These arguments, for and against a standing army, are timeless, as good or bad today as they were in 1787 and probably will be in 2087. Hamilton, Madison, and the other advocates of Congress's power to create such armies as it thought the nation needed, in peace and war, prevailed. But the framers did borrow from the British a device for keeping the genie in the bottle: No appropriation for the Army should be for a longer term than two years. In theory at least, the size and very existence of the standing army depend on affirmative action by each successive Congress of the United States.

But the other great controversy of 1787 seems to have been decided not so much by the Constitution as by history. That dispute was over the role of the state militias in the military polity of the United States. Hamilton, in one of the Federalist letters in which he urged that Congress be granted unlimited authority to provide for the common defense in time of peace as well as war, wearily noted that, "Here I expect we shall be told that the militia of the country is its natural bulwark, and would be at all times equal to the national defence."[26] Indeed he was told so, for those who regarded the traditional citizenry in arms as a shield against invasion, which, unlike the sword of a standing army, could not be used for foreign adventures and could not be turned against those whom it was supposed to protect, were numerous and influential enough to secure the adoption of the militia clauses, which to this day are cited as arguments against the power of Congress to raise armies by conscription.[27] But even in 1787, when most citizens had in fact some degree of military knowledge, and when the weapons of war were relatively cheap, simple, and available, the evidence of experience was against reliance on the militia to be either available when needed or well enough trained to face regular troops. Hamilton said, "This doctrine, in substance, had like to have lost us our independence."[28] Washington was still blunter: "If I was called upon to declare upon Oath, whether the Militia have been most serviceable or hurtful upon the whole; I should subscribe to the latter."[29] Although the Constitution left Congress the option of calling on the militia "to execute the Laws of the Union, suppress Insurrection and repel Invasion," the militia has in fact played a very small part in American military operations since the War of 1812, when the New York militia, concluding that a British invasion from Canada had been repelled, and strictly construing the Constitution, refused to follow the enemy across the Canadian border.[30] In the Mexican, Civil, and Spanish Wars, the President and Congress supplemented the regular army with volunteers. Since 1916 the state militiamen have, in essence, acquired a dual status, as members of the State National Guards and also of the "federally recognized" National Guard of the United States, which is a component of the organized reserve.[31] When in state rather than federal service, the militiamen are subject to the military law of the states, most of which have military codes more or less patterned on the federal Uniform Code of Military Justice; state courts-martial are rare, although not unknown.[32] When called into active federal service, the guardsmen are, of course, in the same legal position as other reservists or regulars on active duty.

If the militia clauses can fairly be described as dead letters, the clauses that permit Congress to create an army (which includes an air force) and navy and to "make Rules for the Government and Regulation of the land and naval Forces" are very much alive. From the latter has been derived the whole elaborate system of American military justice, with which the next chapters will deal.

Notes to Chapter One

[1]There are now about two and a half million people in the armed services; in 1969, at the height of the Vietnam war, there were about 3,300,000, according to the Statistical Abstract of the United States. "Push-button" war might further reduce the number, but this does not seem to be the trend of modern warfare.

[2]Many of the leaders of the American peace movement see nothing to criticize in the maintenance and use of large military establishments by peace-loving democracies, such as North Korea and North Vietnam. Outspoken Russian pacifists are few and mostly in corrective labor camps or lunatic asylums. If any Chinese hold such views, they have sufficient prudence to keep them to themselves.

[3]MOMMSEN, HISTORY OF ROME, Bk. II, Ch. 8, at 561 (Dickson transl. 1889).

[4]For a good modern account of what is known of Roman military law under the empire, *see* BRAND, ROMAN MILITARY LAW (1968).

[5]7 Edw. 1.C.1.

[6]These and other examples of early military justice are reprinted in appendices to WINTHROP, MILITARY LAW AND PRECE-

DENTS (2d ed. 1896), the classic American treatise. It is hereinafter cited as "WINTHROP."

[7]Thus, article 138 of Gustavus Adolphus ordained "that there be two Courts in our Leaguer; a high Court and a lower Court." Succeeding articles prescribed their composition and procedure. Article 159 provided that the high court should have a secretary to "take diligent notice in writing of all things declared before the Court" and that the accused "shall have liberty to answer for himself, until the Judges be thoroughly informed of the truth of all things."

[8]1 MACAULAY, HISTORY OF ENGLAND 231 (1856 ed.). The long struggle between the King and the Parliament over the former's prerogative to discipline soldiers by "martial law" is concisely summarized in Fairman, *The Law of Martial Rule and the National Emergency,* 55 HANS. L. REV. 1253, 1257–59 (1942).

[9]See 1 CLODE, MILITARY FORCES OF THE CROWN 22–24 (1869).

[10]Mutiny Act, 1689, 1 W & M, C.5. preamble.

[11]It should, however, be noted that the first Mutiny Act did not limit the jurisdiction of the military, under the King's authority, to try and punish offenses committed by soldiers in places outside the jurisdiction of English civil courts. Later Articles of War have applied equally to soldiers at home and abroad. *See* WINTHROP, at 20.

[12]The history of military law in England is set forth in Part II of the British Manual of Military Law (1958). *See also* O'Connell, *The Nature of British Military Law,* MILITARY LAW REVIEW, January, 1963, at 141.

[13]Ex parte Milligan, 71 U.S. 2, 141 (1866).

[14]Art. I, § 8.

[15]Art. I, § 10.

[16]Art. II, § 2.

[17]Art. II, §§ 2, 3.

[18]Art. II, § 3.

[19]*See* Selective Draft Law Cases, 245 U.S. 366, 377 (1918).

[20]*See* Prescott, Drafting the Federal Constitution 515–525 (1941).

[21]Jefferson wanted the Bill of Rights to include "protection against standing armies." *See* 12 THE PAPERS OF THOMAS JEFFERSON 438, 440 (Boyd ed. 1955).

[22] *See* 2 FARRAND, THE RECORDS OF THE FEDERAL CONVENTION 640 (1911).

[23] THE FEDERALIST, No. 41 (Madison).

[24] Elbridge Gerry would have added to the power to raise and support armies a proviso that "in time of peace the army shall not consist of more than three thousand men." Prescott, Drafting The Federal Constitution 515–16 (1941). George Washington is supposed to have suggested a further proviso, that no invader should be allowed to bring more than two thousand men with him.

[25] THE FEDERALIST, No. 41 (Madison). Similar arguments, even more strongly phrased, were made by Hamilton. *See, e.g.,* THE FEDERALIST, Nos. 8, 22, 23 and 25.

[26] THE FEDERALIST, No. 25 (Hamilton).

[27] In both the Civil War and World War I, courts heard and rejected the argument that the power of Congress to compel service in the armed forces of the United States is inconsistent with the militia clauses, since it would enable Congress to deprive the states of their militias by drafting the militiamen. Kneedler v. Lane, 45 PA. ST. 238 (1864); Selective Draft Law Cases, 245 U.S. 366 (1918). Undiscouraged, the opponents of conscription made the same argument in World War II and in the Korean and Vietnam wars. *See* Ch. 5, *infra*.

[28] THE FEDERALIST, No. 25 (Hamilton).

[29] 6 THE WRITINGS OF GEORGE WASHINGTON 112 (Fitzpatrick ed. 1932).

[30] *See* AMERICAN MILITARY HISTORY 129 (published by the Chief of Military History, United States Army, 1969).

[31] *See* Maryland, for Use of Levin v. United States, 381 U.S. 41 (1965). The story of the decline of the militia clauses into innocuous desuetude is comprehensively and competently told in Wiener, *The Militia Clause of the Constitution*, 54 HARV. L. REV. 181 (1940).

[32] *See, e.g.,* Miller v. Rockefeller, 327 F. Supp. 542 (S.D.N.Y. 1971).

CHAPTER TWO

The Court-Martial System: How Military Justice Works

Whether military justice is better or worse than the civilian variety is debatable, and debated. There is no doubt that it is *different.* The difference is on the whole less than the difference between an American criminal trial and, say, a French one, but it is great enough to make the more extreme critics of the court-martial system insist that it ought simply to be abolished.

In the eyes of professional staffers of the American Civil Liberties Union, for example, the typical court-martial is a kangaroo proceeding in which a wretched conscript is dragged before a panel of sadistic martinets, convicted on the basis of perjured evidence and his own confession (which has been extracted by torture), and sentenced to fifty or sixty years of solitary

19

confinement, chained to the wall of a subterranean dungeon, and fed on bread and water. Although this stereotype is somewhat inaccurate, it is still reasonable to ask why there should be a separate system of criminal justice for members of the armed forces. Why not try them in the civilian courts, with civilian process and civilian juries? From the constitutional standpoint, it would be perfectly possible for Congress to repeal the Uniform Code of Military Justice, add to the United States Penal Code sections covering purely military offenses, and leave the trial of rogues military to the federal and state courts, which have always had, and often exercised, jurisdiction to try soldiers who violate civilian penal law.

The experiment has been tried in other countries. Under the *Grundgesetz* (the "Basic Law," essentially a constitution) of the Federal Republic of Germany, for example, the trial and punishment of members of the armed forces for all but petty offenses, including such purely military crimes as absence without leave and disobedience of orders, is left to the civilian courts.[1] The draftsmen of the West German Basic Law were, of course, reacting against a monstrous overdose of militarism, at a time when Germany had no armed forces and no spokesmen for the military point of view. For similar reasons, Japan's "self-defense forces" get along with a minimum of military justice. But in England, France, Russia, and the United States, as in practically all of the other major military powers, soldiers are subjected to a distinctive code of military justice administered by military courts, although, in these countries, there may be review by civilian appellate judges. The reasons usually adduced in support of such a system, other than mere adherence to ancient custom, may be summarized as follows:

1. Military discipline cannot be maintained by the civilian criminal process, which is neither swift nor certain. Estimates of the percentage of civilian crimes which in this country go unpunished range from 80 to 95 per cent. There is some evidence that in the West German army the incidence of absence without leave, desertion, and insubordination is so high as to raise serious doubt of its ability to defend the country.[2] An army without discipline is in fact more dangerous to the civil population (including that of its own country) than to the enemy. The public interest in discipline is therefore entitled to greater weight, and the rights of the accused to lesser weight, in the military than in the civilian context. There has, indeed, been a great deal of rhetoric, some of it judicial, suggesting that soldiers are not entitled to anything properly describable as justice. "The machinery by which courts of law ascertain the guilt or innocence of an accused citizen, is too slow and too intricate to be applied to an accused soldier. For, of all the maladies incident to the body politic, military insubordination is that which requires the most prompt and drastic remedies . . . For the general safety, therefore, a summary jurisdiction of terrible extent must, in camps, be entrusted to rude tribunals composed of men of the sword."[3] The Supreme Court of the United States, in considering the constitutionality of an amendment to the Articles of

War passed by Congress during the Civil War,[4] which gave courts-martial jurisdiction (although only in time of war, insurrection or rebellion) over murder, robbery, arson, burglary, rape, and other common crimes, said much the same thing: "It is a matter well known that the march even of an army not hostile is often accompanied with acts of violence and pillage by straggling parties of soldiers, which the most rigid discipline is hardly able to prevent. The offenses mentioned are those of most common occurrence, and the swift and summary justice of a military court was deemed necessary to restrain their commission."[5] In modern times the Court has often stressed (not to say overstressed) the idea that military justice must of necessity be, in the words of Mr. Justice Hugo L. Black, "a rough form of justice, emphasizing summary procedures, speedy convictions and stern penalties."[6] Justice William O. Douglas, who is at times disposed to accept at face value the polemics of the New Left, spoke in a recent case of "so-called military justice."[7]

Such language might indeed have been applied with approximate fairness to many courts-martial of the eighteenth and nineteenth centuries, or even to those of the two World Wars. Shortly after World War I, Professor John H. Wigmore, that towering legal scholar, made the argument in stronger terms than any Judge Advocate would use today. Military justice, he said, *"knows what it wants"*—i.e., discipline—"and it systematically *goes in and gets it."* This clarity of purpose he compared favorably to the uncertainty of the civilian penal system as to whether it wants retribution, or prevention, or deterrence.[8] Civilian criminal jurisprudence seems today no more sure of its goals than it was in 1921; indeed, it seems to have communicated some of its infirmity of purpose to the military.

Today, as lawyers with any knowledge of military law are well aware, the procedure prescribed by the Uniform Code is not appreciably rougher or more summary than civilian criminal process; in some respects (notably, pretrial disclosure of the prosecution's evidence and the provision of automatic appellate review and free appellate counsel) it gives the accused more substantial protection. It is unlikely that soldiers today run much, if any, greater risk of unjust conviction than do civilians.

The best statement of the "military discipline" argument today might be that its demands justify a procedure that does lessen the chance of unjust acquittal, while it need not, and should not, increase the possibility of unjust conviction, In civilian jurisprudence the number of guilty men who are not punished is far, far greater than the number of innocent men who are, and few of us would have it otherwise. But the doctrine that it is better that ninety-nine (or nine hundred and ninety-nine) guilty men go free than that one innocent be convicted is not easily squared with the need to maintain efficiency, obedience and order in an army, which is an aggregation of men (mostly in the most criminally prone age brackets) who have strong appetites, strong passions, and ready access to deadly weapons. Moreover, there are some types of conduct

—desertion and insubordination, for example—which are not crimes at all in civilian life but whose deterrence is essential to the very existence of an army. If a soldier who runs away is punished, in Voltaire's expressive phrase, *pour encourager les autres,* the heartening effect is much diminished if 99 per cent of deserters get away, because some jurors do not approve of restrictions on personal freedom, or have disagreeable memories of tough First Sergeants, or merely dislike the Army.

2. Another aspect of the discipline argument: Since discipline is a responsibility of the military commander, he should have some control of the machinery by which it is enforced—to decide, for instance, whether a particular offender should be prosecuted and what degree of clemency will best promote the efficiency of his command.[9]

3. Military offenses—absence without leave, desertion, insubordination, cowardice, mutiny and the like—have no civilian analogues: The adjudication of guilt or innocence and the assessment of appropriate punishment may require experience and knowledge not commonly possessed by civilian judges and jurors.[10]

4. Soldiers may be stationed and commit crimes in places outside the jurisdiction of American civilian courts. There is probably no constitutional reason why federal district courts could not be given jurisdiction to try soldiers for offenses committed in foreign countries. Federal courts have long had extra-territorial jurisdiction over certain offenses—treason, for example, and some types of fraud on the government

—committed by American citizens abroad. To be sure, the exercise of such jurisdiction is on its face hard to square with the Sixth Amendment's requirement that in all criminal prosecutions, the accused shall enjoy the right to trial "by an impartial jury of the State and district wherein the crime shall have been committed." But the Supreme Court has long read into this requirement an exception, analogous to that explicitly made to the Fifth Amendment's requirement of grand jury indictment, for military trial of cases "arising in the land or naval forces."[11] The Court might well apply similar reasoning to civilian trials of soldiers for offenses committed overseas. If Congress has constitutional power to declare offenses committed in foreign countries triable at all in federal courts,[12] the Sixth Amendment's jury provision is obviously impossible to apply.

But Congress has never attempted to exercise its power to give the federal courts jurisdiction over crimes committed by American servicemen outside the United States. One obvious reason is the difficulty of bringing before a court sitting in this country witnesses who live thousands of miles away.[13] Both the ends of justice and of the public fisc are better served if a trial can be held in the place where the crime was committed.

Whatever its reasons, Congress has since 1775 provided Articles of War, and, for nearly as long, Articles for the Government of the Navy; since 1950 they have been fused in the Uniform Code of Military Justice.

Revisions of the military code (the most important of which were enacted in 1776, 1786, 1806, 1874, 1916, 1920, 1950, and 1968) have made the procedures of military justice progressively more complex and the rights of defendants progressively greater. But the distinctively military character persists. A brief description of American courts-martial and their procedure, which I shall try to keep as free as possible from technicality, will serve to show the ways in which they differ from, and the ways in which they resemble, civilian criminal courts. In the interests of brevity and comprehensibility, I shall mention only the most salient and distinctive features of military trial procedure. The details can be found in the Uniform Code, the *Manual for Courts-Martial* (a bulky volume), and, of course, in the decisions of the military appellate courts.

Although most federal crimes, from income tax cheating to robbing national banks, are tried in district courts of the United States, the states typically provide different criminal courts for the trial of serious and petty offenses. Similarly, the military has general courts-martial, which can try any offense and impose any sentence, including (in theory, although of late years not in practice) death, and special courts-martial, which can impose no sentence more severe than six months' confinement (with corresponding forfeitures of pay) and a Bad Conduct Discharge.[14]

Civilian criminal courts are created by statute and their judges elected or appointed for life or fairly long terms. Juries, whose principal job is to find the crucial fact of guilt or innocence, are drawn from panels of citizens who, in theory and frequently in fact, are a cross-section of the community. But the Code authorizes military commanders to convene courts-martial for the trial of members of their command whom they have reason to believe guilty of violations of the Code. A court-martial is an *ad hoc* tribunal, to which the convening authority may refer only a single case or a few cases for trial.

General courts-martial can be convened only by those high in the military hierarchy—the President himself, the Secretary of a military Department, a general or a flag officer commanding a large unit, and a commander of a major installation.[15] The commander of a smaller unit or installation, such as a regiment or naval vessel, is empowered to convene a special court.[16]

As a general proposition, the convening authority has the power to pick the officers of his command (a minimum of five for a general court and three for a special court) who will sit as members of the court to try the case or cases he refers to it, and who will not only determine guilt or innocence, but assess the sentence. This is *the* major difference between military and civilian practice, for in the latter the state has no more control than the defense over the selection of the jury. Of course, as in civilian trials, the defense and the prosecution can challenge any member of the panel for cause, if he can show facts casting doubt on the prospective juror's impartiality.[17] But the Code allows him only one peremptory challenge (used when counsel suspects that the member is biased, but can't prove it), which is less than he would have in most civilian courts. "Command influence" is naturally the best and favorite target of the critics of military justice.[18]

The Code does place some limits on the commander's freedom to determine the composition of the court, but these limits hardly guarantee that the members will represent a cross-section of the military community. Although the members are normally commissioned officers, an accused enlisted man may request that at least one third of them be enlisted men.[19] Since general courts often consist of five or seven members, and since the conviction and sentencing of those who plead not guilty requires a two thirds vote,[20] this would on its face appear to give enlisted men a strong voice in the trial of their peers. But in fact accused enlisted men rarely claim the privilege, for the enlisted men appointed to a court-martial are almost always senior non-commissioned officers, whom most soldiers believe, probably rightly, to be even less sympathetic to military delinquents than commissioned officers. The practice of appointing Sergeants-Major, First Sergeants, and Chief Petty Officers as enlisted members has been held consistent with the convening authority's duty, under Article 25 of the Code, to detail to courts-martial "such members of the armed forces as, in his opinion, are best qualified for the duty by reason of age, education, training, experience, length of service, and judicial temperament.[21]

The Code's very general, not to say platitudinous, criteria[22] obviously leave the commander who appoints a court-martial a lot of leeway to select the sort of members most likely to do what he regards as justice—*i.e.,* to pack the "jury". It is easier to say what he *cannot* do. Obviously, he cannot put on the court the accuser, or a person who has acted as an investigating officer or counsel in the case, or a witness.[23] It is very doubtful that he can explicitly make rank a qualification[24] and virtually certain that he cannot make race a test of eligibility. There appears to be no case in which there has been a convincing showing that a commander had deliberately excluded blacks, or whites, from the membership of a court-martial, but the Court of Military Appeals once had to consider the problem presented when a convening authority in effect ordered that a court trying a Negro soldier have a minimum number of black members. Two of the three judges thought that the deliberate *inclusion* of members of the accused's race was discrimination in his favor and thus could not prejudice his rights under either the Code or the Constitution.[25] The dissenter thought that *any* form of discrimination based on race violated the Code and possibly the Constitution as well. But all three made it clear that *exclusion* from a court-martial on the basis of race would be illegal.

Civilian criminal courts can, and often do, commit errors which invalidate their convictions, but there is rarely any doubt about the legality of their existence or their power to try any offense within their jurisdiction. Not so with courts-martial. "A court-martial is the creature of statute, and, as a body or tribunal, it must be convened and constituted in entire conform-ity with the provisions of the statute, or else it is without jurisdiction"—and its verdict, therefore, a nullity.[26] Thus, to this day the Court of Military Appeals has to deal with a fair number of cases in which it is contended, sometimes successfully, that a conviction must be set aside, not because of any lack of evidence or error in the trial, but because of some defect in the composition of the court-martial—because, for example, the court was convened by an officer other than the authorized commander[27] or because officers not appointed in proper form sat as members[28] or because the general who convened the court, having himself been the victim of one of the accused's burglaries (although that burglary was not included in the charges), had an interest other than an official interest in the prosecution of the accused, and so was an "accuser," whom Article 22(b) of the Code bars from convening a court-martial.[29] The verdict of a court may be set aside if the members' relationship to the commander who appointed them suggests to the military appellate courts that they were handpicked to ensure conviction.[30] The intricacies of devolution of command, delegation of authority, and similar snarls of military red tape add a special complexity to these distinctive problems of military jurisdiction.

A long step in the process of assimilating military trials to the civilian variety has been the creation and expansion of the powers of the Military Judge, who resembles a civilian trial judge much more closely than the members of the court resemble jurors. A Military Judge must sit on every general court;[31] a special court to which no Military Judge has been detailed cannot (unless no judge was available because of "physical conditions or military exigencies," which is rarely the case) sentence the accused to a Bad Conduct Discharge.[32] The Military Judge must be a qualified lawyer as well as a commissioned officer (usually in the Judge Advocate General's Corps); although he is "detailed" to the court by the convening authority, he must first be "designated" by the Judge Advocate General of the service concerned, to whose office he is assigned and to whom alone he is directly responsible. Neither the convening authority nor members of that commander's staff report on his efficiency or play any role in his promotion.[33] Unlike a federal judge, he does not hold office for life, during good behavior, but he is not subject to the influence of the commander who convenes the court.

Like a civilian judge, he rules upon questions of law arising before and during the trial, such as challenges to members of the court, the legal sufficiency of the charges, the admissibility of evidence and the like.[34] He can dismiss a charge for legal insufficiency, although the convening authority (acting, of course, on the advice of his personal legal adviser, the Staff Judge Advocate) can disagree and order it tried anyhow,[35] if he is willing to buck the odds that the military appellate courts will agree with the Military Judge and reverse a conviction on that charge. If the Judge's ruling amounts to a directed verdict of not guilty—*e.g.,* the granting of a motion to dismiss because of the accused's lack of mental responsibility, or because the evidence is legally insufficient for conviction—his action is final.[36]

A major difference between the Military Judge and his civilian analogue is that in the military practice it is the members of the court who decide the penalty; the Military Judge can only instruct them on the kind and degree of punishment that can legally be imposed. The rule in civilian practice (although there are exceptions in many states) is, of course, that the jury's duties and power end with the determination of guilt or innocence; it is left to the judge to determine the appropriate sentence.[37]

On the other hand, the Military Judge may, if the accused so elects, sit as both judge and jury—that is, determine, sitting alone, whether the accused is guilty or not and, if he finds him guilty, what his punishment should be.[38] (Under Article 18, however, a Military Judge cannot try an offense for which the death penalty may be adjudged unless the convening authority has directed that it be tried as a non-capital case.) In practice, this means that in the great majority of courts-martial the accused can eliminate such danger as really exists, or he thinks exists, that the commander will influence the result of the trial by hand-picking or otherwise influencing the "jury." Since the introduction of this option in the Military Justice Act of 1968, a large majority of those tried by court-martial in all the services have in fact elected to be tried by Military Judges. (It may be suspected that those who do not—or their counsel—are gambling that more than one third of the members of the court will have some sympathy for them.) This option is one not open to a criminal defendant in the federal courts (where his right to trial by a judge requires agreement not only by the judge himself but also by the prosecution) or in the courts of most of the states.

Other powers of the convening authority are not likely to operate to the prejudice of the accused. He cannot overturn an acquittal or increase a sentence; he can reduce sentence or nullify conviction. Power to choose prosecuting attorney ("trial counsel") places the accused in no worse position than the defendant in a civilian case where the public prosecutor typically both decides whether charges will be pressed and which lawyer on his staff will prosecute the case. If the military accused cannot afford to hire his own lawyer, his defense counsel will be appointed by the convening authority. But that defense counsel must be a qualified lawyer if the trial is by general court-martial; defense counsel in a special court-martial need be a lawyer only if the trial counsel is one, or if the court is to be empowered to sentence the accused to a Bad Conduct Discharge, in addition to six months confinement and forfeitures of pay.[39] The accused has a right to be represented by free "military counsel of his own selection if reasonably available;"[40] in practice the "availability" of a particular military lawyer requested by the defendant is pretty much left to the discretion of the commander. But it is equally true, as a practical matter, that the civilian defendant who has no money must also take such legal talent as he is given by the court or the public defender. The Supreme Court's decisions have given the civilian accused a right to a lawyer when he faces imprisonment, but not a right to insist that that lawyer be Edward Bennett Williams.

It is intrinsically impossible to prove or disprove the charge, so regularly made by the critics of military justice that most of them have probably come to believe it, that defense counsel are (a) systematically selected for incompetence and (b) too afraid of the commander's displeasure to make a vigorous defense. I can only say that military lawyers vigorously deny the charge, and that I have seen very little evidence of such incompetence or timidity in the records I have examined. For what it is worth, it is a violation of Article 37 of the Code for a commander preparing an efficiency report to "give a less favorable rating . . . because of the zeal with which [the person being rated] as counsel represented any accused before a court-martial." Such an injunction is obviously difficult or impossible to enforce; but military defense counsel seem to me to raise as many defenses, and push them as hard, as lawyers in civilian trials. In recent years, comparatively few of the younger Army lawyers have been career officers; since they are merely fulfilling their military service obligation by three years or so of active duty, they are neither bucking for promotion nor in much fear of the commander's displeasure. However, the practical ending of the draft may mean that most military lawyers will be career officers. Thus, there is much to be said for the suggestion that appointed military defense counsel, like military judges, should be assigned to a central organization, independent of the command which convenes the court-martial.[41] Such a change would remove both the potential and the appearance of improper command influence.

In so-called political cases in which the accused's conduct was motivated by dislike of the military or the United States government in general, and which have been the occasion of most of the fervid diatribes against military justice, the accused typically has no trouble obtaining the services of as many anti-Establishment lawyers as can manage to clamber aboard, sometimes in such numbers as to get in each other's way. A petition for a writ of certiorari to the Supreme Court, filed in the court-martial of Captain Howard Levy, was signed by no less than eight of them, of varying degrees of eminence and ability.[42]

The grand jury is, of course, unknown to military law. But it is doubtful that its denial is much of a loss to those charged with military crime, for the grand jury, despite its prominent position in the Bill of Rights, does not usually offer significant protection to those suspected of crime. It is an *ex parte* proceeding; not merely does the accused have no right to be represented by counsel, he need not be present or even be informed that the proceeding has been instituted.[43] The military equivalent is the investigation which Article 32 of the Code requires to be made before a charge can be referred to a general court-martial. In such an investigation the accused must be informed of the charges against him, and of his right to a lawyer; moreover, he is entitled to cross-examine witnesses, and to be informed of any other evidence against him.[44] He thus gets what the civilian defendant rarely gets—advance notice of the prosecution's case against him.

Overall, a civilian lawyer defending his first court-martial will find more that is familiar than strange. Plea-bargaining—the exchange of a guilty plea for a reduction in the charge or sentence—is as common in military as in civilian practice, with the difference that the bargain is more binding in the military: the civilian prosecutor cannot bind the judge, who may hand out a stiffer sentence than the prosecutor recommends, whereas the convening authority, who makes the deal in military practice, can cut down a court-martial's sentence to reflect that deal. The rules of evidence are about the same in courts-martial as in federal criminal trials. Article 36 of the Code empowers the President to prescribe the procedure and the rules of evidence in trials by military courts (which is done in the Manual for Courts-Martial) but enjoins him "so far as he considers practicable, [to] apply the principles of law and the rules of evidence generally recognized in the trial of criminal cases in the United States district courts." The accused can, as in civilian courts, require the government to produce (and pay for) witnesses whose evidence is material to his case. Though requests for subpoenas or the production of witnesses (sometimes stationed at distant posts) must be made to the prosecutor, disagreements between him and the defense as to the accused's need for the particular testimony are resolved by the Military Judge.[45] Astute defense counsel request, not infrequently, witnesses whose attendance will be difficult and expensive to procure, hoping that a grant of the request will induce the convening authority to abandon the prosecution, or that a denial will lead to reversal of a conviction.

There are, of course, many differences of detail, but I think it fair to say that most of them give the military accused a slightly better break than he would get in a civilian trial. Thus, although the Supreme Court's landmark holding in *Miranda* v. *Arizona*,[46] that the police cannot constitutionally question a suspect in their custody until he has been informed of his rights to remain silent and consult a lawyer, is as applicable to military as civilian police,[47] it upset the MP's far less than it did the civilian cops, for the guardians of military law had long been required to give such warnings, and, indeed, to give them even in circumstances such as demand for a sample of a suspect's handwriting where the Supreme Court has refused to extend such protection to civilian suspects.[48]

There are some differences—for example, although soldiers are covered by the Fourth Amendment's prohibition of "unreasonable" search and seizure,[49] and evidence obtained by such searches is excluded in courts-martial, searches that might be unlawful if civilians were involved may be "reasonable" for military persons and premises. Such searches are normally authorized by the military commander having jurisdiction of the premises, or his delegate, rather than by a warrant issued by a judge or United States Magistrate, and they may cover more people and places than could be searched under a civilian warrant.[50] An interesting example of the broader discretion of the military authorities to search military personnel is a case in which a civilian court, trying a member of the Air Force for the federal offense of transporting a stolen car from one state to another, admitted in evidence a set of car keys discovered by the Air Police in the course of a "strip search" for weapons, on the ground that a search which might have been unreasonable if the subject had been a civilian was allowable where military personnel on a military post were concerned.[51] But by and large, it is fair to say that in most matters of procedure and evidence the rights of the soldier defendant, if they differ from the civilian's, are likely to differ for the better.

This is clearly true of appellate review[52] unless we accept at face value the loud and dogmatic assertions of some critics that the agencies which review court-martial convictions, including the Courts of Military Review and the Court of Military Appeals, are spineless creatures of the Pentagon, ready to rubber stamp any travesty of justice.[53] But the record does not seem to support such anathemas; regular perusal of the reported decisions of the military appellate courts leaves the reader pretty well convinced that their judges are by and large as independent, conscientious, and fairminded as those of state and federal courts.[54]

From the standpoint of sheer quantity and availability of appellate review, the military convict is plainly better off than the civilian. Even the least serious cases —those in which the sentence does not exceed six months' confinement—must be reviewed by the convening authority and his Staff Judge Advocate or (if he has none) by a military lawyer in a higher command.[55] Of such automatic review it may at least be said that it is free, that it is more than the accused would get in civilian courts, and that he has nothing to lose. While the convening authority may (and sometimes does) disapprove a conviction or reduce a sentence, acquittals are final and sentences cannot be increased.[56] The minor offender is not entitled, as a matter of right, to further review; but the Judge Advocate General of the service may, on petition, vacate or modify a verdict if he finds "error prejudicial to the substantial rights of the accused."[57]

More serious sentences—those which include a punitive discharge (whether or not suspended by the convening authority) or as much as a year's confinement—must be reviewed by a Court of Military Review, consisting of three military or civilian judges (in practice almost always military), and located in the Office of the Judge Advocate General of the service concerned, which is empowered to reduce the sentence, dismiss charges, or order a new trial if it finds error in the proceedings.[58] From its decision a final appeal lies to the Court of Military Appeals, the "Supreme Court of Military Justice," whose three judges are "appointed from civil life by the President, by and with the advice and consent of the Senate,"[59] and are, of course, in no way subject to the control or influence of anyone in the military establishment. COMA is *required* by the Code to review only those decisions of the Courts of Military Review in which the sentence affects a general or flag officer (*i.e.,* an admiral),[60] or in which a death sentence is affirmed, and cases in which the Judge Advocate General in effect asks COMA to review the lower court's decision on a question of law. It may, on petition by the accused, review any decision of a Court of Military Review which the judges think presents a substantial question of law. In proceedings before appellate courts, the accused is entitled to free counsel, who is not the same lawyer who represented him at the trial and who is consequently quite free to question the tactics, and even the competence, of the trial lawyer.[61] The Supreme Court has yet to hold that an indigent civilian must be furnished appellate counsel.

It should, moreover, be noted that the scope of review by the military authorities is much broader than is common in civilian practice. Only the Court of Military Appeals is limited to matters of law; it, like a civilian court, may reverse on the facts only if it finds that the evidence is legally insufficient to support a conviction.[62] Civilian appellate judges cannot reverse a conviction merely because they themselves, had they been sitting as jurors, would have had a reasonable doubt as to guilt. But the convening authority, his Staff Judge Advocate, and the Court of Military Review, unlike civilian appellate courts, judge for themselves the strength of the evidence and the credibility of witness and, in theory and occasionally in fact, reverse if perusal of the record does not convince *them* that the accused is guilty beyond a reasonable doubt.[63] Again, the charge that the military review is no more than a perfunctory rubber-stamping of convictions is easy to make, and hard to prove or disprove; all that can be said is that conscientious military appellate judges, if we admit the possibility that such men may exist (and even that they may not be very exceptional), have broader power than their civilian counterparts to set aside a conviction which strikes them as unjust. By the same token, they have practically unlimited discretion to reduce sentences.[64] In most civilian jurisdictions, on the other hand, the severity or leniency of punishment—given the wide gap between statutory minimums and maximums—depends in very large part on the particular trial judge's attitude toward the offense and the offender;[65] it is notorious that astute criminal lawyers will go to great lengths to calendar their cases in such a way as to avoid Judge A, who is known to be death (figuratively speaking) on tax evasion or drug offenses, and bring the case before Judge B, who is full of liberal principles and the milk of human kindness. Inequality of sentences, although a source of just complaint in both military and civilian criminal process, is probably somewhat less so in the former. On the other hand, the greater equality in sentencing that is promoted by the military's elaborate system of review is to some extent counteracted by the tendency of courts-martial, relying on that review and aware that their sentences can only be decreased, to hand out penalties that leave plenty of room for clemency. This habit, incidentally, contributes to the common opinion that military punishments are savage; the news media, if they pay any attention at all to a court-martial, will report the original sentence, but not as a rule the subsequent reductions in that sentence. The fifteen-year terms awarded some of the Presidio mutineers (a group of privates who in 1968 staged a disorderly, but not very violent, protest against conditions in the stockade at that post in San Francisco) were indeed harsh—even though mutiny is the ultimate military crime, this, as mutinies go, was a picayune affair—but few of the honest liberals who were properly shocked seem to have learned of the reduction, first to seven years and then to two, of those sentences as they traveled up the line,[66] nor did they learn that the Court of Military Review, concluding that the evidence did not support a conviction of mutiny, but only the lesser offense of willful disobedience of a lawful order, further reduced the sentence to one year.[67]

In theory, the action of the highest military appellate tribunal is final. Article 76 of the Code provides that "the proceedings, findings and sentences of courts-martial as approved, reviewed, or affirmed as required by [the Code] . . . are final and conclusive. Orders publishing the proceedings of courts-martial and all action taken pursuant to those proceedings are binding upon all . . . courts . . . of the United States." Nevertheless, the federal courts have developed techniques for policing the fairness of courts-martial that are very similar to those which they apply to convictions in the criminal courts of the states. Those techniques are discussed in Chapter IV. Here I need only note that in this respect also the military defendant is about as well off as the civilian, although the peculiar nature of some military punishments creates peculiar problems for civilian courts trying to devise appropriate relief.

This last is the final important difference between military and civilian penal law—the character of the punishments which can be imposed. Courts-martial do, of course, have power to inflict the ordinary penalties: fine, imprisonment, and possibly death. But there are also distinctively military punishments: punitive discharges, which deprive the subject of the various benefits, including pension, to which he would otherwise be entitled and which make it hard for him to find civilian employment; forfeitures of pay; reduction in rank; and reprimand. So far as the Code is concerned, a general court-martial can impose any sentence (except death, for which explicit statutory authorization is required) for any offense. In practice, the President's Table of Maximum Punishments[68] places limits on their discretion which, where common crimes are concerned, approximate civilian norms.

The picture that emerges from this rather summary description is one of a criminal process that differs radically from the civilian in only one respect: the role of the military commander, the convening authority, whose responsibility it is to maintain discipline in the command, who decides which cases shall be prosecuted, and who selects the "jury" that will decide guilt and assess punishment. There is no doubt that his unique interests and powers create at least a possibility of unfairness. Even if the accused elects trial by a Military Judge sitting alone, as he usually does, that Judge is an officer of the service, with a professional interest in its discipline, and he is not altogether independent of the Judge Advocate General and the civilian officers of the Department. These are major differences, and they give importance to the questions next to be considered—the scope of the military courts' jurisdiction, and the constitutional rights of the soldier accused of crime.

Notes to Chapter Two

[1]The *Grundgesetz* permits military courts to exercise complete criminal jurisdiction over members of the armed forces in time of war, or when they are stationed outside Germany or on naval vessels at sea. So far as I know, no use has yet been made of this authority. Military commanders can inflict minor "disciplinary" punishments, of which the most severe is three weeks confinement, and Military Service Courts can impose "career punishment," including reduction in rank and pay and dishonorable discharge, on career soldiers. *See generally* Moritz, *The Administration of Justice within the Armed Forces of the German Federal Republic*, MILITARY LAW REVIEW, January, 1960, at 1; Krueger-Sprengel, *The German Military Legal System*, 57 MIL. L. REV. 17 (1972); Sherman, *Military Justice Without Military Control*, 82 YALE L. J. 1398, 1408–13 (1973).

[2]"The Disintegrating Army," *The Economist*, March 18, 1972, at 34, 37

[3]MACAULAY, HISTORY OF ENGLAND 35 (1856 ed).

[4]Act of March 3, 1863, ch. 75, § 30, 12 Stat. 736.

[5]Coleman v. Tennessee, 97 U.S. 509, 513 (1878).

[6]Reid v. Covert, 354 U.S. 1, 35–36 (1957).

[7]O'Callahan v. Parker, 395 U.S. 258, 266 (1969). He quoted, with apparent approval, a polemicist's assertion that "None of the travesties of justice perpetrated under the UCMJ is really very surprising, for military law has always been, and continues to be, primarily an instrument of discipline, not justice." Glasser, *Justice and Captain Levy*, 12 COLUMBIA FORUM 46, 49 (1969). Douglas's rhetoric did not sit well with the members of a panel which considered the problems of military justice at the American Bar Association's 1970 convention.

[8] *See* WIGMORE, *Lessons from Military Justice*, 4 J. AM. JUD. SOC'Y. 151 (1921).

[9]"The exercise of military jurisdiction is also responsive to other practical needs of the armed forces. A soldier detained by the civil authorities pending trial, or subsequently imprisoned, is to that extent rendered useless to the service. Even if he is released on bail or recognizance, or ultimately placed on probation, the civil authorities may require him to remain within the jurisdiction, thus making him unavailable for transfer with the rest of his unit, or as the service otherwise requires." Harlan, J., dissenting in O'Callahan v. Parker, 395 U.S. 258, 282–83 (1969).

[10]"It is true that military personnel because of their training and experience may be especially competent to try soldiers for infractions of military rules. Such training is no doubt particularly important where an offense charged against a soldier is purely military, such as disobedience of an order, leaving post, etc." United States *ex rel.* Toth v. Quarles, 350 U.S. 11, 18 (1955).

[11] *See, e.g.,* O'Callahan v. Parker, 395 U.S. 258, 262 (1969); Reid v. Covert, 354 U.S. 1, 37 (1957); Duke & Vogel, *The Constitution and The Standing Army*, 13 VANDERBILT L. REV. 435, 441 (1960).

[12]Section 2 of article III of the Constitution, which deals with the judicial power of the United States, provides that "The trial of all Crimes . . . shall be by Jury; and such Trial shall be held in the State where the said Crimes shall have been committed; but when not committed within any State, the Trial shall be at such Place or Places as the Congress may by Law have directed." The Supreme Court has never questioned the power of Congress to make offenses committed by American citizens outside the United States triable in whatever federal court is most convenient, such as that in whose district he is first found or brought. United States v.

Bowman, 260 U.S. 94 (1922); Jones v. United States, 137 U.S. 202 (1890); *see* Toth v. Quarles, 350 U.S. 11, 22 (1955). The Court of Military Appeals recently held that the provisions of article III have no application to courts-martial. Chenoweth v. Van Arsdall, 22 U.S.C.M.A. 183 (1973).

[13]The Court of Claims, considering the constitutional justification for court-martialing servicemen who commit crimes against civilians in foreign countries, recently suggested that statutory provision for the trial in American courts "of crimes of violence committed against foreign nationals on the streets of foreign cities would encounter very serious problems of constitutional law and international law. . . . How could the testimony of eye witnesses be obtained?" Gallagher v. United States 423 F.2d 1371, 1374–75 (Ct. Cl. 1970), *cert. denied* 400 U.S. 849 (1970).

[14]Articles 16 and 20 of the Uniform Code authorize summary courts-martial, consisting of a single officer, with authority to impose as much as 30 days' confinement. But under the 1968 amendments a summary court cannot try a serviceman without his consent, and it seems likely that in future the bulk of the petty offenses formerly dealt with by summary courts will be tried by special court-martial or, if the accused does not demand trial by court-martial, as he usually does not, dealt with by "commanding officer's nonjudicial punishment" under Article 15, which authorizes punishments nearly as severe as those which a summary court could inflict. The trend is likely to be accelerated by a recent holding of a civilian court that a soldier tried by summary court-martial is constitutionally entitled to the services of a lawyer. Daigle v. Warner, 348 F. Supp. 1074 (D. Hawaii 1972). Although the judges of the Court of Military Appeals are of several minds on the subject, the Army and Air Force now furnish counsel to the accused in summary court-martial proceedings. *See* Alderman, 22 U.S.C.M.A. 298 (1973).

Article 15 and its workings are described in Note, *The Unconstitutional Burden of Article 15*, 82 YALE L. J. 1481 (1973), which argues, I think wrongly, that it is unconstitutional under the doctrine of United States v. Jackson, 390 U.S. 570 (1968), because the accused, if he wants a formal trial and counsel, must risk a court-martial which could inflict punishment more severe than is allowable under article 15.

[15]Art. 22, UCMJ. The Supreme Court has said that the Presi-

dent, as Commander in Chief, would have power to create a court-martial even if Congress did not confer it upon him. Swaim v. United States, 165 U.S. 553 (1897).

16Art. 23, UCMJ.

17Art. 41, UCMJ. *See* Manual for Courts-Martial United States 1969 (Revised edition), ¶ 62f. The Manual is hereinafter cited as MCM.

18 *See, e.g.,* SHERRILL, MILITARY JUSTICE IS TO JUSTICE AS MILITARY MUSIC IS TO MUSIC, 76 and *passim* (1970); Sherman, *Military Injustice,* The New Republic, March 9, 1968, at 21.

19Art. 25(c), UCMJ. The French and German military codes had similar provisions in the nineteenth century, but American courts-martial were limited to commissioned officers until 1948. *See* WINTHROP, at 70. The article provides that enlisted members must belong to a "unit" (normally a company, ship's crew, or equivalent body) other than the accused's and that such a request need not be granted if eligible enlisted members "cannot be obtained on account of physical conditions or military exigencies." Although it might be impossible to obtain enlisted men of other units on board a ship at sea, or even in an isolated military post, it would rarely be impossible to postpone a court-martial until the accused can be returned to a place where other units are stationed. Cases in which a convening authority has denied an accused's request that enlisted men be appointed to the court are extremely rare. The convening authority cannot, of course, appoint enlisted members unless the accused so requests. White, 21 U.S.C.M.A. 583 (1972).

20Art. 52, UCMJ. Death sentences require a unanimous vote, and sentences to confinement in excess of ten years the votes of three quarters of the members.

Some Military Judges have recently ruled that since, under the Uniform Code, the choice between death and life imprisonment in murder cases is left to the members of the court, the imposition of a death penalty is unconstitutional under the Supreme Court's decision in Furman v. Georgia, 408 U.S. 238 (1972). *See* New York Times, Nov. 2, 1972, at 8.

21Crawford, 15 U.S.C.M.A. 31 (1964); *see also* Kemp, 22 U.S.C.M.A. 152 (1973).

22Similar qualifications are commonly specified for civilian jurors. *E.g.,* 28 U.S.C. § 1861; *see* United States v. Dennis, 183 F.2d

201 (2d Cir. 1950), *aff'd* 341 U.S. 494 (1951). But in civilian practice there is no person equivalent to the convening authority who selects prospective members of the jury.

[23]Art. 25(d) (2), UCMJ. The Code, in terms, disqualifies only witnesses for the prosecution, but the convening authority would be highly unlikely to detail prospective witness for the defense; if he did, the prosecutor would presumably challenge for cause.

[24]*Compare* Greene, 20 U.S.C.M.A. 232 (1970), in which the Court of Military Appeals strongly suggested that it was improper for a convening authority to order that only field-grade officers (majors, lieutenant colonels and colonels) be detailed to general courts. The commander's intent was benign; the order was motivated by his belief that company-grade officers—*i.e.*, lieutenants and captains—had demonstrated a tendency to impose unduly harsh sentences. Article 25(d) (1) provides that "when it can be avoided, no member of an armed force may be tried by a court-martial any member of which is junior to him in rank or grade," but is otherwise silent on the subject.

[25]Crawford, *supra* note 21. Civilian courts are not in harmony on the question. *Compare* Collins v. Walker, 329 F.2d 100 (5th Cir. 1964), which found an unconstitutional discrimination against a Negro defendant when a number of Negroes were deliberately included in the panel of grand jurors which indicted him, with Dow v. Carnegie-Illinois Steel Corp., 224 F.2d 414 (3d Cir. 1955), *cert. denied* 350 U.S. 971 (1956).

[26]McClaughry v. Deming, 186 U.S. 49, 62 (1902). The conviction of a volunteer officer by a court-martial composed of regulars was held void, because the Articles of War in those days prohibited regulars from sitting on courts which were to try volunteers. *See also* Runkle v. United States, 122 U.S. 543, 555–56 (1887). But the *Deming* case has been read as "reaching only laws that govern the convening of courts-martial. An error of law not affecting the constitution of the court, its jurisdiction over person and subject matter, or the validity of its sentence, does not cause the court-martial to 'lose' jurisdiction." Allen v. Van Cantfort, 436 F.2d 625, 628 (1st Cir. 1971), *cert. denied* 402 U.S. 1008 (1971).

[27]Bunting, 4 U.S.C.M.A. 84 (1954).

[28]Harnish, 12 U.S.C.M.A. 443 (1961). *See also* White, *supra* note 19.

[29]Gordon, 1 U.S.C.M.A. 255 (1951). Other interesting exam-

ples of the sort of personal interest which has been held to make the convening authority an "accuser" are Shepherd, 9 U.S.C.M.A. 90 (1958) (charges arising out of the accused's making false official reports as to his progress in reducing his weight from 300 to 200 pounds pursuant to the commanding general's pet "fat-boy" program) and Marks, 19 U.S.C.M.A. 389 (1970), in which the convening authority had himself set the trap that caught the accused and thus was disqualified from reviewing the conviction.

[30]Hedges, 11 U.S.C.M.A. 642 (1960).

[31]Art. 16, UCMJ.

[32]Art. 19, UCMJ.

[33]Art. 26, UCMJ. *See generally* Moorehead, 20 U.S.C.M.A. 574 (1971).

[34]Arts. 41, 51, UCMJ. The Military Judge, like a civilian trial judge, also rules on various pleas in bar which, if granted, would obviate trial of the issues—*e.g.*, pleas that the statute of limitations has run, former jeopardy, pardon, or condonation, denial of speedy trial and so forth. *See* MCM, ¶ 68.

[35]Art. 62(a), UCMJ: Priest v. Koch, 19 U.S.C.M.A. 293 (1970).

[36]Art. 62(b), UCMJ.

[37]Under the criminal codes of some states, such as California and New York, the jury may determine the penalty for certain offenses, such as murder. This is not the case in the federal courts.

[38]Art. 16, UCMJ.

[39]Arts. 19, 27, UCMJ. The 1968 amendment of the Code, depriving special courts of jurisdiction to adjudicate Bad Conduct Discharges unless the accused was furnished lawyer counsel, effectively ended a lively judicial controversy, in both military and civilian courts, as to whether the accused in such cases had a constitutional right to legally qualified counsel. A majority of the Court of Military Appeals, and the federal Court of Appeals for the Tenth Circuit, held that there was no such right. Culp, 14 U.S.C.-M.A. 199 (1963); Kennedy v. Commandant, 377 F.2d 339 (10th Cir. 1967). The latter decision overruled an earlier decision to the contrary by a district court. Application of Stapley, 246 F. Supp. 316 (D. Utah 1965). But the argument is still going on as to summary courts, in which the Code makes no provision for counsel. *See supra*, note 14.

[40]Art. 38(b), UCMJ.

[41] *See* Schiesser & Benson, *Modern Military Justice*, 19 CATHOLIC U.L. REV. 489, 508 (1970).

[42]The case of Captain Levy, a medical officer who was convicted of disobeying a lawful order and of making various disloyal statements to enlisted men, must have been litigated more extensively, in both military and civilian courts, than any court-martial (I might almost say any criminal case) in the history of the United States. It is the Jarndyce v. Jarndyce of military law. A partial list of the reported decisions includes Levy v. Corcoran, 389 F.2d 929 (D.C. Cir. 1967), cert. *denied* 389 U.S. 960 (1967); Levy v. Resor, 17 U.S.C.M.A. 135 (1967); Levy v. Resor, 384 F.2d 689 (4th Cir. 1967), *cert. denied* 389 U.S. 1049 (1968); United States v. Levy, 39 C.M.R. 672 (1968); Levy v. Dillon, 286 F. Supp. 593 (D. Kans. 1968), *aff'd* 415 F.2d 1263 (10th Cir. 1969); Levy v. Parker, 316 F. Supp. 473 (M.D. Pa. 1970), *rev'd* 478 F.2d 772 (3d Cir. 1972). The Third Circuit found that the charge of making "disloyal" statements was unconstitutionally vague and that his conviction and sentence on a second charge of disobeying a lawful order might have been tainted by the unconstitutional charge. What the Supreme Court will hold is unclear.

[43] *See generally* 1 ORFIELD, CRIMINAL PROCEDURE UNDER THE FEDERAL RULES §§ 6:75, 6:118 (1966); Calkins, *Grand Jury Secrecy,* 63 MICH. L. REV. 455 (1965); Note, *Discovery by a Criminal Defendant of His Own Grand-Jury Testimony,* 68 COLUM. L. REV. 311 (1968).

[44]*See* Tomaszewski, 8 U.S.C.M.A. 266 (1957); DeLauder, 8 U.S.C.M.A. 656 (1958); Moyer, *Procedural Rights of the Military Accused: Advantages over a Civilian Defendant,* 22 MAINE L. REV. 105 (1970).

[45]MCM,¶ 115; *see* Jones, 21 U.S.C.M.A. 215 (1972); McElhinney, 21 U.S.C.M.A. 436 (1972). Similar disputes can arise when the accused seeks to require the government to pay for psychiatrists and other expert witnesses. MCM, ¶ 116; *see* Johnson, 22 U.S.C.M.A. 424 (1973).

[46]384 U.S. 436 (1966).

[47]Tempia, 16 U.S.C.M.A. 629 (1967).

[48]United States v. Wade, 388 U.S. 218 (1967); Gilbert v. California, 388 U.S. 263 (1967). For descriptions of the military practice in "custodial interrogation," *see* Penn, 18 U.S.C.M.A. 194

(1969); Quinn, *Some Comparisons Between Courts-Martial and Civilian Practice*, 15 U.C.L.A. L. REV. 1240 (1968).

[49]Hartsook, 15 U.S.C.M.A. 291 (1965).

[50] *See* Harman, 12 U.S.C.M.A. 180 (1961), for a description of the "shakedown search" of the effects of every soldier in a barracks.

[51]United States v. Miller, 261 F. Supp. 442 (D. Del. 1966). To similar effect *see* United States v. Grisby, 335 F.2d 652 (4th Cir. 1964), where the court found no violation of the fourth amendment in the search of a military man's quarters located on a military post.

[52]For detailed descriptions of the process of review of convictions under the Uniform Code, *see* Moyer, *supra* note 44, at 127–33, and, of course, MCM, Chs. XVII–XX.

[53] *E.g.*, SHERRILL, *supra* note 18, at 213–15. The author's reasoning is in essence that affirmance of a court-martial conviction of which he disapproves—a category which includes practically all of them—is conclusive evidence of incompetence or prejudice on the part of the appellate judges.

[54] *See* Schiesser & Benson, *Modern Military Justice*, 19 CATHOLIC U.L. REV. 489, 502 (1970). Although both authors are Army Judge Advocates, their approach to military justice seems to be characterized by objectivity rather than uncritical admiration.

[55]Arts. 60–65, 69, UCMJ; MCM, ¶¶ 84–91, 94–103.

[56]Art. 62, UCMJ: Christopher, 13 U.S.C.M.A. 231 (1962).

[57]Art. 69, UCMJ.

[58]Arts. 65(b), 66, UCMJ. The Military Justice Act of 1968 changed the name of these tribunals from Boards of Review to Courts of Military Review but did not significantly change their jurisdiction or powers. Under article 69 the verdict of a general court-martial, even if the sentence is not stiff enough to require consideration by a Court of Military Review, must go to the Judge Advocate General, who may refer it to such a court.

[59]Art. 67, UCMJ.

[60]A federal Court of Appeals has rejected an argument that this discrimination in favor of the top brass is unconstitutional. Gallagher v. Quinn, 363 F.2d 301 (D.C. Cir. 1966), *cert. denied* 385 U.S. 881 (1966). Congress was probably motivated not so much by special solicitude for officers of high rank as by its judgment,

which has much historical justification, that such proceedings—which have, of course, been infrequent—are likely to have a high political content.

⁶¹*See* MCM, ¶ 102; Horne, 9 U.S.C.M.A. 601 (1958). If the accused retains his own lawyer that lawyer may, of course, appear for him at any and all stages of the proceeding.

⁶²It did not, however, take the Court of Military Appeals long to discover the ease with which questions of fact can be converted into questions of law. O'Neal, 1 U.S.C.M.A. 138 (1952); *see* Goulet, *The United States Court of Military Appeals and Sufficiency of the Evidence,* 42 GEO. L. J. 108 (1953).

⁶³MCM, ¶¶ 86, 100; Arthur, 9 U.S.C.M.A. 81 (1958).

⁶⁴Arts. 64, 66, UCMJ: Caid, 13 U.S.C.M.A. 348 (1962).

⁶⁵*See generally* American Bar Association Project on Minimum Standards for Criminal Justice, Standards Relating to Appellate Review of Sentences (Tentative Draft, 1967); Frankel, Criminal Sentences: Law without Order (1973).

⁶⁶*See* Moyer *supra* note 44, at 132. Robert Sherrill, attributing the reductions entirely to the Army's fear of an aroused public opinion, cites them as another example of the military reviewing authorities' lack of independence, servile deference to the wishes of higher authority, and general unscrupulousness. SHERILL, *supra* note 18, at 58–59. In Mr. Sherrill's court, the Army has no chance of either acquittal or clemency.

⁶⁷*E.g.,* Sood, L42 C.M.R. 635 (1970).

⁶⁸MCM, Ch. XXV.

CHAPTER THREE

The Jurisdiction of Courts-Martial

*I*F THE JUSTIFICATION FOR A separate system of military justice is the need to maintain discipline among soldiers, there is no reason for courts-martial to try civilians, and no compelling reason why they should try even soldiers for crimes that have no effect on military discipline. This proposition has led the Supreme Court in recent years to shear away much of the sweeping jurisdiction that Congress had granted to courts-martial. Three things the Court has made clear in recent years about the jurisdiction of courts-martial:[1]

1. A court-martial can try any member of the armed forces on active duty for a "service-connected" offense.

2. In time of peace a court-martial cannot try any civilian.

3. A court-martial cannot try a soldier for an offense that is not "service-connected"—at least if the offense is triable by jury in an American civilian court.

These constitutional limitations on military jurisdiction were far from obvious—particularly to Congress —until the Court spoke. Congress had, in fact, for years been engaged in a steady expansion of that jurisdiction. In 1787 the traditional competence of the military courts was limited to soldiers and a very loosely defined category of civilian camp-followers. The first American Articles of War, faithfully copying the British, provided that "All suttlers and retainers to a camp, and all persons whatsoever, serving with the continental army in the field, though not enlisted soldiers, are to be subject to the articles, rules, and regulations of the continental army." But this jurisdiction over civilians, of some antiquity even then, had always been restricted to time of war and usually to places in which active hostilities were being carried on.[2]

The truth is that Congress, during the Civil War and before and after World Wars I and II, developed a habit of solving what it thought were military problems by an erratic subjection of various types of civilians to military justice, sometimes at the urging of the Judge Advocates General and sometimes over their strenuous objection. In the Civil War, indeed, it went much farther than it has gone—or tried to go—at any time since. The Congress of 1862, presumably acting

on the premise that civilian due process was a great
deal too good for the slippery and prehensile entre-
preneurs who were then supplying the Union armies
with decayed beef, shoddy pantaloons, and worn-out
muskets at extortionate prices, provided that civilian
contractors for arms, munitions, and supplies should
be "deemed and taken as a part of the land or naval
forces . . . for which . . . [they] shall contract to furnish
said supplies." There seem to have been a number of
courts-martial under this unique provision[3] (whose
application to the modern military-industrial complex
would certainly produce an unprecedented and grati-
fying prosperity among military lawyers), but its con-
stitutié ality was considered on only one occasion by
a civilian court. That court, though plainly of the opinion that a civilian whose only tie to the armed services
was a contract to sell them supplies could not constitutionally be subjected to their criminal jurisdiction,
managed to dodge the constitutional issue by the familiar judicial technique of twisting the statute into the
shape of a pretzel—in this case, by construing the
word "contractor" as intended to include only persons who were in fact members of the armed forces,
such as "military storekeepers".[4]

The Congress of 1863 invented another variety of
peacetime jurisdiction over civilians that proved considerably more durable. Aimed primarily at the military opposite numbers of dishonest contractors, it
permitted courts-martial to try various frauds against
the government, despite the accused's subsequent
separation from the service, and without regard to

whether he could also be tried in a civilian court. Courts-martial under these Articles were by no means rare, and the inferior federal courts almost never questioned their legality.[5]

In World War II a cluster of sensational and widely publicized cases gave Congressmen a graphic demonstration of the possibility that American servicemen could commit serious crimes in foreign parts, conceal them until their discharge from the service, and thereafter thumb their noses at the law. The federal courts could try a very limited number of offenses, such as treason and certain frauds against the government committed by American citizens in foreign countries; courts-martial could try discharged servicemen only for frauds against the United States. Thus, Chief Petty Officer Harold Hirshberg, who had been convicted of mistreating fellow Americans in a Japanese prisoner of war camp, went free because the Supreme Court construed the old Articles for the Government of the Navy as cutting off court-martial jurisdiction to try an offense committed prior to an honorable discharge, even though Hirshberg had re-enlisted the very next day.[6] The conviction of Captain Kathleen Nash Durant, who stole the crown jewels of Hesse, was sustained only because the Army's investigators worked overtime, so that charges could be served on her, and her terminal leave revoked a couple of days before she would have kissed the Army goodbye forever.[7] Sergeant Carl George LoDolce, charged with shooting Major William Holohan (after a dose of cyanide in his soup had caused the hardy Major merely to feel somewhat queasy) while the two were on a secret mission behind the German lines in Northern Italy, could not be court-martialed, for he had returned to the United States and been honorably discharged three years before the Italian police recovered the weighted sack containing Major Holohan's body from the lake where it had been sunk.[8]

Congress could, of course, have plugged the loophole by giving the federal courts jurisdiction to try such cases. It chose, instead, to expand the old jurisdiction over frauds against the government by authorizing the court-martialing of ex-servicemen for offenses that were good for more than five years in prison and could not, under existing law, be tried in an American state or federal court.[9] It may be noted that the jurisdiction was thrust on the Army over the objection of its Judge Advocate General, who concurred in Colonel Winthrop's flat opinion[10] that a civilian in peacetime cannot constitutionally be made liable to military jurisdiction.

Congress had earlier expanded military jurisdiction over civilians in other directions. In 1916 General Enoch Crowder, then the Judge Advocate General of the Army and a powerful lawyer,[11] persuaded Congress to expand the Articles of War to cover civilians accompanying the armed forces outside United States territory, even in time of peace. The provision, which was re-enacted and even broadened as Article 2(11) of the Uniform Code, was hardly questioned by the federal courts prior to 1955, largely because it was generally assumed, despite the authority of Colonel Winthrop, that any case "arising in the land or naval forces" could be tried by court-martial, whether or not the accused was a member of those forces.[12] The Uniform Code of 1950 marked the zenith of military jurisdiction over civilians. Article 2(10) preserved the old wartime jurisdiction over "persons serving with or accompanying an armed force in the field"; Article 2(11) added to this the power to try civilians, such as employees or dependents, accompanying the armed forces outside the United States, even if peace prevailed and the forces were not "in the field"; and Article 3 subjected to court-martial honorably discharged veterans who had committed serious offenses not triable in an American civil court before their separation from the service. Civilians could not, of course, commit the purely military offenses, such as absence without leave or mutiny; it would, for example, never have been possible to court-martial striking civilian employees. But under the Code the military's jurisdiction over offenses was even broader than its jurisdiction over persons. As will shortly be chronicled, Congress had steadily expanded the scope of military justice in this area too. By 1950 the constitutional power to make rules for the government and regulation of the land and naval forces had been stretched to the breaking point; all soldiers and millions of civilians were triable by court-martial for just about any offense, including, at least in theory, a violation of the Internal Revenue Code or the antitrust laws.

At this point the Supreme Court intervened. In a series of decisions between 1955 and 1969 it held that the constitutional foundation would not bear the edifice that Congress had raised upon it. The Court began with the case of Airman Robert Toth, convicted by a general court-martial of a murder committed in Korea, which did not come to light until after he had been honorably discharged.[13] The Justices held this conviction a nullity: the Congressional power to make rules for the government and regulation of the land and naval forces could not cover a man who had wholly severed his connection with those forces and become, as Justice Black put it, a "civilian ex-soldier." In the ensuing years Congress has done nothing to close the jurisdictional gap thus created—which suggests that, in practice, most serious crimes committed by American soldiers overseas are either discovered before the culprit's discharge or are never discovered at all. (Of course the country in whose territory the crime is committed has jurisdiction, unaffected by the malefactor's discharge from the armed forces of the United States—but only if it can extradite or otherwise lay its hands on him.)

The decision in Toth's case encouraged a couple of ladies who had been convicted by courts-martial of murdering their soldier husbands in Great Britain and Japan, respectively, to seek writs of habeas corpus in the federal courts.[14] The Supreme Court at first upheld the military jurisdiction, though only by a 5 to 4 vote.[15] Thereupon the ladies' lawyer, Colonel Frederick Bernays Wiener, whose "Civilians Under Military Justice" I have already cited, achieved something so rare and difficult that lawyers regard it as approximately impossible; he petitioned for rehearing and reconsideration, got it, and persuaded the Court to reverse itself. By this time two of the original majority, Justices Stanley Reed and Sherman Minton, had retired, Mr. Justice William Brennan had been added to the Court, and Justice John Marshall Harlan had changed his mind—the latter a remarkably rare phenomenon on the Supreme Court. The upshot was a lopsided (6–2) holding that these civilians could not be court-martialed in time of peace.[16] But loose ends were left; Justices Felix Frankfurter and Harlan limited their concurrence to capital cases; they thought, in effect, that it might be "necessary and proper" for the regulation of the land and naval forces that Congress give the military the power to jail accompanying civilians, but not that there be committed to courts-martial power to invoke the "awesome finality" of hanging them. Moreover, the opinion left open the possibility that the military's interest in disciplining civilian *employees,* as distinct from dependents, might be great enough to justify their subjection to military justice. But in a string of succeeding cases all of these questions were resolved against the Government, and Article 2(11) was held void in its entirety,[17] although not without several dissents.

The decisions, though clear enough as far as they went, left unanswered a number of questions, some of them important. For one thing, none of the civilian dependents or employees had been tried "in time of war." But both civilian and military courts have managed to avoid the question of the constitutionality of Section 2(10) of the Code, which gives courts-martial jurisdiction "in time of war, [over] persons serving with or accompanying an armed force in the field." The United States Court of Appeals for the District of Columbia Circuit dodged the question by holding that an able-bodied civilian seaman on a civilian tanker, who stabbed a shipmate in Mamasan's Beach Bar in Da Nang East, was not so closely connected with the Navy as to be "serving with or accompanying" it in the field.[18] The Court of Military Appeals and the Court of Claims achieved the same result by holding that "time of war" meant only a war declared by Congress.[19]

A question of greater practical importance is the status of several classes of military-civilian hybrids— persons who are primarily civilians but who have some sort of connection with the military.[20] Examples are reservists, of various types, and retired regulars.

The problems raised by the court-martialing of reservists not on active duty are intricate, interesting to specialists in military and constitutional law, but have not so far been of great practical significance, for such trials have been few and far between. Article 2(3) of the Code permits the court-martialing of reservists who misbehave themselves during inactive duty training—the ordinary weekly or weekend drill—if orders "voluntarily accepted" specify that the reservist shall be subject to the Code. But only the Navy has so far made any use of the power, and it has done so but rarely. Although a recent decision of a Circuit Court of Appeals seems to assume that the jurisdiction is constitutional,[21] and two of the judges of the Court of Military Appeals have said as much by way of dictum,[22] its legislative history suggests that Congress intended to confine the jurisdiction to those reservists whose training involved equipment, such as aircraft, whose misuse might entail disastrous consequences.[23]

Probably the most important case in which a criminal's reserve status deprived him of immunity from prosecution was that of Airman Wallace Wheeler, which demonstrated that military murderers who are not discharged and who do not sever every tie to the armed services should not place too much reliance on the *Toth* case. Wheeler, who knifed a casual female acquaintance in Wiesbaden and failed to disclose the fact until after his return home, could not quite cut every tie: when he was released from active duty he had still a residual obligation under the Selective Service Act and so was transferred to the standby reserve. He proceeded to find a civilian job and generally to civilianize himself as thoroughly as was possible without an actual honorable discharge. But murder will out, and this one did. Five months later Wheeler was questioned by the Air Force's criminal investigators and freely confessed. More, he volunteered to return to active duty for the sole purpose of standing trial, though he was motivated less by pangs of conscience than by intense fear—probably ill-founded—of being extradited and tried in a German court.[24] Wheeler's enthusiasm for court-martial seems to have evaporated almost as soon as he saw the charges against him, but both a civilian court[25] and the Court of Military Appeals[26] upheld military jurisdiction. The civilian judge and one of the judges of the Court of Military Appeals thought that his membership in the inactive reserve, by itself, gave him sufficient military status to distinguish him from Mr. Toth, even if he had not returned to active duty; the other two judges of COMA went no farther than to hold Article 3(a) constitutional as to a soldier who was on active duty at the time he was tried as well as when he committed the crime. By the same token, soldiers who commit murders overseas, keep them secret until their enlistments expire, and are honorably discharged, should never, never reenlist.[27]

The question of the constitutionality of court-martial jurisdiction over dishonorably discharged inmates of military prisons (Article 2(7) of the Code allows courts-martial to try "persons in custody of the armed forces serving a sentence imposed by a court-martial") is equally interesting to the scholar, but of even less practical importance. It should not, in fact, arise at all, for if a military convict is so poor a prospect for rehabilitation that the execution of his discharge is not suspended, his connection with the military should be (and usually is) totally severed by incarcerating him in a federal pen rather than a disciplinary barracks, whose purpose (in theory and often in fact) is to restore him to duty. Under Article 58(a), "a sentence of confinement adjudged by a court-martial . . . may be carried into execution by confinement in any place of confinement under the control of any of the armed forces or in any penal or correctional institution under the control of the United States . . ." But the courts, including the Supreme Court, have consistently held that military prisoners even when they are just as conclusively discharged as Mr. Toth retain a sufficiently intimate relationship with the armed services to distinguish them from him, and the Supreme Court a few years ago preferred to ignore a broad hint from a Circuit Court of Appeals that it ought to reconsider the matter in the light of the *Toth* case.[28] Military prisoners whose discharges have been suspended, with a view to remission if they behave themselves, present no constitutional difficulty; not only do they have as much military status as other soldiers, but they would have trouble committing a crime that was not service-connected.

In short, as of now the military cannot try a veteran who gets an honorable discharge and stays out; but if there is merely a hiatus in his subjection to the Uniform Code, his sin (if it is serious enough to bring him within Article 3(a) and not triable in any other American court) may find him out.

A far bigger problem, at least potentially, is posed by the Code's subjection to courts-martial of "retired members of a regular component of the armed forces who are entitled to receive pay." There are now about a million of them—a number that has tripled in the past ten years. It is estimated that there will be about 1.6 million by the end of the century. Regulars can retire at half-pay after twenty years, plus an additional 2.5 percent of their base pay for each additional year, up to a maximum of 75 percent after thirty years. The average age at retirement is forty-one—which means a life expectancy of rather more than thirty years. It is obvious that we have here a very large number of citizens who deeply desire to retain their military status. But that status, and the pension that goes with it, can be terminated by sentence of a court-martial—and in virtually no other way. A retired regular who misbehaves himself can be court-martialed, sentenced to discharge or dismissal, and thus deprived of his pension: in effect, he is sentenced to a money penalty of monstrous proportions having no necessary relation to the gravity of his offense. That offense, to be sure, must meet the "service-connection" criterion discussed below, but old soldiers may not find it very difficult to commit offenses that fall within the tests so far developed. They tend to live in the vicinity of military posts and to maintain business and social connections with other military men, active and retired. They frequently get jobs with defense contractors and deal with procurement officers.

The Army, as a matter of policy, does not court-martial retired personnel and has, in fact, gone on record as favoring amendment of the Code to abolish the jurisdiction.[29] But Naval courts-martial have on several occasions sentenced retired regulars to dismissal and financial disaster, and the Air Force has done so at least once. So far, the lower courts have held the proceedings constitutional, and the Supreme Court has declined to intervene. The temptation to economize by chopping evildoers off the payroll is powerful and may grow as the pension item in the military budget grows. (It is now something over $4.5 billion a year and may reach $22 billion in another twenty-five years.)[30] Sooner or later the Supreme Court will have to decide the question. Its importance seems great enough to justify a description—as brief as possible—of its history and constitutional merits.

The constitutionality of such jurisdiction has, at any rate, whatever solidity derives from long congressional acquiescence; the amenability of retired regulars to court-martial—though unknown to the founding fathers—is as old as the retired list itself, which was also unknown to them. The concept of retirement dates from 1861, a year in which the problem of debridement from the military corpus of physically and mentally decrepit officers presented itself forcibly to the attention of Congress.[31] For the next fifty-five years, although the jurisdiction remained on the books, few subjects seem to have concerned Congress less than the constitutional rights of retired regulars— in large part, no doubt, because there were very few of them by modern standards,[32] still fewer who engaged in conduct sufficiently flagitious to call for criminal prosecution, and hardly any who were actually court-martialed.

Woodrow Wilson seemed to think that he could not function as Commander in Chief without the power to court-martial old soldiers. When the Senate in 1916— as part of a comprehensive and badly needed reorganization of the military establishment, including a revision of the Articles of War—inserted a rider abolishing the jurisdiction, Wilson's outrage was such that he forced Congress to restore it by vetoing the entire bill, including the appropriation for the Army. He accompanied his action with an eloquent message, full of genuine Wilsonian rhetoric; if retired officers were exempt from court-martial, he warned, the retired list might become "a source of tendencies which would weaken the discipline of the active land forces and impair that control over those forces which the Constitution vests in the President."[33] Apparently, his thought was that if retired officers were left to civilian laws and courts they would become a hotbed of dreamers of military *coups d'état* and hopeful men on horseback. Such fears are not, of course, pure fantasy, as is convincingly demonstrated in the histories of the Weimar Republic, the Second, Third and Fourth French Republics, and other polities too numerous to mention. But although our own history is not devoid of generals (and an admiral or so) who have rather easily been persuaded to see themselves as saviors of the country, in our case all of them who amounted to anything have attempted or accomplished the salvation by running for office in the usual way. Whatever danger there may be in electing to high office former military men, the danger is not likely to be alleviated by subjecting these men to court-martial before they reach that office. True, Article 88 of the Uniform Code, which subjects to punishment "any commissioned officer who uses contemptuous words against the President, the Vice President, Congress, the Secretary of Defense, the Secretary of a military department, the Secretary of the Treasury, or the Gover-

nor or legislature of any State, Territory, Commonwealth, or possession in which he is on duty or present," would if strictly applied considerably inhibit the
ordinary conduct of one afflicted with the itch for elec-
tive office.[34] But, aside from its dubious constitutionality, it has not in fact been so applied. For one thing,
it has not been construed to cover polemics that express contempt of the subject in his official capacity or
of his official policies and conduct. Strong language
may be employed so long as it is not directed *ad homi-
nem:* if not personally contemptuous, "adverse criticism of one of the officials or groups named in the
article in the course of a political discussion, even
though emphatically expressed, may not be charged as
a violation of the article."[35] It has, of course, no application to an officer who has resigned from the service and would clearly be unconstitutional if it purported to do so. Even if the man of destiny thinks to
attain his goals by "inciting to riot" in Oxford, Mississippi, or other violent means, and is reluctant (in case
the putsch fails) to surrender his pension by resigning,
it is doubtful that subjecting him to military jurisdiction adds anything to the civilian law's protection
against subversion and sedition, except to the extent
that it avoids local juries favorable to the brand of
sedition involved. The history of those countries in
which military subversion or sedition is a common-
place feature of the governmental process shows that
the real danger comes from those officers who are very
much in active service; the ex-general will not get far
unless he has the support of the officers who actually

command the armed forces. If he has that support, he is not likely to be much deterred by the threat of being brought before a court-martial drawn from their ranks.

President Wilson had, however, other reasons grounded not merely upon solicitude for the national welfare but upon concern for the retired officers themselves. After adverting to "the wholesome and unifying effect of . . . subjection to a common discipline," he said

> I am persuaded that officers upon the retired list would themselves regard as an invidious and unpalatable discrimination which in effect excluded them from full membership in the profession to which they have devoted their lives, and of which by the laws of their country they are still members.[36]

The syntax is execrable, but the meaning is clear and perhaps not altogether without psychological validity. The middle-aged and elderly gentlemen who constitute the retired list undoubtedly cherish their military status, and some of them may feel (if they stop to think about it) that subjection to the military code, no less than the right to wear the uniform and print their rank upon their calling cards, is one of the essential distinctions between them and a civilian population to which they do not wish to be completely homologized. One is reminded of the episode in which Caesar scotched a mutiny in the Tenth Legion by addressing the soldiers as "*Quirites,*" (a term usually translated as "citizens," though its actual meaning seems more closely approximated by "voters"), a shocking expedient that

instantly recalled them to their duty.[37] But it is probable that the comfort retired officers derive from subjection to military jurisdiction dissipates rather rapidly
when that jurisdiction is actually invoked. President
Wilson's psychology certainly lacks experimental
verification, for those retired officers who have in recent years been court-martialed seem to have derived
very little satisfaction from the experience; their challenges to the jurisdiction indicate strongly that they
found it both invidious and unpalatable.

However dubious his supporting arguments, Wilson's veto stuck, and Congress has not troubled itself
with the problem since 1916. The courts, as noted
above, have rejected challenges to the jurisdiction by
retirees whose pensions had been cut off by court-
martial. The leading case is that of Admiral Selden
Hooper, which was litigated to the bitter end, in every
available forum.

The Admiral, who had retired in 1948 after an honorable and distinguished career, resided in California,
where he devoted his golden years to homosexual
affairs with enlisted members of the Marine Corps and
Navy, in violation of both the California Penal Code
and the Uniform Code. California seems not to have
concerned itself with the Admiral's lovelife. Not so the
Navy; indeed, it was the Navy, using methods that,
though they may not have violated the Fourth Amendment, added very little to the dignity of the service,
which uncovered the evidence against him.[38] On April
15, 1957, he was charged with violations of Articles
125 (sodomy), 133 (conduct unbecoming an officer

and gentleman), and 134 (conduct of a nature to bring discredit upon the armed forces) of the Uniform Code. On May 6 and 7 he was tried by general court-martial, convicted, and sentenced to be dismissed from the service and to total forfeiture of pay. The Navy's Board of Review affirmed, making short work of the accused's contention that he could not constitutionally be tried unless recalled to active duty,[39] which the law did not permit to be done without his consent.[40]

At this point, and before the Court of Military Appeals had acted,[41] Admiral Hooper attempted a flanking maneuver, petitioning a federal district court for injunctive relief and for the convening of a three-judge court to pass on the constitutionality of Article 2(4). That court denied relief, on the ground, *inter alia,* that the petitioner had not exhausted his military appellate remedies.[42] But the court's conclusions of law included a flat statement that Article 2(4) "appears to be constitutional without doubt, to the extent that no substantial issue of its unconstitutionality is sufficiently presented as to require the convening" of a three-judge court. The Circuit Court of Appeals, though it remarked that "very interesting questions lurk here," concluded that "the doctrine of exhaustion of remedies . . . is implicit in the trial court's judgment" and on this ground alone affirmed the dismissal.

Meanwhile, the Court of Military Appeals had held unanimously that the exercise of jurisdiction under Article 2(4) did not necessitate the retired officer's recall to active duty, and that Article 2(4), as so construed, could constitutionally be applied to Hooper. In effect, COMA refused to draw a constitutional line between members of the armed forces on active duty and those who have put their uniforms in mothballs:

> Officers on the retired list are not mere pensioners in any sense of the word. They form a vital segment of our national defense, for their experience and mature judgment are relied upon heavily in times of emergency. The salaries they receive are not solely recompense for past services, but a means devised by Congress to assure their availability and preparedness in future contingencies. This preparedness depends as much upon their continued responsiveness to discipline as upon their continued state of physical health. Certainly, one who is authorized to wear the uniform of his country, to use the title of his grade, who is looked upon as a model of the military way of life, and who receives a salary to assure his availability, is a part of the land or naval forces.[43]

On January 7, 1961, President Eisenhower, cleaning up the papers on his desk, approved the sentence and ordered it executed. Admiral Hooper, having exhausted his military remedies, proceeded to test the constitutionality of the court-martial by bringing suit for his pension in the Court of Claims. But that court too, despite "certain doubts," held that a court-martial could constitutionally try and dismiss a retired officer.[44] (The judges were still less sure that the Constitution would have permitted a court-martial to inflict any punishment beyond dismissal and loss of pay —but, of course, that issue was not before them.) The

Supreme Court, despite the lower court's hinted invitation, refused to review the Admiral's case. His last hope flickered out when the Court of Military Appeals held that the Supreme Court's decision in *O'Callahan* v. *Parker* (shortly to be discussed), which held that offenses without a "service connection" could not be tried by court-martial, was not to be retroactive. One judge concurred on the ground that the military status of Hooper's inamorati provided a sufficient "service connection" to put his case outside the rule of *O'Callahan* v. *Parker.*[45] In the only other case to reach a civilian court, a district judge similarly concluded that a Navy court-martial could sentence a retired officer to dismissal and expressed similar doubt whether the court could impose other penalties.[46]

The constitutional validity of this variety of military jurisdiction, potentially so troublesome to so many pensioners, must in the last analysis depend on whether the armed services have an interest in the conduct, or misconduct, of their retired members sufficient to make their subjection to court-martial a "necessary and proper" incident to the government and regulation of the Army, Navy, and Air Force. What reason (other than economy) had the Navy for court-martialing Admiral Hooper, instead of leaving him to the state of California?

In the first place, of course, his conduct directly affected enlisted men on active duty. That, at least, provided a service connection. But, after all, that would have been true had Hooper been a retired bond salesman, and in that case, there would have been nothing for the Navy to do if the California authorities refused to act. Perhaps his naval rank and status may to some extent have facilitated his liaisons. To the extent that it was known that one entitled to call himself "Admiral" and wear the uniform was engaged in such delinquencies, the naval service might be brought into disrepute. Certainly sailors and marines who knew the Admiral, directly or by reputation, were likely to lose their awe of flag officers. In short, the Navy's principal (and only proper) objective was to strip Hooper of his rank and status: but for reasons more than a century old, rooted in history that has no relevance to modern conditions, the Navy could get rid of him in no other way than by sentence of a court-martial; and it could not take away his rank without taking away his pension.

Until shortly after the Civil War, the President could fire any officer from the service summarily, with or without cause. But one of the by-products of Congress's vendetta against Andrew Johnson was the Tenure of Office legislation of 1866 and 1867, which *inter alia* prohibited the peacetime dismissal of an officer of the armed forces by presidential action, except pursuant to sentence of a general court-martial.[47] Although the constitutionality of such a congressional limitation on the power of the Commander in Chief has never been directly adjudicated by the Supreme Court, it may well be doubted.[48] There are, of course, elaborate statutory and administrative provisions for the elimination of unfit military personnel on active duty.[49] Deliberately or not, Congress has made no comparable provision for those who are retired. Unless the President had chosen to challenge the constitutionality of the Tenure of Office Act, Hooper could not have been dismissed by executive action. One of the statutes does empower the President at any time to "drop from the rolls" (including, of course, the payroll) of any of the armed forces any officer, active or retired, but only if he is finally convicted of an offense by a civilian court and sentenced to confinement.[50] Not even this very limited exception to the general congressional failure to provide an administrative method of separating officers on the retired list was available to the Navy in Admiral Hooper's case, for he had not been convicted and sentenced to confinement by a civilian court.

The upshot is that the Navy or the Army or the Air Force if it wishes to strip a retired officer of a rank and uniform on which he is reflecting no credit, in itself a reasonable enough objective, can do so only by bringing into action a jurisdictional weapon of far greater destructiveness than is necessary to the achievement of the limited objective. The general court-martial could inflict imprisonment; and it must if it dismisses the officer and at the same time deprives him of his pension.[51]

Whether retired pay can lawfully be cut off, even as a punishment for crime, is doubtful. A few years ago the Court of Claims, which over the years had handed down a series of irreconcilable decisions and dicta—sometimes in the same case—respecting the nature of retired pay,[52] decided that such pay is not a "gratuity or mere pension" but something the serviceman has earned, whose forfeiture or reduction Congress could not authorize without raising a serious constitutional question.[53] But nearly forty years ago the Supreme Court said that "pensions . . . and other privileges accorded to former members of the army and navy . . . are gratuities. They involve no agreement of parties, and the grant of them creates no vested right. The benefits conferred by gratuities may be redistributed or withdrawn at any time in the discretion of Congress."[54] That view of a pension, or at least of one paid pursuant to a provision in force during the recipient's employment and which is morally, if not technically, a part of his contract of employment, was somewhat old-fashioned even when Justice Brandeis expressed it.[55] The latest opinion of the Court of Claims, that retired pay is earned, corresponds much more closely to present-day concepts. Nevertheless, it could not be safely predicted that the Supreme Court would today hold that retired pay is a vested right of which the pensioner cannot constitutionally be deprived, particularly if the deprivation is pursuant to the sentence of a court, military or otherwise.[56]

All things considered, I do not think that the Supreme Court is likely soon to hold that retired soldiers, sailors, and airmen cannot be court-martialed and stripped of their pensions. But something ought to be done, for the jurisdiction contains the seeds of injustice and hardship. One solution is an act of Congress permitting an administrative separation of retired officers which would strip them of their rank and status, but not of the pension earned by honorable service. Alternatively, the same power could be given to courts-martial.

Despite such tangles, however, the services today have small jurisdiction, and exercise less, over people who are essentially civilians,[57] which is as it should be. Military justice should have no greater scope than is absolutely required to maintain military discipline. As the Court said in the *Toth* case, the military should have "the least possible power adequate to the end proposed."[58]

But a second conclusion flows from this premise— one that did not become manifest until nearly fifteen years after *Toth* had been decided. If the preservation and enhancement of discipline does not justify the court-martialing of civilians, what need is there to take out of the civilian courts soldiers whose transgressions have no military aspect?

The second conclusion was perhaps not quite so plain as the first one. It certainly was not plain to the Supreme Court, which, even as it held that "the test for jurisdiction . . . is one of *status*, namely, whether the accused in the court-martial proceeding is a person who can be regarded as falling within the term 'land and naval Forces'," added that "the power to 'make Rules for the Government and Regulation of the land and naval Forces' bears no limitation as to offenses."[59] In the light of these clear and categorical pronouncements, so uncharacteristic of the Court, plus the fact that his commanders may have felt a legitimate interest in a soldier even when he was off-post and engaged in totally unauthorized and unmilitary pursuits, the services could hardly be blamed for continuing to try soldiers who met the Court's status test for all sorts of civilian offenses, from bouncing checks to bigamy.

All this pleasing certainty evaporated in 1969.

In an opinion filled with maddening muddle and obscurity, whose basis and reasoning, if any, are nearly impossible to decipher, Mr. Justice Douglas and four of his brethren held that a court-martial cannot constitutionally try a soldier for an offense that is not "service-connected,"—except maybe sometimes. The only thing about the decision that was definite was the result in the actual case before the court—that it was unconstitutional to court-martial Sergeant James O'Callahan for attempting while on leave, off-post, and clad in civilian clothes to rape a fourteen-year-old tourist in Honolulu.[60] Such was the ambiguity of the Douglas opinion that the Court of Military Appeals has had to puzzle over its application to various other factual situations in more than sixty cases, as of this writing. In one form or another, the problem has arisen in more than a dozen cases in the inferior federal courts; the law review articles attempting to figure out its basis and meaning are past counting.

Despite the ambiguity of the opinion, the *result* can be defended. To begin with, the idea that courts-martial should confine themselves to military crimes is not without historical support, although that support is by no means so strong and convincing as Justice Douglas assumed, since the history which the framers of the

Constitution were familiar with is at best unclear. The Mutiny Act of 1689 covered only offenses having an obvious relation to military discipline—mutiny, desertion, and sedition—but the British Articles of War (applicable outside the Kingdom and, after 1718, at home) were much broader. The British Articles of 1765, from which the first American Articles of War were lifted, not only covered malicious destruction of "any Property whatsoever belonging to any of our subjects," but included the grandfather of the present general article, making court-martial offenses of "all Crimes not Capital, and all Disorders or Neglects, which Officers and Soldiers may be guilty of, to the Prejudice of good Order and Military Discipline."[61] The British *practice* seems usually to have been to turn over to the civilian authorities soldiers accused of ordinary crimes, committed within the kingdom, against civilians or their property: indeed, another of the Articles of 1765 required officers to turn over accused soldiers on demand of the civil authorities. But, as has been pointed out by critics of the Douglas opinion in *O'Callahan*,[62] Parliament's disposition to limit military jurisdiction in the seventeenth and eighteenth centuries was based on a disposition to limit the power of the *Crown* and increase its own; it does not necessarily follow that the framers of the American Constitution, having given *Congress* the power to govern the armed forces, intended to confine that power within narrow limits. The early American history of the exercise of such jurisdiction is at best ambiguous. Certainly, plenty of heroes of the Revolution were court-martialed for stealing the pigs and poultry, and molesting the wives, daughters, and maid-servants of farmers. Justice Douglas dismissed these precedents by remarking that many of the trials took place between 1773 and 1783—i.e., in time of war—and of the others, that "in almost every case . . . it appears that some special military interest existed." But the evidence is not really so clear; as Douglas himself recognized in a later part of his opinion, many of the cryptic court-martial reports "simply recite the offender and the offense, and give no basis for judging the relationship of the offense to military discipline." As to the wartime cases, it can certainly be argued that, under campaign conditions, any variety of looting or mistreatment of the civil population inevitably has an evil effect on military efficiency.

It *is* fairly clear that, after the War of 1812, the practice of the United States Army was not to try common crimes under the general article unless they had some sort of impact on military discipline—unless, for instance, the victim was a fellow soldier, or the crime was committed on a military post.[63] Colonel Winthrop noted, however, that military commanders were allowed broad discretion in deciding which offenses against civilians affected discipline, and that "especially as the civil courts do not readily take cognizance of crimes when committed by soldiers, military commanders generally lean to the sustaining of the jurisdiction of courts-martial in cases of crimes so committed against civilians, particularly when committed on the frontier, wherever the offence can be viewed as affecting, *in any material though inferior degree,* the discipline of the command."[64] In many cases, of course, a soldier who committed a common crime, triable as such in the civilian courts, simultaneously committed a plainly military offense. A famous example is that of Sergeant John Mason of Battery B of the Second Artillery, the Jack Ruby of his day; detailed to guard Charles Guiteau, the assassin of President Garfield, he attempted to avenge his Commander in Chief by firing his musket at Guiteau, through the window of the latter's cell. He missed. A court-martial convicted Mason of violating the general article, which in those days was still worded in terms almost identical with those of the British Articles of 1765, and sentenced him to eight years confinement at hard labor. The Supreme Court, when he sought habeas corpus, upheld the sentence, pointing out that he had been convicted not of the civilian offense of assault with intent to kill, but of "an atrocious breach of military discipline."[65]

Nevertheless, the power to try under the general article essentially civilian offenses, even in time of war, and outside the United States, was sufficiently doubtful so that in 1847, General Winfield Scott resorted to the device of creating "military commissions," to try both civilians and soldiers accused of "assassination, murder, poisoning, rape" and a long list of other offenses, including most of the common felonies.[66] Scott seems to have been exercising his powers under international law as the military governor of occupied territory; but it is not clear why he—or his Judge Advocate—did not refer at least some of the charges to

84 / *JUSTICE UNDER FIRE*

courts-martial to be tried as violations of the general article. The puzzle is illustrated by the case of one Captain Foster, of a Georgia infantry battalion, accused of murdering Lieutenant Goff of the Pennsylvania volunteers in occupied Mexico. Foster was tried by a military commission, but decided not to await its verdict; he escaped his guard and fled to Georgia. When the Governor of Pennsylvania asked President Polk what the United States proposed to do about it, Attorney General Toucey opined that nothing could be done, for the military government of Mexico, its courts and its laws, had ceased to exist.[67] Toucey seems to have assumed that the military commission could also be regarded as a court-martial trying a violation of the Articles of War; but Captain Foster's unit had been disbanded and mustered out of the service, and the military commission had been dissolved and could not be revived. No civil court of the United States could then or now try a murder committed in Mexico. So Captain Foster remained at liberty, perhaps to shoot more Pennsylvania volunteers a few years later.

The problem recurred, of course, in the Civil War. In occupied Confederate territory, General Scott's solution would have been available; but large Union armies trained and campaigned in loyal states, and some of the boys in blue drew no distinction between the stealable property of loyal citizens and that of rebels. (The Colonel of a regiment of New York Zouaves, recruited mostly in the neighborhood of the Bowery, is said to have remarked on the departure of his unit that the city might as well disband its police force, for he hadn't left a crook or a blackguard behind him. It was also reported of this unit that on parade every officer took care to keep more than arm's length from his company, lest his pockets be picked.[68]) In the early part of the war such offenders were handed over to the state courts for trial,[69] but this had its inconveniences: It placed a heavy burden on the local authorities, and it meant that the accused soldier, even if he were innocent or his offense petty, was temporarily or permanently lost to the Army. Congress included in the Act of March 3, 1863,[70] which also instituted the nation's first draft, a provision empowering courts-martial to try, in time of war, insurrection or rebellion, a number of ordinary felonies—murder, robbery, arson, burglary and rape, for example. The provision (which was retained in the Articles of 1874) was considered by the Supreme Court in the bizarre case of Private Pryor Coleman, a soldier in the Union army which occupied Tennessee in 1865. A court-martial convicted him of murdering a girl with the melodious and lovely name of Mourning Ann Bell. He was sentenced to be hanged, but, like Captain Foster, escaped before the penalty was executed. In 1870 he applied for and obtained an honorable discharge; computerized interference with privacy had not yet been invented, and his name rang no bells in the Office of the Adjutant General. But in 1874 Tennessee law caught up with him; he was convicted of the murder in the courts of that state. The Supreme Court held that Coleman, as a member of an occupying army, could not be tried by the courts of the occupied enemy state, and on that ground reversed his conviction.[71] His victory was, however, an empty one, for the Court ordered him to be turned over to the Army, "to be dealt with as required by law."[72] The Supreme Court obviously had no doubt of the constitutionality of military trial of a soldier in wartime for the murder of a civilian; indeed the Justices assumed that Congress could have made that jurisdiction exclusive, had it wished to do so.

But the peacetime practice was not changed until 1916, when Judge Advocate General Crowder persuaded Congress to amend the Articles of War to cover most of the ordinary felonies, except for the capital offenses of murder and rape, which courts-martial still could not try in the United States in peacetime. Even these were included in the Uniform Code. The punitive articles of the Code specifically denounce, in addition to the purely military offenses, such ordinary crimes as drunken or reckless driving, riot and breach of the peace, murder, manslaughter, rape, larceny, robbery, forgery, drawing checks without sufficient funds, maiming, sodomy, arson, extortion, assault, burglary, housebreaking, perjury and frauds against the United States. And almost every other imaginable type of misbehavior can be charged under one or both of the general articles.

These articles are another unique feature of military justice, and one which is almost as great a favorite of its critics as command influence. They do in truth read as if they were intended to permit the punishment of almost any type of conduct that displeases a commanding officer. Article 133, applicable only to commissioned officers and cadets, covers "conduct unbecoming an officer and a gentleman";[73] Article 134, "all disorders and neglects to the prejudice of good order and discipline in the armed forces, all conduct of a nature to bring discredit upon the armed forces, and crimes and offenses not capital." The "Devil's Articles," although they are not in practice quite so sweeping as they look, do cover some types of conduct which for a civilian might be unethical or immoral, but not criminal. Thus, "dishonorable" failure to pay debts, or failure to support one's family, can be charged under either article—a jurisdiction which has sometimes threatened to turn the armed services into nationwide collection agencies, although a failure to pay which results from honest impecuniosity is not an offense.[74]

The sweep of the general articles, whose phraseology may fairly be described as downright nebulous, has recently led one Circuit Court of Appeals to hold both of them, in their entirety, to be unconstitutionally vague—too broad and general in their wording to give fair warning of what sort of conduct they prohibit.[75] Another Circuit Court, for similar reasons, held void for vagueness the first two clauses (but not the "crimes and offenses not capital" clause) of Article 134.[76] What the Supreme Court will say is hard to predict.

It is, however, fair to say that in actual practice, the articles are not nearly so vague as they look. Almost all of the acts actually charged under these articles, notably drug offenses, are of a sort which ordinary soldiers know, or should know, to be punishable. Common crimes not covered by any of the specific articles—bigamy, for example—are chargeable as violations of one or both of the general articles, so long as they have a service connection. "Crimes and offenses not capital" has come to be, by long construction, simply an assimilative crime act; it covers only "those acts or omissions, not made punishable by another article, which are denounced as non-capital crimes or offenses by enactments of Congress or under authority of Congress and made triable in the Federal civil courts"[77]—for example, the transportation of a stolen vehicle across a state line, in violation of the Dyer Act. Violations of state or foreign law, not covered by any of the specific articles, are usually chargeable as conduct of a nature to reflect discredit upon the armed forces, if in fact the circumstances were such that the armed forces were likely to be discredited—if, for instance, the offender was in uniform at the time he decided to take his pet pig into a mosque. Virtually all of the other transgressions which have normally been charged under the general articles —assaults, indecent acts with children, false swearing, and so forth and so on—are spelled out in some detail in the *Manual for Courts-Martial.*[78]

Occasionally a soldier manages to think up a shenanigan so original and novel that it is neither forbidden by any of the services' thousands of regulations and standing orders nor mentioned in the Manual's catalogue of sins chargeable under the article.

Naval Airman David Sadinsky, for example, posed a pretty problem when he won a bet by doing a backflip from the flight deck of the carrier *Intrepid*, then under way in a heavy sea, and put the Navy to the expense and trouble of detaching a destroyer to fish him out. The Board of Review reversed his conviction, on the ground that Sadinsky's dive, not being prejudicial to good order and discipline, was not a violation of the Code. The Court of Military Appeals thought otherwise and held, moreover, that the general article, as so construed and applied, was not unconstitutionally vague.[79] The basis of the "void-for-vagueness" doctrine applied by the civilian courts is simply the individual's right to know in advance that particular conduct is punishable: "The test is whether the language conveys sufficiently definite warning as to the proscribed conduct when measured by common understanding and practices."[80] By this test, Sadinsky had no just complaint, for his efforts to make his leap look accidental showed that he was well aware that the Navy would take a very dim view of the episode if it found out that his abandonment of the ship was voluntary.

In other cases, the Court of Military Appeals has held that the military's discretion to decide what sort of dubious conduct is unbecoming an officer and a gentleman, or prejudicial to good order and discipline, or of a nature to bring discredit on the armed forces, however broadly worded, is not unlimited. Thus, a second lieutenant, ordered to Vietnam but given a month's leave and instructions to await "port call orders," who simply praised God and stayed home when the orders, lost in administrative foul-up, failed to arrive, was not guilty of "conduct unbecoming" merely because he made no officious effort to find out what happened to his orders. Clearly he could not be charged with absence without leave, and, said the Court of Military Appeals, "the general articles . . . cannot be used as catchalls to proscribe as criminal conduct activities which would be innocent if charged under any other article."[81] In short, there seem to be few, if any, of those convicted under the general articles who can fairly claim surprise. Whether the Supreme Court, weighing all these factors, will uphold the lower courts' invalidation of the articles, remains to be seen.

Constitutional or not, the general articles in their present form seem at best unnecessary. There is no need to punish ungentlemanly conduct as a crime, even if there were universal agreement on standards of conduct among gentlemen. If an officer displays traits of character which make him unfit to command —and it may be remarked in passing that Alexander, Julius Caesar, and Napoleon were none of them paragons of veracity, chastity, and sobriety—he can be eliminated from the service without being convicted of crime. The genuine crimes usually charged under the general articles could as easily, and with much clearer constitutionality, be covered by explicit articles of the Code. One such article, for example, might simply replace the "crimes not capital" clause of Article 134 by incorporating by reference the federal penal code. If Congress wants to court-martial military personnel who indulge in cheating at cards or indecent acts with children (with a service connection), it might just as well say so explicitly, whether or not the courts compel it to do so.

Thus, immediately prior to June 2, 1969, when *O'Callahan* was decided, a soldier could be tried for just about any offense, if not under one of the specific articles, then under one or both of the general articles. The practice of the services was generally to turn over to the civil authorities, state or federal, soldiers whose offenses had no direct impact on discipline. But that practice was far from invariable. Civilian prosecutors, who had their hands full keeping up with the criminous proclivities of the residents of their own communities, were frequently only too glad to let the Army take care of its own criminal population—as in the *O'Callahan* case itself—and the Army, for its own reasons, was often willing to oblige.

All these arrangements and assumptions were, of course, knocked into the proverbial cocked hat by O'Callahan's case. The majority concluded that "the crime to be under military jurisdiction must be service-connected," but it gave few hints as to what might constitute a sufficient service-connection; the opinion seemed to suggest that the main reason for limiting military jurisdiction was to preserve, for as many offenders as possible, the presumed benefits of grand and petty juries; it emphasized that the holding was limited to peacetime offenses, triable in American civilian courts, and not involving "any question of the flouting of military authority, the security of a military post, or the integrity of military property."

Even if the *O'Callahan* decision were broadly and generously construed, it would leave courts-martial plenty to do. Obviously, the pure military offenses, not triable by civil courts, are still within military competence, including those (like Sergeant Mason's) which also involve violations of civilian penal codes. So, presumably, are most of the crimes which before 1916 could have been charged under the general articles as conduct unbecoming an officer and gentleman, or prejudicial to good order and discipline. But military appellate courts have shown no disposition to apply *O'Callahan* in such a way as to limit narrowly the jurisdiction of military courts. Thus, they have found sufficient service-connection whenever the victim was another serviceman, even if the crime occurred off-post.[82] (COMA has not, however, been inclined to stretch the definition of "fellow serviceman" for this purpose; it has held that soldiers could not be court-martialed merely because their victims happened to be civilian dependents or even a retired major.[83]) Offenses committed within a military reservation, where the commander has primary responsibility for the maintenance of order, are *ipso facto* service connected, even if the victims are pure civilians, though it is not enough that the accused may have brought on the post property stolen elsewhere.[84] (On the other hand, the offense of driving a stolen car across a state line, in violation of the Dyer Act and therefore of the general article, has been held service-connected if the accused stole the car on the post, even though the crossing took place outside the military reservation.[85]) Offenses whose commission is facilitated by the accused's military status, such as victimizing civilians by running up a hotel bill, or cashing a stolen check with a forged endorsement on the strength of a uniform and a service identification card,[86] are service-connected. Since drugs make soldiers less fit for duty, the use, and even the possession, of marijuana (and, *a fortiori*, more potent drugs) on or off post, on or off duty, is said by COMA to be service-connected.[87] Conspiring to turn over classified documents to the First Secretary of the Soviet Embassy "offends against the government and discipline of the military state" and is thus service-connected;[88] by an extension of this reasoning, so is the making of "disloyal statements" in violation of the general article—though civilian courts have held such a charge unconstitutionally vague, particularly where there was no showing that the peace leaflets in question posed any substantial threat to discipline.[89]

These offenses would also have been triable by jury in civilian courts as violations of state or federal law; the courts-martial could be justified only by finding a substantial impact on military discipline and security. But the Court of Military Appeals, believing that the principal reason for reversing O'Callahan's conviction was that he had been denied the benefits of trial by jury, has carved out two exceptions still larger. A crime committed outside the United States is not triable in an American court, unless it violates one of the rare sections of the United States Penal Code which have extraterritorial effect. Thus, an American soldier who commits a rape, robbery, or murder in a foreign country must be tried either by court-martial or in the courts of that country—which, of course, are not bound by the Constitution of the United States and in most cases do not regard a jury (which is by and large a peculiarity of Anglo-American law) as essential to justice. Assuming that the country in question is willing to waive its primary jurisdiction,[90] the soldier charged with a non-service connected offense in a foreign country loses nothing if he is court-martialed.[91] The Court of Military Appeals managed to reach the same conclusion in the case of Specialist Fourth Class Stuart Goldman, whose offense, possession of counterfeit United States currency, although committed in Vietnam, *was* triable in a District Court of the United States.[92] Although neither the majority nor the dissenting opinion makes the point clear, the decision can be justified only on the ground that Goldman, unlike O'Callahan, was operating in "a zone of conflict," and his case was thus excluded from the ambit of that decision by Justice Douglas's observation that it dealt only "with peacetime offenses, not with authority stemming from the war power." But this basis, too, seems unsound: even if the Vietnam hostilities are considered "war" for this purpose, there was no visible military reason, beyond the convenience of the Government in obtaining witnesses, why Goldman could not have been shipped to the United States to stand trial. The argument that the exigencies of the Vietnam war required military control of soldiers more complete than would be needed in peacetime, proves too much; it would follow that during the Vietnam conflict courts-martial could have tried, without regard to service-connection, even offenses committed in the United States—which the Judge Advocates never argued and the military courts never held.

The reasoning that *O'Callahan* limits jurisdiction only when the accused would otherwise be entitled to trial by jury likewise led COMA to decide that the Marine Corps could try Private First Class Michael Sharkey by special court-martial for being drunk and disorderly in a public place,[93] since "petty" offenses, punishable by no more than six months in the cooler, are not within the Sixth Amendment's guarantee of trial by jury.[94] Special courts-martial, for minor offenses, are far more common than general courts. But for many offenses, a special court can award not merely six months confinement and corresponding forfeitures of pay, but a Bad Conduct Discharge; Sharkey himself drew one. A BCD has, of course, no analogue in civilian jurisprudence, but it is plainly so serious a penalty (for, like a Dishonorable Discharge, it involves loss of substantial rights) that an offense for which it can be imposed seems rather more than "petty."

Thus, the military courts, taking advantage of the ambiguities and exceptions with which the *O'Callahan* decision is lavishly supplied, have construed it in such a way as to permit courts-martial to try most of the nonmilitary crimes that they would have been likely to try before that decision. The civilian courts have thus far taken a generally similar line. The Supreme Court itself agreed (unanimously, for a wonder) that Corporal Isiah Relford, who raped a pair of civilians, one visiting and one employed at Fort Dix, within the confines of that post, could constitutionally be court-martialed, though he might also have been tried in the courts of New Jersey: "When a serviceman is charged with an offense committed within or at the geographical boundary of a military post and violative of the security of a person or property there, that offense may be tried by a court-martial."[95] It will be noted that the Supreme Court did not quite say that the location of the offense on the reservation is by itself sufficient grounds; Relford's crimes also affected the safety of others on the post. A soldier who concocted a fradulent income tax return while sitting at his desk in the headquarters building would probably still be entitled to whatever benefit there might be in a civilian trial.

The civilian courts, like the military, have found service-connection where the victims were servicemen; the Court of Appeals for the Fifth Circuit so held in the case of a Navy lieutenant charged with a series of homosexual rapes, at pistol point, of naval enlisted men, though the gallant officer wore civilian clothes and the rapes occurred outside the base.[96] (The fact that offenses, when committed on post or against the persons and property of other servicemen, or government property, may be tried by court-martial does not, however, mean that they *must* be so tried: When soldiers stationed at Fort Leavenworth were put on trial in a civilian court for stealing government property, and noted with dismay that the maximum penalty under the United States Penal Code was twice as long as that under the Manual for Courts-Martial's Table of Maximum Punishments, the civilian court made short work of their attempt to read *O'Callahan* backwards by contending that since their offense was service-connected, it could be tried *only* by a military court.[97])

Civilian judges, considering that the invalidation of military jurisdiction to try soldiers accused of crimes against the inhabitants of foreign countries would get the accused nothing more than a trial in the local courts and confinement in the local jails, have joined their military brethren in concluding that *O'Callahan* does not apply to such cases.[98] One district court decided that, since Okinawa is in a foreign country, that exclusion applied there too, despite the fact that the accused could have been tried in the civilian courts of the former American Military Government of that island, whose procedures generally resembled those of American courts—including both grand and petty juries.[99] Civil courts have had less occasion to consider the propriety of military jurisdiction over petty offenses, for the recipient of a sentence of six months or less is likely to be out of jail before he can attack his conviction in the civil courts, but at least one district court, refusing to enjoin a military trial on charges of smoking marijuana on the post, has indicated agreement as to the inapplicability of *O'Callahan* to petty offenses.[100] In short, about the only significant note of disagreement between military and civilian judges are holdings by the latter that the mere possession or use of marijuana by a soldier, not on duty or on military premises, is not service-connected within the meaning of *O'Callahan*.[101]

The Supreme Court has not passed on these questions, although it has agreed to review the off-post marijuana law. Its opinion in the *Relford* case emphasized that challenges to military jurisdiction over offenses would be approached *ad hoc*, on a case by case basis. Justice Blackmun, not unsympathetic to the difficulties of military prosecutors and the lower courts, admitted that

> [A]ny *ad hoc* approach leaves outer boundaries undetermined. *O'Callahan* marks an area, perhaps not the limit, for the concern of the civil courts and where the military may not enter. The case today marks an area, perhaps not the limit, where the court-martial is appropriate and permissible. What lies between is for decision at another time.

If this left military lawyers little wiser than they were before, Justice Blackmun did at least begin to sort out the confusion by listing no less than a dozen distinct factors on which the *O'Callahan* decision was based and whose presence or absence would be relevant to the decision of future cases—the serviceman's proper absence from the base; the crime's commission away from the base; its commission at a place not under military control; its commission within our territorial limits and not in an occupied zone of a foreign country; its commission in peacetime and its being unrelated to authority stemming from the war power; the absence of any connection between the defendant's military duties and the crime; the victim's not being engaged in the performance of any duty relating to the military; the presence and availability of a civilian court (he did not say an *American* court) in which the case can be prosecuted; the absence of any flouting of military authority; the absence of any threat to a military post; the absence of any violation of military property; and the offenses being among those traditionally prosecuted in civilian courts. What he did not indicate, of course, was the weight to be attached to each of these circumstances and what would happen when some are present and others not. Since the permutations and combinations are almost, if not quite, infinite, it is obvious that *O'Callahan* will be troublesome for years to come.

The Supreme Court did, however, clear up one large question on which the Circuit Courts of Appeal had split, when a majority held (although the Justices did not agree on the reasons for the holding) that *O'Callahan* was not retroactive—*i.e.*, that it did not invalidate convictions that had become final before the date of its decision.[102] Had the case gone the other way, hundreds and maybe thousands of prisoners would have been sprung, and thousands more military convicts would have been entitled to honorable discharges and possibly to back pay.

Whether *O'Callahan* v. *Parker* is a right reading of the Constitution is at least debatable; Justice Harlan's dissent seems very persuasive to me. But as a matter of *policy*—although such questions ought in theory to be left to Congress rather than the Court—there is much to be said for it. If only for reasons of public relations, it is just as well that the military courts confine themselves to cases having military significance. I doubt that soldiers who indulge their criminous proclivities, or are accused of doing so, will be better off than they were before. So long as the soldier has the option of trial by a military judge, with a minimum of "command influence," he gets much the same process he would get, for instance, in the courts of Japan or France or Germany, whose juryless criminal justice is, *pace* Justice Douglas, no less civilized than ours. Soldiers who are stationed in communities with bad civilian-military relations, and perhaps Negro soldiers stationed in some of the states of the old Confederacy, may be less than overjoyed by their liberation from military justice. But it must be remembered that court-martial jurisdiction over nonmilitary offenses has never been exclusive,[103] and that many or most such cases would probably have been tried in the local courts even before *O'Callahan.*

But regardless of the relative merits of civilian and military criminal process, the public seems to agree with the Supreme Court that the power of the military should generally be confined as straitly as is compatible with the discipline and efficiency of the armed forces. It is hard to argue that much harm is done to military efficiency by removing from military control the sort of soldier who typically gets in trouble with the civilian authorities. If he is innocent, he is returned to the service; if he is guilty, the Army can probably get along without him.

Once we say that military courts have jurisdiction

over the accused and the offense, it is not clear what constitutional rights he *does* have; and indeed, the Supreme Court has yet to hold squarely that he has any at all. To this problem we turn next.

Notes to Chapter Three

[1]The problems of the trial of civilians by other types of military tribunal, under international law or in domestic emergencies, are discussed in Chapters V, VI, and VII.

[2] *See generally* WIENER, CIVILIANS UNDER MILITARY JUSTICE (1967) for a scholarly, comprehensive, and eminently readable account of the British practice before, during and since the American Revolution.

[3] *See* WINTHROP, at 98, n. 83.

[4] *Ex parte* Henderson, 11 Fed. Cas. 1067 (No. 6349) (C.C.D. Ky. 1878). The case was actually decided in 1866, though not reported until twelve years later. *See* WINTHROP, at 106.

[5] *E.g., In re* Bogart, 3 Fed. Cas. 796 (No. 1596) (C.C.D. Cal. 1873); Kronberg v. Hale, 180 F.2d 128 (9th Cir. 1950),*cert. denied* 339 U.S. 969 (1950); Marino v. Hildreth, 61 F. Supp. 667 (E.D.N.Y. 1945); *Ex parte* Joly, 290 Fed. 858 (S.D.N.Y. 1922).

[6]United States *ex rel.* Hirshberg v. Cooke, 336 U.S. 210 (1949). There had been much inconclusive debate on the point, although the Army since 1862, and the Navy until 1932, had taken the position that an honorable discharge cut off liability to military

punishment for any and all offenses theretofore committed. The position was based on the Supreme Court's holding in United States v. Kelly, 82 U.S. 34 (1873), that an honorable discharge was "a formal final judgment passed by the government upon the entire military record of the soldier, and an authoritative declaration by it that he had left the service in a status of honor." *See Ex parte* Drainer, 65 F. Supp. 410 (N.D. Cal. 1946), *aff'd* 158 F.2d 981 (9th Cir. 1946). This was true enough in the Kelly case, where the issue was whether Kelly, who had deserted, returned voluntarily, made good the time lost and been given an honorable discharge, was entitled to a bounty as an honorably discharged veteran of the Civil War. But this explanation of the rule made little sense when the honorable discharge was based simply on ignorance. There were many puzzling varieties of the problem of the effect on court-martial jurisdiction of a hiatus in military status between the crime and the trial, all calculated to test the ingenuity of Judge Advocates: For example, did a so-called "short discharge," conditioned on reenlistment, wash away the recipient's sins? The Court of Military Appeals a few years ago abolished a great deal of esoteric legal learning by holding that any kind of honorable discharge, though followed by reenlistment, insulates the soldier from prosecution by the military—unless his offense is one of those covered by Article 3 of the Code, discussed below. Ginyard, 16 U.S.C.M.A. 512 (1967).

[7]Hironimus v. Durant, 168 F.2d 288 (4th Cir. 1948), *cert. denied* 335 U.S. 818 (1948). Her husband, Colonel Jack Durant, whose romance blossomed from their common interest in the collection of historic gems, stayed in jail for similar reasons. Durant v. Hiatt, 81 F. Supp. 948 (N.D. Ga. 1948), *aff'd sub nom.* Durant v. Gough, 177 F.2d 373 (5th Cir. 1949).

[8]*In re* LoDolce, 106 F. Supp. 455 (W.D.N.Y. 1952). The decision rejected, on dubious grounds, the Italian government's request for extradition.

[9]Art. 3(a), UCMJ.

[10]WINTHROP, at 105.

[11]Justice Felix Frankfurter, who as a young man had served as a Judge Advocate and known Crowder well, described him as "one of the best professional brains I've encountered in life" and "a heroic character." *See* Felix Frankfurter Reminisces (1960).

[12] *See* WIENER, CIVILIANS UNDER MILITARY JUSTICE 305–308 (1967). This reasoning, as Colonel Wiener points out, rested on the idea, prevalent among both military and civilian lawyers before the *Toth* Case, that the fifth amendment's *exception* from the grand jury requirement was a *grant* of jurisdiction.

[13] United States *ex rel.* Toth v. Quarles, 350 U.S. 11 (1955).

[14] The conviction of one of them, Mrs. Clarice B. Covert, had been reversed by the Court of Military Appeals, 6 U.S.C.M.A. 48 (1955), but when she filed her petition the Air Force still held her in custody for retrial.

[15] Kinsella v. Krueger, 351 U.S. 470 (1956); Reid v. Covert, 351 U.S. 487 (1956).

[16] Reid v. Covert and Kinsella v. Krueger, 354 U.S. 1 (1957).

[17] Kinsella v. Singleton, 361 U.S. 234 (1960) (dependent could not be tried for noncapital offense); Grisham v. Hagan, 361 U.S. 278 (1960) (employee could not be tried on capital charge of murdering his wife, Dolly Dimples Grisham); McElroy v. Guagliardo, 361 U.S. 281 (1960) (employee not triable for noncapital offense).

[18] Latney v. Ignatius, 416 F.2d 821 (D.C. Cir. 1969).

[19] Averette, 19 U.S.C.M.A. 363 (1970); Robb v. United States, 456 F.2d 768 (Ct. Cl. 1972). COMA's decision is not easy to reconcile with an earlier one which held that hostilities in Vietnam made November 3, 1964, "time of war" for the purposes of Article 43 of the Code, which suspends the statute of limitations on desertion in time of war. Anderson, 17 U.S.C.M.A. 588 (1968).

[20] *See generally* Bishop, *Court-Martial Jurisdiction over Military-Civilian Hybrids: Retired Regulars, Reservists and Discharged Prisoners,* 112 U. PA. L. REV. 317 (1964).

[21] Wallace v. Chafee, 451 F.2d 1374 (9th Cir. 1971), *cert. denied, sub nom.* Wallace v. Warner, 409 U.S. 933 (1972).

[22] Schuering, 16 U.S.C.M.A. 324 (1966). Judge Homer Ferguson had his doubts. The conviction of Schuering, a marine reservist who had stolen government property during a weekend drill, was reversed because the Navy had no power to order him to active duty in order to court-martial him.

[23] *See* S. Rep. No. 486, 81st Cong., 1st. Sess. 4–5, 7 (1949).

[24] The Extradition Treaty with Germany, like most such treaties, probably did not cover American citizens. *Cf.* Valentine v.

United States *ex rel.* Neidecker, 299 U.S. 5 (1936).

[25]Wheeler v. Reynolds, 164 F. Supp. 951 (N.D. Fla. 1958).

[26]Wheeler, 10 U.S.C.M.A. 646 (1959).

[27]Gallagher, 7 U.S.C.M.A. 506 (1957); Atkinson v. Kish, 176 F. Supp. 820 (M.D. Pa. 1959).

[28]Simcox v. Madigan, 298 F.2d 742 (9th Cir. 1962), *cert. denied* 370 U.S. 964 (1962). *See* Kahn v. Anderson, 255 U.S. 1 (1921). The Court of Military Appeals is of like opinion. Peebles v. Froehlke, 22 U.S.C.M.A. 266 (1973); Nelson, 14 U.S.C.M.A. 93 (1963); Ragan, 14 U.S.C.M.A. 119 (1963).

[29]*See Committee on the Uniform Code of Military Justice, Good Order and Discipline in the Army, Report to Honorable Wilber M. Brucker, Secretary of the Army* 175 (1960).

[30]*See* Wall Street Journal, Dec. 29, 1972, at 4.

[31]Act of August 3, 1861, ch. 42, 12 Stat. 287. The primeval congressional provisions for retirement distinguished between those who were "wholly retired" (with a year's pay) and who thereupon became pure civilians, not subject to the Articles of War, and those who were merely retired from active service, retaining both their entitlement to pay and their subjection to the Articles. *See* 29 OPS. ATT'Y GEN. 397, 401–02 (1912); WINTHROP, 746–47. The connection between pay status and subjection to the Articles of War is still reflected in the Uniform Code.

[32]The Army's retired list was for many years limited to 300. Act of July 15, 1870, ch. 294, § 5, 16 Stat. 317; see Runkle v. United States, 122 U.S. 543, 549 (1887). By 1895 retired officers and enlisted men together aggregated only 1,562. *See* WINTHROP, at 87.

[33]53 Cong. Rec. 12844–45 (1916). Wilson's veto message is quoted *in extenso* in Hooper, 9 U.S.C.M.A. 637, 643–45 (1958).

[34]During the course of the Senate hearings on the Uniform Code Senator Estes Kefauver, a Democrat, purported to be somewhat alarmed by the thought that General Dwight D. Eisenhower, Admiral Chester Nimitz, or other members of the retired list might be court-martialed for "calling public officials what they really are." *See Hearings on S. 857 Before a Subcommittee of the Senate Committee on Armed Services,* 81st Cong., 1st Sess. 330 (1949). Senator Leverett Saltonstall, a Republican, did not view the prospect with similar alarm. At that time General Eisenhower was not known to

be a Republican and was, indeed, regarded in some circles as a likely candidate for the Democratic nomination in 1952.

[35]MCM, ¶ 167.

[36]53 CONG. REC. 12845 (1916).

[37]4 MOMMSEN, HISTORY OF ROME 527 (Dickson transl. 1889). *See also* SUETONIUS, THE LIVES OF THE TWELVE CAESARS 43 (Forester transl. 1903).

[38]No fewer than four agents of the Office of Naval Intelligence, two of them commissioned officers, established a stakeout on the roof of a neighboring house, whence they could observe, with the aid of binoculars, the goings-on in the Admiral's bedroom.

[39]WC NCM 57–00988 (unpublished), Sept. 10, 1957. The Board, referring to the "time-honored jurisdiction of courts-martial to try retired regular personnel," ruled that Hooper's case was one arising in the naval forces within the meaning of that clause of the Fifth Amendment and that he was "still an officer of the Navy." It held further that his pay was in the nature of salary, rather than a pension for past services of which he could not constitutionally be deprived.

[40]10 U.S.C. § 6481.

[41]Since the accused had flag rank, review by that court was mandatory under article 67(b) (1) of the Code.

[42]Hooper v. Hartman, 163 F. Supp. 437, 441–42 (S.D. Cal. 1958), *aff'd* 274 F.2d 429 (9th Cir. 1959).

[43]Hooper, 9 U.S.C.M.A. 637, 645 (1958). COMA reaffirmed its holding in a subsequent case involving a retired Air Force sergeant. Bowie, 14 U.S.C.M.A. 631 (1964).

[44]Hooper v. United States, 326 F.2d 982 (Ct. Cl. 1964), *cert. denied* 377 U.S. 977 (1964).

[45]Hooper v. Laird, 19 U.S.C.M.A. 329 (1970).

[46]Chambers v. Russell, 192 F. Supp. 425 (N.D. Cal. 1961).

[47]Act of July 13, 1866, ch. 176, § 5, 14 Stat. 92; 10 U.S.C. § 1161(a). *See* Wallace v. United States, 257 U.S. 541, 545 (1922); Blake v. United States, 103 U.S. 227, 234–35 (1881); Allen v. United States, 91 F. Supp. 933, 935 (Ct. Cl. 1950); BURNS, THE DEADLOCK OF DEMOCRACY 74 (1963); Colby, *The Power of the President To Remove Officers of the Army*, 15 GEO. L. J. 168 (1927).

[48]*Cf.* Myers v. United States, 272 U.S. 52 (1926), which held

unconstitutional a statute providing that postmasters could be removed only with the advice and consent of the Senate. Even Justice Louis D. Brandeis, who dissented, recognized that there might be a stronger case for the President's power to dismiss Army and Navy officers.

[49] *See, e.g.,* 10 U.S.C. §§ 3781–87, 3791–97, 6384, 8781–87, 8791–97. The history of these statutes and regulations, and the administrative practice under them, were exhaustively described in the course of Senate hearings in 1962. *See Hearings on Constitutional Rights of Military Personnel Before the Subcommittee on Constitutional Rights of the Senate Committee on the Judiciary,* 87th Cong., 2d Sess. 736–73, 800–02 (1962).

[50] 10 U.S.C. § 1161(b). (Navy Regulations provide for the exercise of this authority. 32 C.F.R. § 714.5 (1972). There seems to be no corresponding Army or Air Force Regulation.) There appears to be no similar statute respecting enlisted men. But, since the Tenure of Office Act places no restriction on their separation, the President's authority to discharge a retired enlisted man is presumably intact. The Hiss Act, 5 U.S.C. §§ 8311–8322, cuts off the retired pay of persons convicted of various offenses against national security. But even that statute, though originally passed at a time when Congress was far from finicky about the rights of subversives, real or suspected, never cut off retired pay the right to receive which had accrued prior to its enactment, and it has been held unconstitutional, as an *ex post facto* law, insofar as it attempted to cut off retirement benefits, to whose receipt the recipient was not yet entitled when the bill was passed, because of an offense committed prior to that date. Hiss v. Hampton, 338 F. Supp. 1141 (D.D.C. 1972).

[51] "Upon ceasing to hold the office, the right to pay, being an emolument thereof and dependent thereon, likewise ceases." Hooper v. Hartman, 163 F. Supp. 437, 441 (S.D. Cal. 1958), *aff'd* 274 F.2d 429 (9th Cir. 1959).

[52] *Compare* Geddes v. United States, 38 Ct. Cl. 438, 445 (1903) *with* Steelman v. United States, 318 F.2d 733, 734 (Ct. Cl. 1963).

[53] Berkey v. United States, 361 F.2d 983, 990 (Ct. Cl. 1966).

[54] Lynch v. United States, 292 U.S. 571, 576–77 (1934). The Court cited United States v. Teller, 107 U.S. 64 (1883), Frisbie v. United States, 157 U.S. 160 (1895), and United States v. Cook, 257

U.S. 523 (1922). Only Teller is in point on its facts; the other two are at best dicta. Teller held only that a wounded veteran of the Mexican War, who had been in receipt of a pension under an act of Congress, could not, when that pension was superseded by a larger one under a later pension act which cut off all lesser pensions under previous laws, claim a constitutional right to receive both pensions. Though the Court did state that "no pensioner has a vested legal right to his pension" and that "pensions are the bounties of the government, which Congress has the right to give, withhold, distribute, or recall, at its discretion," 107 U.S. at 68, the pension involved was in fact in the nature of a gratuity, in the sense that Congress had not provided for it until after the pensioner had received his wounds; it could hardly have been regarded as one of the terms of his employment. Lynch itself held that benefits under War Risk Insurance, being bottomed on contract, could not constitutionally be reduced by Congress.

[55] *See* Note, 70 HARV. L. REV. 490 (1957); Note, 53 HARV. L. REV. 1375 (1940).

[56] The Court has held that Congress could constitutionally cut off the Social Security benefits of aliens deported for having been Communists, since the right to such benefits was not an "accrued property right." Flemming v. Nestor, 363 U.S. 603 (1960). The dissenters argued that the termination amounted to punishment without judicial trial. *Id.* at 622, 640.

[57] Another type of civilian in uniform is the youth who enlists by falsely claiming to be over 18 (or, if his parents consent, 17). Since his enlistment is invalid, he remains a civilian who cannot be court-martialed, unless and until he effects a constructive enlistment by voluntarily remaining in the service after he comes of age. *See* Graham, 22 U.S.C.M.A. 75 (1972).

[58] Toth v. Quarles, 350 U.S. 11, 23 (1955).

[59] Kinsella v. Singleton, 361 U.S. 234, 240–41, 246 (1960).

[60] O'Callahan v. Parker, 395 U.S. 258 (1969).

[61] *See* Nichols, *The Devil's Article*, 22 MIL. L. REV. 111 (1963). The general article, probably borrowed from the Articles of Gustavus Adolphus of 1621, first appeared in the British Articles of 1625, in language even broader than that quoted in the text: "All other disorders whatsoever are to be punished, as these formerly nominated."

[62] *See, e.g.*, Harlan, J., dissenting in O'Callahan v. Parker, 395

U.S. at 275; Nelson & Westbrook, *Court-Martial Jurisdiction over Servicemen for "Civilian" Offenses: An Analysis of O'Callahan v. Parker,* 54 MINN. L.REV. 1, 6–19 (1969).

[63]WINTHROP, at 723–724.
[64]*Id.* at 725.
[65]*Ex parte* Mason, 105 U.S. 696 (1882).
[66]WINTHROP, at 832.
[67]5 OPS. ATT'Y GEN. 55 (1848).
[68]*See* HARLOW, OLD BOWERY DAYS (1931), pp. 345–46.
[69]*See* Coleman v. Tennessee, 97 U.S. 509, 514 (1879).
[70]Ch. 75 § 30, 12 Stat. 736.
[71]Coleman v. Tennessee, 97 U.S. 509 (1879).
[72]The Secretary of War, apparently concerned about the effect of the honorable discharge, sought the advice of the Attorney General, who ruled that, since it rested on fraud, it was a nullity and Coleman simply a military convict awaiting the execution of his sentence. But, considering the lapse of time, he recommended to President Hayes that that sentence be commuted to life imprisonment. 16 OPS. ATT'Y GEN. 349 (1879).
[73]For this purpose a female officer is a gentleman. MCM, ¶ 212. Conduct that is unladylike is even harder to define than that which is ungentlemanly.
[74]MCM, ¶ 213(f) (7). *See* Note, *Imprisonment for Debt: In the Military Tradition,* 80 YALE L. J. 1679 (1971).
[75]Levy v. Parker, 478 F.2d 772 (3d Cir. 1972).
[76]Avrech v. Secretary of the Navy, 477 F.2d 1237 (D.C. Cir. 1973). A district court had earlier held that the specification of making a "statement disloyal to the United States" in violation of article 134 was unconstitutionally vague, especially since it impinged on the sensitive area of freedom of speech, but it stopped short of holding unconstitutional the general article itself. Stolte v. Laird, 353 F. Supp. 1392 (D.D.C. 1972).
[77]MCM, ¶ 213(e). *See* Grafton v. United States, 206 U.S. 333 (1907).
[78]MCM, ¶¶ 212, 213.
[79]Sadinsky, 14 U.S.C.M.A. 563 (1964).
[80]Jordan v. DeGeorge, 341 U.S. 223, 231–32 (1951); *see* Wiener, *Are the General Military Articles Unconstitutionally Vague?,* 54 A.B.A.J. 357 (1968).
[81]Hale, 20 U.S.C.M.A. 150, 158 (1970).

[82]*E.g.*, Rego, 19 U.S.C.M.A. 9 (1969); Cook, 19 U.S.C.M.A. 13 (1969).

[83]*E.g.*, Henderson, 18 U.S.C.M.A. 601 (1969); Armes, 19 U.S.C.M.A. 15 (1969); Snyder, 20 U.S.C.M.A. 102 (1970).

[84]Riehle, 18 U.S.C.M.A. 603 (1969).

[85]Swisher v. Moseley, 442 F.2d 1331 (10th Cir. 1971).

[86]*E.g.*, Frazier, 19 U.S.C.M.A. 40 (1969); Fryman, 19 U.S.C.M.A. 71 (1969).

[87]*E.g.*, Beeker, 18 U.S.C.M.A. 563 (1969); Castro, 18 U.S.C.M.A. 598 (1969). COMA recently stuck to its position, rejecting the reasoning of civilian courts which had held the contrary. Rainville, 22 U.S.C.M.A. 464 (1973).

[88]Harris, 18 U.S.C.M.A. 596 (1969).

[89]Levy v. Parker, 478 F.2d 772 (3d Cir. 1972); Stolte v. Laird, 353 F. Supp. 1392 (D.D.C. 1972).

[90]As a matter of international law, the sovereign in whose territory a crime is committed has the primary right to try one accused of the crime, regardless of his nationality or status as a member of the armed forces of a friendly country, unless it agrees to waive that right. Wilson v. Girard, 354 U.S. 524 (1957); United States *ex rel.* Stone v. Robinson, 431 F.2d 548 (3d Cir. 1970). Under most of the Status of Forces Agreements which regulate jurisdiction over American servicemen stationed in foreign countries, the host country has the primary right to try offenses against its nationals or their property, but may waive it. *See generally* SNEE & PYE, STATUS OF FORCES AGREEMENTS AND CRIMINAL JURISDICTION (1957). A soldier who contends that his trial in a foreign court did not meet the standards of fairness required by the Status of Forces Agreement, and that the United States is thus under no duty to surrender him to the foreign authorities, must address the argument to the military and diplomatic authorities, for the courts will not interfere with their discretion. Holmes v. Laird, 459 F.2d 1211 (D.C. Cir. 1972), *cert. denied* 409 U.S. 869 (1972).

[91]Keaton, 19 U.S.C.M.A. 64 (1969); Weinstein, 19 U.S.C.M.A. 29 (1969).

[92]Goldman, 18 U.S.C.M.A. 389, and *on petition for rehearing* 18 U.S.C.M.A. 516 (1969). Judge Ferguson dissented.

[93]Sharkey, 19 U.S.C.M.A. 26 (1969).

[94]*See, e.g.*, Duncan v. Louisiana, 391 U.S. 145 (1968).

[95]Relford v. Commandant, 401 U.S. 355, 369 (1971), fol-

lowed in Harkcom v. Parker, 439 F.2d 265 (3d Cir. 1971). Other federal courts of appeals had already come to a similar conclusion. Diorio v. McBride, 431 F.2d 730 (5th Cir. 1970); Zenor v. Vogt, 434 F.2d 189 (5th Cir. 1970), *cert. denied;* 401 U.S. 995 (1971); King v. Moseley, 430 F.2d 732 (10th Cir. 1970).
  [96]Silvero v. Chief of Naval Air Basic Training, 428 F.2d 1009 (5th Cir. 1970). *Accord:* Zenor v. Vogt and King v. Moseley, *supra* note 95.
  [97]United States v. Bixler, 321 F. Supp. 268 (D.Kans. 1971).
  [98]Bell v. Clarke, 437 F.2d 200 (4th Cir. 1971); Hemphill v. Moseley, 443 F.2d 322 (10th Cir. 1971); Gallagher v. United States, 423 F.2d 1371 (Ct. Cl. 1970), *cert. denied* 400 U.S. 849 (1970); Wimberley v. Laird, 472 F.2d 923 (7th Cir. 1973); Williams v. Froehlke, 356 F. Supp. 591 (S.D.N.Y. 1973).
  [99]Williamson v. Alldridge, 320 F. Supp. 840 (W.D. Okla. 1970); *cf.* Jacobs v. Froehlke, 334 F.Supp. 1107 (D.D.C. 1971) *aff'd on other grounds* 481 F.2d 540 (D.C. Cir. 1973). In O'Callahan's case Justice Douglas had in fact stressed that "the offenses were committed within our territorial limits, not in the occupied zone of a foreign country."
  [100]Diorio v. McBride, 306 F. Supp. 528 (N.D. Ala. 1969), *aff'd on other grounds* 431 F.2d 730 (5th Cir. 1970).
  [101]Cole v. Laird, 468 F.2d 829 (5th Cir. 1972); Councilman v. Laird, 481 F.2d 613 (10th Cir. 1973) (off-base sale of marijuana to another serviceman held not service-connected, *cert. granted* Dec. 17, 1973); Moylan v. Laird, 305 F. Supp. 551 (D.R.I. 1969); Lyle v. Kincaid, 344 F. Supp. 223 (M.D. Fla. 1972), modified 352 F. Supp. 81 (M.D. Fla. 1972); Schroth v. Warner, 353 F. Supp. 1032 (D. Hawaii 1973).
  [102]Gosa v. Mayden and Warner v. Flemings, 935. Ct. 2936 (1973).
  [103]Caldwell v. Parker, 252 U.S. 376 (1920). The Court did not hold that Congress could not give the military exclusive jurisdiction over soldiers, but merely that it had not chosen to do so. In an earlier case the Court, while coming to the same conclusion about the intent of Congress, plainly assumed that it had constitutional power to bar civilian courts from trying soldiers. Coleman v. Tennessee, 97 U.S. 509 (1879). It should be noted that in each of these cases the crime was committed in wartime.

CHAPTER FOUR

The Bill of Rights and the Serviceman

"*T*HE POWER OF CON-
gress, in the government of the land and naval
forces," said Chief Justice Chase more than a century
ago, "is not at all affected by the fifth or any other
amendment."[1] If this were the law—and the Supreme
Court has never said plainly that it is not—soldiers
would have no more rights than slaves had, and Congress would be free to make the military code as summary and cruel as the criminal law of Nazi Germany or
Stalinist Russia.

The language of the Bill of Rights does little to
resolve the question. Only one of its protections is
explicitly denied to soldiers: the Fifth Amendment excepts from its requirement of grand jury indictment in
cases of "capital or otherwise infamous crimes"—

which is in reality not a very valuable right[2]—"Cases arising in the land or naval Forces." All the Amendments which spell out our basic rights are, on their faces, as applicable to soldiers as to civilians. Yet all of the Articles of War and Articles for the Government of the Navy which have been enacted since the birth of the Republic contained provisions obviously inconsistent with the Bill of Rights. The Uniform Code, which for the first time gave soldiers most of the procedural protections included in the first ten Amendments, has no provision for either trial by jury or bail, and (in recognition of the fact that soldier witnesses are more likely to move away or be killed than are civilian witnesses) it allows the prosecution to introduce written depositions in noncapital cases,[3] which would violate a civilian defendant's Sixth Amendment right to confront the witnesses against him. The Supreme Court long agreed with Congress that where military men and courts were concerned, the First, Fourth, Fifth, Sixth, and Eighth Amendments are irrelevant. The Court has never to this day squarely held that a soldier has any constitutional rights when he is court-martialed, or indeed that he has any constitutional rights of any variety. The more excitable and less learned critics of military justice have a simple explanation of the apparent paradox; the Justices, from Bushrod Washington and John Marshall to Holmes, Brandeis, Cardozo, and Hughes, ignored their oaths and conspired with Congress to perpetrate a deliberate and outrageous nullification of the Constitution.[4]

The contention has indeed been made, and in the august pages of the Harvard Law Review at that, that the framers of the Bill of Rights did mean those Amendments to apply to soldiers and sailors.[5] But, as an eminent constitutional lawyer observed, "within the year, two massive articles by Frederick Bernays Wiener showed otherwise."[6] It is as certain as any historical proposition can be that men who were contemporaries of the framers of the Bill of Rights (*e.g.*, the Congressmen who enacted the Articles for the Government of the Navy of 1799 and the Articles of War of 1806), and the framers themselves, never supposed that soldiers were included within its protection. In 1814, for example, General William Hull was court-martialed for having surrendered Detroit without firing a shot, in the preceding year. Hull claimed that the Sixth Amendment entitled him to have his counsel examine witnesses and address the court. If he had he been tried in a civil court, he would clearly have been right; but the military court, unwilling to have justice obfuscated by the pettifoggery of civilian lawyers, ruled against him. He was found guilty and sentenced to the firing squad. President Madison, who certainly knew as much as any living man about the intentions of the framers of the Bill of Rights, approved the sentence without comment, though he allayed such qualms as General Hull may have suffered by remitting its execution.[7]

The assumption that the Bill of Rights was not for soldiers was certainly shared by the Supreme Court, at least for the Republic's first century and a half. Chief

Justice Chase's quoted statement was only dictum, for the issue in the case was whether a civilian could constitutionally be tried by a military commission, and he made it in a concurring opinion, rather than an opinion of the Court. But none of his brethren contradicted him. Indeed, the Court had little occasion to consider the matter until modern times, for few soldiers or lawyers saw any hope in arguing that the Bill of Rights had anything to do with courts-martial. On the rare occasions when they made the extraordinary contention that it did, they got short shrift from the Justices. Consider, for example, *Keyes* v. *United States,*[8] a suit by a cashiered second lieutenant in the Fifth Cavalry to collect his pay, on the ground that the court-martial which sentenced him to dismissal from the service was too unfair to be valid. The "mere errors" in that case, as found by the Court of Claims, included the facts that the colonel commanding the regiment had preferred one of the charges, had appeared as a prosecution witness, and, sitting as a member of the court-martial, had voted to convict and cashier. The Supreme Court affirmed the dismissal of Keyes' petition on the uncomplicated ground that, since "the court-martial . . . had cognizance of the charges made, and had jurisdiction of the person of the appellant . . . whatever irregularities or errors are alleged to have occurred in the proceedings, the sentence of dismissal must be held valid when it is questioned in this collateral way." Even Captain Oberlin Carter, an indefatigable long-distance litigant, could find no chink or cranny in the wall between military and civilian justice, though he devoted nearly forty years of almost monomaniacal effort to attempts to secure the nullification of his court-martial sentence, and ended by alleging nothing less than personal prejudice on the part of the Assistant Judge Advocate General and the members of the court-martial; intimidation of defense witnesses, abstraction of defense documentary evidence, use by the prosecution of evidence known by it to be false, and sundry other irregularities, which, if they really occurred (and no court ever decided that they did not), would certainly seem to have given the proceedings some hint of unfairness. He never won a round.[9]

The Second World War saw armies of a size unprecedented in the history of the United States and, as a necessary corollary, courts-martial in numbers theretofore unimaginable. Despite large scale postwar clemency,[10] there remained in federal penal institutions a great number of men who were there pursuant to sentences of Army or Navy courts-martial.[11] Being no more anxious to stay in jail than their civilian counterparts, they presently took to the courts by squads and platoons. Few of the petitioners could adduce the orthodox grounds of collateral attack, for in practically every case, it was plain that the court-martial had had jurisdiction over the person and the offense, and power to impose the sentence; but it was inevitable, given the frequently amateur personnel of wartime courts-martial and the stresses and strains under which they operated, especially overseas, that some of the petitioners could tell startling, and some-

times apparently truthful, tales of unfairness calculated to cause a federal judge of average fairmind-
edness to chafe under the restrictions of the traditional rules, and make him receptive to the heterodox
proposition that even a soldier was entitled to some
sort of due process, whether by virtue of the Constitution or by the Articles of War, the denial of which
could make his court-martial conviction a nullity. In
Hicks v. *Hiatt*[12], for example, a senior circuit judge,
sitting as a district judge, granted a writ of habeas
corpus to a soldier convicted by general court-martial,
on the stated ground that the accumulation of errors
at the trial—notably in the admission and exclusion of
evidence—was so gross that the "procedures of the
military law were not applied to Hicks in a fundamen-
tally fair way."[13] Another circuit judge, also sitting as
a district judge, detonated with an ear-shattering ex-
plosion. Starting with the mild observation that "the
trial . . . in the eyes of both the prosecution and the
defense was wholly obnoxious and repulsive to their
fundamental sense of justice," he had "no difficulty in
finding that the court which tried this man was satu-
rated with tyranny; the compliance with the Articles of
War and with military justice was an empty and farcical
compliance only . . ."[14] The petitioner went free, at
least temporarily.[15] There were a number of other
cases in which inferior federal courts undertook to
conduct a searching review of allegedly unfair proceedings of courts-martial,[16] though in all probability
none of them got up quite as great a head of steam as
the judge just quoted.[17]

Despite these mutterings of discontent among the judicial proletariat, the Supreme Court was far from ready to open the safety valve. In *Humphrey* v. *Smith*,[18] the convict sought to impeach a court-martial verdict not only on the ground that the inadequacy of the pretrial investigation required by the Articles of War had deprived the court-martial of jurisdiction, but on the further ground that the incompetence of his counsel and errors in the admission of evidence had had that effect. The District Court, although disclaiming any intent to examine the record for error, did in fact review it carefully and found no merit in any of the contentions.[19] Basing its decision solely on the inadequacy of the pretrial investigation, the Court of Appeals ordered the writ granted.[20] Mr. Justice Black and five other Justices, reversing on the ground that the requirement of pretrial investigation was not jurisdictional, nevertheless went out of their way "at once [to] dispose of" Smith's other contentions,[21] citing the uncompromising decision, nearly half a century before, in Captain Carter's case. Yet a close observer might have discerned that the door was not quite slammed shut, for Mr. Justice Black, perhaps casually and perhaps with meticulous care, limited the holding to a "court-martial conviction resulting from a trial fairly conducted"[22]—a qualification which, however cautious, had not been adumbrated by anything in the language of earlier opinions. Moreover, although Smith's contentions went not only to the alleged absence of evidence sufficient to support his conviction, but also to the alleged unfairness of his trial, all that

Mr. Justice Black actually said was that, while the evidence "was in sharp dispute . . . our authority in habeas corpus proceedings to review court-martial judgments does not permit us to pass on the guilt or innocence of persons convicted by courts-martial"[23] —a proposition which, assuming the presence of some evidence to support the finding, is equally true of collateral review of civilian convictions. Finally, perusal of the district court's review of the record leaves one pretty well persuaded that Smith *was* guilty, a circumstance which in practice may not be altogether irrelevant; none of the Justices could have lost much sleep over the hardness of his case. Thus, the Smith case afforded no reliable basis for prophecy about what would happen if a really hard case reached the Court. In *Wade* v. *Hunter,* a case decided the same day, the Court refused to exclude the possibility that at least the double jeopardy provision of the Fifth Amendment was applicable to court-martial proceedings, though it found that Wade had not in fact been put twice in jeopardy.[24]

What seemed to a district court and a court of appeals a sufficiently hard case did in fact reach the Court the following year—a case in which the lower courts had directed the release of a military convict named Eugene Brown because the record was so "replete with highly prejudicial errors and irregularities" as to amount to a denial of due process in violation of the Fifth Amendment.[25] The Supreme Court unanimously[26] reversed and did so in terms calculated sharply to remind the errant lower courts that their function in military habeas corpus proceedings was only to examine the court-martial's authority to try the person and the offense, and to impose the sentence.

Nevertheless, it would strain the ordinary judicial conscience to ignore such errors as were found by the lower courts in Brown's case; those errors included: conviction of murder on "evidence that does not measure to malice, premeditation, or deliberation"; incompetence and lack of preparation of appointed defense counsel; "gross" incompetence of the court's law member; and "total misconception of the applicable law" by the military reviewing authorities.[27] If the proceedings had been concerned with a conviction by a civil court, such findings would certainly have presented a substantial question of denial of constitutional due process.

If the Brown case was a longish step to the rear, the Court later in the same term took a half pace forward. In *Whelchel v. McDonald*,[28] a case in which the petitioner in substance contended that he had been denied due process by the military reviewing authorities' rejection of his claim of insanity, Mr. Justice Douglas duly recited the conventional propositions that the only issue was "jurisdiction" and that the military's errors in evaluating the evidence of insanity did not affect its jurisdiction; but he added that the accused was entitled to an *opportunity* to present the defense of insanity and that a denial of that opportunity would have gone to jurisdiction. Whelchel had had that opportunity. There is nothing in the opinion to suggest that the result would have been different if the court-martial had found him mentally responsible after hearing a panel of seven psychiatrists unanimously testify that Whelchel was a hopeless lunatic; the error would have been only an error in evaluating the evidence. It was later said that *Whelchel* expanded the concept of "jurisdiction" in habeas corpus review of courts-martial,[29] but the expansion is measurable only with a micrometer.

But no matter what the draftsmen of the Constitution intended, and no matter what the Supreme Court may have said and done between 1791 and the Korean War, I think it safe to say that soldiers today have constitutional rights, although it would be most unsafe to dogmatize about the precise extent of those rights. *Brown* v. *Board of Education*[30] showed that neither the understanding of those who drafted and enacted the Fourteenth Amendment nor the prior holdings of the Supreme Court could preserve segregation by law when social conditions and public opinion had radically changed. The principle is, of course, quite as applicable to the constitutional rights of soldiers as to those of Negro children. Chief Justice Warren, speaking off the bench, put it very well in 1962:

I suppose it cannot be said that the courts of today are more knowledgeable about the requirements of military discipline than the courts in the early days of the Republic. Nevertheless, events quite unrelated to the expertise of the judiciary have required a modification in the traditional theory of the autonomy of military authority.

These events can be expressed very simply in numerical terms. A few months after Washington's first inauguration, our army numbered a mere 672 of the 840 authorized by Congress. Today, in dramatic contrast, the situation is this: Our armed forces number two and a half million; every resident male is a potential member of the peacetime armed forces; such service may occupy a minimum of four per cent of the adult life of the average American male reaching draft age; reserve obligations extend over ten per cent of such a person's life; and veterans are numbered in excess of twenty-two and a half million. When the authority of the military has such a sweeping capacity for affecting the lives of our citizenry, the wisdom of treating the military establishment as an enclave beyond the reach of the civilian courts almost inevitably is drawn into question.[31]

The reexamination has been under way for the last decade or so, in the White House and the Pentagon, in Congress, and in the federal courts, including the Supreme Court.

The process may be said to have begun, in an uncertain, hesitant, and confusing way, with *Burns* v. *Wilson*.[32] Chief Justice Warren, who was not yet a member of the Court when *Burns* was decided, spoke (in the address above-quoted) about as charitably of that decision as possible: "The various opinions of the members of the Court in *Burns* are not, perhaps, as clear on this point as they might be. Nevertheless, I believe they do constitute recognition of the proposition that our citizens in uniform may not be stripped of basic rights simply because they have doffed their civilian clothes." Since *Burns* is still the principal lighthouse in these trackless waters, however low its candlepower, and since the several opinions of the Justices represented most of the possible judicial points of view and will certainly be quoted when and if the Court finally clears up the question, the case deserves examination.

Burns and another airman had been convicted by general court-martial of a "particularly brutal" rape and murder and sentenced to death. Having exhausted the procedures of military review, they petitioned for writs of habeas corpus in the District of Columbia, which had jurisdiction over the respondent, the Secretary of Defense.[33] Burns and his copetitioner made a number of allegations, supported by possibly truthful affidavits and other evidence outside the record, which raised in the mind of one circuit judge such "serious doubt whether 'the whole course of events' from apprehension to conviction did not amount to a serious denial of fundamental fairness" that he wanted the case remanded for a hearing on the merits.[34] The petitioners alleged that they had been illegally detained; that their confessions had been coerced; that they had been denied the effective assistance of counsel; that favorable evidence had been suppressed and perjured testimony knowingly used; and that the trial was conducted in an atmosphere of "hysteria and terror." The district court summarily dismissed the petitions on the traditional ground that a civil court could investigate only the court-martial's jurisdiction over the person, the crime and the sentence—not whether it had denied the accused a fair trial. The Court of Appeals, though it examined the record in detail, affirmed—essentially on the ground that these issues of fact had been presented to and fully explored and resolved by the military authorities upon "substantial evidence."

In the Supreme Court four different opinions were filed; none was supported by a majority of the Court. In what many lower courts seem to have mistaken for a majority opinion, the largest faction, consisting of Chief Justice Fred M. Vinson and Justices Tom C. Clark, Harold H. Burton, and Stanley Reed, voted to affirm, stating that:

1. "The constitutional guarantee of due process is meaningful enough, and sufficiently adaptable, to protect soldiers—as well as civilians—from the crude injustices of a trial so conducted that it becomes bent on fixing guilt by dispensing with rudimentary fairness. . . ."

2. "But in military habeas corpus the inquiry, the scope of matters open for review, has always been more narrow than in civil cases." If the Uniform Code's provision (Article 76) that the determinations of military tribunals shall be final and binding on all courts does not altogether preclude habeas corpus jurisdiction, yet "these provisions do mean that when a military decision has dealt fully and fairly with an allegation raised in that application, it is not open to a federal civil court to grant the writ simply to reevaluate the evidence."

3. Thus, in the Burns case, "had the military courts manifestly refused to consider" the petitioners' allegations of fundamental unfairness, the district court

might have evaluated for itself the question of due process. But, since the record showed that the military courts "have heard petitioners out" on these matters, nothing remained for the civil courts to do.

Justices Robert H. Jackson and Sherman Minton concurred in the result. The former wrote no opinion, and the latter registered his pronounced and explicit disapproval of the idea that "the federal courts sit to protect the constitutional rights of military defendants," beyond satisfying themselves of the existence of jurisdiction in the traditional sense; he attested his orthodoxy by citing *In re Grimley*, [35] in which the Court, some sixty years before, had flatly stated that "no mere errors in [court-martial] proceedings are open to consideration" by the civil courts. Justice Felix Frankfurter cast a vote in favor of more light; he was unwilling either to affirm or reverse without more argument of the "questions of great delicacy and difficulty" that the case presented. Nevertheless, he did not wait for a fuller canvass of the problem to make the essentials of his position pretty clear:

> I cannot agree that the only inquiry that is open on an application for habeas corpus challenging a sentence of a military tribunal is whether that tribunal was legally constituted and had jurisdiction, technically speaking, over the person and the crime. Again, I cannot agree that the scope of inquiry is the same as that open to us on review of State convictions; the content of due process in civil trials does not control what is due process in military trials. Nor is the duty of the civil courts upon habeas corpus met simply when it is found that the military sentence has been reviewed by the

military hierarchy, although in a debatable situation we should no doubt attach more weight to the conclusions reached on controversial facts by military appellate courts than to those reached by the highest court of a State.

On petition for rehearing he added a significant gloss to his first opinion; demanding "well-focused argument and careful deliberation before enunciating the principle that a conviction by a constitutional court which lacked due process is open to attack by habeas corpus while an identically defective conviction when rendered by an *ad hoc* military tribunal is invulnerable," he made it clear that he saw no reason for treating the principle that jurisdiction may be "lost" by a denial of whatever process the Constitution required in the circumstances, as any less applicable to military than to civil courts.

Justices Hugo L. Black and William O. Douglas, though what they had to say seems at bottom not very different from the Frankfurter dictum, simply dissented. No reargument was needed to persuade them that some, if not all, of the rights conferred by the Fifth and Sixth Amendments applied to soldiers;[36] if not, they asked, why did the draftsmen of the Fifth think it necessary explicitly to except cases arising in the land or naval forces from the requirement of a presentment or indictment of a grand jury? The Court, they went on to say, had held in *Wade* v. *Hunter* that the double jeopardy provision of that Amendment was applicable to military proceedings; and surely, the right not to be compelled to be a witness against oneself is no less fundamental. Therefore, it was not enough that the military authorities might have given fair consideration to the constitutional question; the petitioners were entitled to a judicial hearing on the circumstances surrounding their confessions and to have those circumstances tested by the standards of due process formulated by the Supreme Court—not merely by whatever standards might have been formulated by Congress in the Uniform Code of Military Justice.

Unfortunately, the reasoning of the dissent lent little or no force to its conclusion, however right that conclusion may be. In the first place, the argument based on the explicit denial of the grand jury right is very infirm, if only because it proves a great deal too much. By a parity of reasoning, it could be shown that the framers of the Bill of Rights intended to apply to courts-martial the Sixth Amendment's requirement for "all criminal prosecutions" of an "impartial [petty] jury of the State and District wherein the crime shall have been committed"—which even Justices Black and Douglas conceded was not the case.[37] Secondly, *Wade* v. *Hunter* simply is not authority for the proposition for which the dissenters cited it, for what it actually held was no more than that "under the circumstances shown, the Fifth Amendment's double jeopardy provision did not bar petitioner's trial before the second court-martial," because even *if* that part of the Bill of Rights applied to courts-martial, that second trial "was not the kind of double jeopardy within the intent of the Fifth Amendment." (Four years later,

indeed, in *Reid* v. *Covert,* Justice Black, in an opinion
in which Justice Douglas concurred, buttressed his
conclusion that courts-martial could not constitutionally be used for the trial of civilians by animadverting
on the inadequate constitutional protection afforded
the accused in such proceedings. By way of illustration, he pointed out that "in *Swaim* v. *United States*
. . . this Court held that the President or commanding
officer had power to return a case to a court-martial
for an increase in sentence. If the double jeopardy
provisions of the Fifth Amendment were applicable
such a practice would be unconstitutional." Since
Wade v. *Hunter* was not so much as mentioned, it may
be inferred that the dissenters in *Burns* had had second
thoughts about the meaning of that case. But then,
Justice Black had not mentioned the Swaim case in his
opinion in *Wade* v. *Hunter.*)

Of all the Justices, I think Felix Frankfurter came
closest to an accurate analysis of the problem and a
prophecy of what the Court will eventually do. It has
long been held that the decisions of military courts
cannot be directly appealed to the Supreme Court (or,
a fortiori, any other court), even when the petitioner
alleges a denial of his rights under the Constitution of
the United States.[38] (Of course, Congress could, if it
wanted, make the decisions of the Court of Military
Appeals reviewable by the Supreme Court in the same
way as the decisions of other federal appellate courts.)
But, as usual, there is more than one legal way to skin
a cat, or a court-martial. The same result can be
achieved by "collateral review" of court-martial con-

victions, which is not limited to the necessarily infrequent cases in which the overworked Supreme Court can be persuaded to grant a petition for a writ of certiorari, but may be initiated in the district courts of the United States, or (when the petitioner seeks to collect the pay of which he was deprived by an allegedly invalid sentence) in the Court of Claims.[39]

There are several pathways to the civilian courts for the military petitioner who believes or hopes that the military courts denied him due process. The most commonly trodden, of course, is the petition for a writ of habeas corpus. The Supreme Court more than twenty years ago refused to construe the Congressional provision that "the proceedings, findings and sentences of courts-martial . . . shall be final and conclusive . . . and binding upon all . . . courts . . . of the United States"[40] as denying the protection of the great writ;[41] even if that is what Congress intended, the Constitution permits suspension of the privilege of the writ only "when in Cases of Rebellion or Invasion the public Safety may require it."[42] Habeas corpus takes care of practically all civilian petitioners whose grievance is unlawful confinement. But the military has punishments, such as punitive discharge, reduction in rank, and forfeiture of pay, for which habeas corpus is not as a rule an appropriate remedy.[43] The Supreme Court has yet to decide whether the Code's finality provision bars other methods of collateral review not explicitly protected by the Constitution. But the inferior federal courts have shown in the last few years a very tolerant attitude in this respect. Thus, military convicts complaining of punitive discharges and forfeitures of pay have been permitted to attack the validity of their convictions and sentences by suits for back pay in the Court of Claims.[44] Other courts have issued writs of *mandamus* to the service secretaries, ordering the substitution of honorable for punitive discharges.[45] And the Court of Appeals for the District of Columbia Circuit (an important court for such purposes, since all of the service secretaries can be, and often are, sued in the District) has held that a petition for a declaratory judgment that a court-martial sentence was void was also an appropriate remedy.[46]

It should be remembered that the analogous jurisdiction of the federal courts to review, in habeas corpus, convictions by state or federal courts which, for whatever reason, cannot be directly appealed, is itself a fairly modern development. Until shortly before World War II the scope of collateral review of civilian criminal proceedings was also very limited; it too was said to go only to "jurisdiction" in the narrowest or "historic" sense.[47] Historically, in fact, courts-martial verdicts were more vulnerable to habeas corpus than were those of the civil courts: "At common law a judgment of conviction rendered by a court of general criminal jurisdiction was conclusive proof that confinement was legal,"[48] while "a court-martial was considered as one of those inferior courts of limited jurisdiction, whose judgment may be questioned collaterally,"[49] and from the earliest times a civil court could properly inspect at least the military court's jurisdiction over the person and offense and the lawfulness of its sentence.[50] Thus, President Lincoln's suspension of the writ of habeas corpus was intended for the benefit of the various types of military tribunal which proliferated during the Civil War—indeed, the original suspension of April 27, 1861, took the form of an executive order delegating to the Commanding General of the United States Army and other military officers authority to suspend the writ.[51] Not until 1867 did Congress cast the habeas corpus jurisdiction of the federal courts in substantially its present form by extending the writ to all cases in which "any person may be restrained of his or her liberty in violation of the constitution, or of any treaty or law of the United States."[52] It is noteworthy that neither that statute nor any amendment differentiates between civil and military tribunals.[53]

But, although historically the scope of collateral review of civilian criminal proceedings was not greater than that of courts-martial, a gradual development, inaugurated by the Supreme Court in 1938,[54] has given new dimensions to the concept of examination in collateral proceedings of the "jurisdiction" of a civilian criminal court. The technical rationale is that jurisdiction, though it existed when the trial began, evaporated because the defendant was somehow denied constitutional due process.[55] This latter is itself an uncertain but expanding concept, which includes such basic unfairness as lack of counsel,[56] or the admission of a coerced confession,[57] or the prosecution's knowing use of perjured testimony[58]—all of which can happen in a court-martial as well as in a civilian trial. If a federal court is satisfied that a state prisoner was, in fact, denied the effective assistance of counsel, or that a coerced confession was in fact admitted in evidence against him, it will grant the writ regardless of what the state courts may have thought about those issues.[59] Whether it is desirable to employ this particular method of vindicating the state prisoner's rights under the federal constitution is not the immediate question.[60] For the present at least, that controversy has been resolved in favor of the proposition that the federal courts can examine, for themselves, the fairness of a petitioner's trial in a state court and can range far beyond the record in the course of that examination. The not less important question with which we are here concerned, and which the Supreme Court will sooner or later have to decide, is whether there is any good reason why military tribunals should not be subject to the same quality of constitutional policing as state criminal courts—emphasizing, however, that procedures which would invalidate a civilian trial may be justified by the special needs of the military. The process that is due a soldier is not necessarily the same as that due a civilian.

The Supreme Court itself has cleared up none of the confusion left in the wake of *Burns* v. *Wilson*. All that can be said with anything approaching confidence is that soldiers tried by court-martial have *some* constitutional rights, however ill-defined, and that those rights, should the military courts fail to recognize them, can be enforced by the federal courts—at least by habeas corpus. The Justices unanimously declined

the most recent invitation to settle some of these questions. Commander Richard Augenblick, convicted of
"an indecent, lewd and lascivious act" and sentenced
to dismissal, and Air Force Sergeant Kenneth Juhl,
convicted of more prosaic black-market offenses and
sentenced to reduction in rank, forfeiture of pay, and
six months confinement, brought suit in the Court of
Claims for the pay of which they said they had unconstitutionally been deprived. Neither could seek habeas
corpus, for the Commander had not been sentenced
to confinement, and the Sergeant had already done his
time. The Commander complained of the Government's failure to produce notes and tape recordings
made by agents interrogating him and the principal
witness against him;[61] the Sergeant, that he had been
convicted on the uncorroborated testimony of an ac-
complice, contrary to paragraph 153 (a) of the Manual
for Courts-Martial. The Court of Claims, in what Justice Douglas called "a conscientious effort to undo an
injustice," ruled in favor of both plaintiffs.[62] But the
Supreme Court chose not to decide the question of
the civilian court's jurisdiction in such cases; it reversed both decisions on the ground that in neither
one did the errors alleged, if errors they were, "rise to
a constitutional level."[63] "A constitutionally unfair
trial," said Justice Douglas, "takes place only where
the barriers and safeguards are so relaxed or forgotten
. . . that the proceeding is more a spectacle . . . or trial
by ordeal . . . than a disciplined contest." Such rhetoric, however picturesque, is not a very helpful definition of "constitutional" error; but it does appear that

common, garden-variety error in the admission of evidence, such as courts daily commit, will not do. Yet, the tone of the opinion strongly suggests that if there *had* been a really serious violation of the rights of the accused, if either case had been "a worthy candidate for consideration at the constitutional level," the Justices would have upheld the Court of Claims' jurisdiction to annul the sentence of the military court.

Shortly thereafter, the Court of Appeals for the District of Columbia Circuit, which had been holding up its decision in another case in the vain hope that the high Court's decision in *Augenblick* would settle the matter, set forth its own view of the law, which much resembles that which Justice Frankfurter expressed in *Burns* v. *Wilson.* Air Force Captain Joseph Kauffman, convicted of failure to report attempts by Soviet and East German agents to obtain military information and sentenced to dismissal, brought suit to have his sentence declared void, and the Secretary of the Air Force ordered to restore him to active duty with full rank and seniority. The court found that the military appellate courts had "fully and fairly considered appellant's claims of constitutional error and disposed of them in accordance with Supreme Court standards."[64] The Court of Military Appeals had, in fact, reversed Kauffman's conviction on the more serious count of conspiring to sell military secrets to the East Germans because it found that that conviction rested on evidence obtained by "massive and deliberate violations" of his constitutional rights, such as illegal search and seizure and bugging his conversations with his lawyer.[65] But the civilian court made it clear that if the military court had not caught these errors, which were unquestionably of constitutional magnitude, Kauffman would have been entitled to relief. Since the court's observations on the jurisdiction of the civilian courts to review military verdicts for constitutional error probably foreshadow what the Supreme Court will say when it has to, they bear quotation:

> We think that the scope of review of military judgments should be the same as that in habeas corpus review of state or federal convictions, and constitutional requirements should be qualified by the special conditions of the military only where these are shown to require a different rule. . . .
> We hold that the test of fairness requires that military rulings on constitutional issues conform to Supreme Court standards, unless it is shown that conditions peculiar to military life require a different rule.[66]

But the scope of review by the civil courts may be even broader where the soldier seeks habeas corpus, for the Habeas Corpus Act authorizes the writ whenever custody is challenged as being "in violation of the Constitution or *laws* or treaties of the United States." Looking at this language and peering into the clouded crystal ball of *Burns* v. *Wilson,* another Circuit Court of Appeals recently concluded that it must consider a military prisoner's contention that the military courts had misconstrued various provisions of the Code, though such errors might be of less than constitutional size.[67]

The Supreme Court will settle those matters sooner

or later—most likely later. The reason for the probable tardiness is simple: as Kauffman's case demon-
strates, a clear and substantial violation of constitutional due process will not often survive review by the
military appellate courts. In the first place, the Uniform Code itself requires courts-martial to afford most
of the protections that the accused would have under
the Constitution. It prohibits compulsory self-incrimination, double jeopardy, and cruel or unusual punishments;[68] the accused must be apprised of the charges
against him;[69] he is to be assisted by counsel of his
choice and to have the benefit of compulsory process.[70] In some respects, the Code, as construed by the
Court of Military Appeals and the President's rules of
procedure and evidence, embodied in the Manual for
Courts-Martial, actually gives the accused rights
rather more extensive than the Supreme Court has yet
read into the Constitution. Thus, the Supreme Court,
having held in *Miranda* v. *Arizona*[71] that a suspect in
police custody could not be interrogated unless he
had been informed of his right to say nothing and see
a lawyer, refused to extend the rule to police obten-
tion of an "identifying physical characteristic," such as
a fingerprint or a specimen of handwriting.[72] But the
Court of Military Appeals, construing Article 31 of the
Code, had held and continued to hold that a handwriting sample obtained from a military accused could not
be used as evidence against him unless the military
investigators had first advised him of his right to *do*
nothing as well as to *say* nothing.[73] When the Supreme
Court held that a statement obtained in violation of

the *Miranda* rules, which could not have been introduced in evidence against the defendant, could, nonetheless, be used to impeach the credibility of his testimony at the trial,[74] COMA adhered to its contrary rule that even such use was impermissible, basing its holding not on the Constitution but on its reading of the Manual for Courts-Martial.[75]

If a court-martial denies a serviceman a right that Congress has granted him in the Code, there is no reason to wade into the constitutional morass. If the error actually prejudiced the accused, COMA will bust the conviction for lack of "military due process," and it will normally treat as prejudicial a denial of one of the more important statutory rights, such as the admission of evidence obtained in violation of the prohibition against self-incrimination contained in Article 31, or failure of the military judge properly to instruct the members of the court.[76] Of course, many errors in procedure or the admission of evidence do the accused no actual harm: A larceny specification charging him with stealing "goods" of a stated value might be insufficiently specific to inform him of the exact nature of the charges against him, but it would not be ground for reversal if the record of trial clearly showed that he and his counsel did in fact know exactly what goods he was supposed to have stolen.[77] A provision of the Manual that COMA finds to be inconsistent with the Code is, of course, a nullity.[78] Moreover, COMA, like the civilian courts, will bend the statute very far to avoid breaking it against the Constitution. It has, for example, avoided a possible conflict with the accused's Sixth Amendment right "to be confronted with the witnesses against him" by reading into Article 49, which permits the use of depositions in noncapital cases, a requirement that the accused and his counsel be allowed to be present and cross-examine when a deposition is taken.[79] Neither COMA nor any other court has ever quite reached the point of holding unconstitutional any of the sections of the Code dealing with procedure and evidence, but there is not much doubt that they would do so if a case should arise in which a conflict with the Constitution could not be avoided by muscular construction of the statute. Perhaps the closest approach is *Tempia*,[80] in which COMA, in order to avoid a collision with *Miranda* v. *Arizona*,[81] which laid out the contitutional rights of people being questioned by the police, overruled its own recent holding[82] that the Code and the Manual did not require that such a suspect be informed that a free lawyer would be appointed upon request. COMA has in the last few years many times reiterated the proposition that the rights contained in the first eight amendments, as interpreted by the Supreme Court, "except those which are expressly or by necessary implication inapplicable," apply to servicemen as well as civilians.[83] "To the extent a particular procedure or right is determined by the Supreme Court of the United States to be constitutionally mandated, this Court is bound by that determination since the Supreme Court is the highest tribunal in the Federal judicial hierarchy."[84]

What is not so clear is *which* parts of the Bill of

Rights are "expressly or by necessary implication" inapplicable.[85] Military cases, are, of course, expressly exempted from the grand jury requirement—and in any case the Code's provision for pre-trial investigation gives the accused more valuable rights (especially the right to know the prosecution's case against him) than he would get if he were indicted by a civilian grand jury.[86] The Supreme Court and virtually everyone else agree that the right to trial by petty jury is excluded "by necessary implication." Bail has never been known in military law; considering the inevitable restrictions on the freedom of even law-abiding soldiers, the practice would obviously be hard to adapt to military circumstances. Although some zealous civilian counsel have thrown in demands for bail along with the rest of their shotgun blasts at military justice, the civilian and military courts have regularly held that the Eighth Amendment's prohibition of "excessive bail," (which implies a right to reasonable bail), has no application to the military.[87]

The Code and the Manual do in fact provide criteria for the accused's rights to freedom pending trial and appeal, which to me make more sense than conditioning his freedom on his ability to raise high bail. In substance, they stipulate that the accused shall not be confined before trial unless it seems necessary to insure his continued presence.[88] After conviction, a sentence to confinement cannot be "executed" until the requisite review has taken place, but the convict can still be subjected to such restraint as is necessary to prevent his fleeing the jurisdiction,[89] which may differ

only in name from the penal confinement to which he
has been sentenced. After Captain Dale Noyd's conviction of disobeying a lawful order was approved by
the convening authority, and while it was pending in
a Court of Military Review, he was moved from
confinement in his comfortable bachelor quarters to
more Spartan accommodations in the Disciplinary
Barracks in Fort Leavenworth. His lawyers promptly
sought habeas corpus to return him to his own apart-
ment, alleging with some plausibility that locking him
up in the latter cheerless institution was not needed to
keep him from fleeing and that, in fact, it amounted to
an "execution" of his sentence. The District Court
agreed, but the Circuit Court of Appeals and the Supreme Court held that the civil court should not have
intervened until Noyd had sought relief in the military
courts;[90] the Court of Military Appeals has jurisdiction
to issue writs of habeas corpus in aid of its jurisdiction
over cases that may eventually come before it.[91] The
hardship imposed on Captain Noyd turned out to be
less severe than it might have been, for his sentence,
not having been suspended, began to run at the time
it was imposed, regardless of whether he was confined
in his quarters or in the Disciplinary Barracks; when
Justice Douglas (the Court being in recess) ordered
Noyd released pending the Court's action on his petition, the sentence had only two days to run. (Justice
White, who had denied the same application the day
before and who may not have been favorably impressed by Douglas' intermeddling, dissented in the
main case on the ground that the issue was so picayune

that the writ should have been dismissed as improvidently granted.) When COMA affirmed the sentence, he had served it. Of course, if the Court of Military Appeals had reversed Noyd's conviction, his grievance would have had real substance.

It is appropriate at this point to digress slightly by remarking that the Supreme Court reemphasized in Noyd's case the rule that the military convict, like the state convict, must normally exhaust whatever remedies he has within the system of justice that tried him before the federal courts will hear his complaints of constitutional unfairness.[92] But there is at least one large exception in military cases; the petitioner, unlike people held for trial by civilian courts, may claim that a court-martial has no right to try him at all, no matter how fair the trial or how clear his guilt. If he claims, for example, that he is a civilian, the federal courts will not require him to languish in military custody until the sometimes lengthy process of military trial and review has been completed.[93] The same reasoning appears to be applicable when a soldier seeks to enjoin his trial on the ground that the *crime* is not one that can constitutionally be tried by a military court; several federal courts have enjoined military trials or granted writs of habeas corpus, without requiring the soldier to exhaust his military remedies, when they found that the Supreme Court's decision in *O'Callahan* v. *Parker* had deprived the military of power to try the non-service-connected offenses charged.[94]

A special, and peculiarly knotty, problem was presented by soldiers who claimed that in the eyes of God, and hopefully of federal judges, they were civilians because, under service regulations, they were entitled to discharge as conscientious objectors.[95] Must such a soldier risk a court-martial for disobeying an order that goes against his conscience? So long as his application for discharge is still in the military administrative works, he runs no great danger, for the same regulations direct that until the Secretary makes a final determination the soldier is to be assigned to duties involving as little conflict as possible with his claimed beliefs; an order to engage in combat training or to embark for an area of combat would thus be an unlawful order which he would be entitled to disobey. If the Secretary rules against him, however, he loses the protection of the regulation and can be subjected to any order that is otherwise lawful. But a civilian court can still order his discharge if it finds that the Secretary's finding that he did not fit the regulation's definition of conscientious objection (which is the same as that of the Selective Service Act) had "no basis in fact." The Supreme Court recently cleaned up a confused tangle of conflicting decisions in the lower courts by holding that a soldier need not await the verdict of a court-martial and the result of military review, before resorting to that remedy; if he persuades the civilian judge that there was no evidence to support the Secretary's finding, he is entitled to immediate discharge[96]—unless, of course, he was charged with an offense, such as stealing another soldier's watch, which had no connection with his conscientious objection to war.[97] But if the denial of his application for discharge is final, in

the sense that no petition for review is pending in the
military administration or the federal courts, he cannot plead the wrongness of the Secretary's decision as
a defense to court-martial charges, for COMA refused
to contemplate the possibility of "a member actually
being in the service . . . who could not be the recipient
of any lawful order."[98]

When and if the Court holds that the First, Fourth,
Fifth, Sixth and Eighth Amendments all apply to soldiers, it is pretty clear that the Amendments will not
confer on them exactly the same rights that they give
civilians; "conditions peculiar to military life"[99] will be
held to justify greater restrictions on the liberty of a
soldier than would be tolerable for a civilian. To start
with a fairly trivial freedom, most courts hold that a
civilian—such as a high school student or even a uni-
formed fireman—has a constitutional right to be as
hirsute as he wishes; if he believes, however wrongly,
that his beauty is increased by a pageboy bob or an
Afro, sideburns, dundrearies, muttonchops, a walrus
mustache, or handlebars, he cannot arbitrarily be sent
to the barber. The burden is on the censor, or tonsor,
to show that there is some reasonable connection between the degree of the citizen's hairiness and the
public welfare.[100] As a matter of history, there seems
to be no correlation between short hair and military
virtue. The cropheaded roundheads beat the cava-
liers; but the Persians, who were amazed to see the
Spartan hoplites at Thermopylae combing their long
hair, soon learned that they faced the bravest and best
disciplined warriors in Hellas.[101] The Civil War was

fought by generals so luxuriantly bewhiskered as to be practically lurking in ambush, many of them both brave and competent. But American military commanders have generally favored short haircuts, and in modern times few of them have sanctioned more facial hair than a discreet and military mustache of the Blackjack Pershing pattern. They have been accorded the broadest discretion to regulate the grooming of their subordinates. The earliest victim of this species of military oppression seems to have been Colonel Thomas Butler, a veteran of the Revolution, who was twice court-martialed, in 1804 and 1805, for refusing to cut off his queue.[102] Colonel Butler (who died shortly after his second conviction, although of yellow fever rather than humiliation) made no effort to vindicate his rights in the civil courts, but a number of contemporary soldiers have done so, with small success.[103]

In principle, it seems clear that the Fourth Amendment protects soldiers from "unreasonable" search and seizure. But it seems equally clear that searches that would be unreasonable for civilians may be proper in the military context.[104] Men who live in barracks simply do not have the privacy that most civilians can expect: they may find a home in the Army, but that home is no castle. The Manual lays down ground rules that are generally similar to those prevailing in the federal courts.[105] The Courts of Military Review and COMA have wrestled with the problem in cases too numerous to cite, not infrequently finding that the commander lacked "probable cause" to authorize the search and that the evidence was consequently inadmissible.[106] But the soldier usually lacks the protection provided the civilian in normal circumstances, that the police must obtain a search warrant from a judge; commanding officers can authorize searches of a soldier's person or property whenever he or it is located in a place subject to military control.[107] Moreover, no "probable cause" is needed for routine "inspections," as distinct from "searches" for particular things, and incriminating evidence accidentally turned up in the course of a genuine inspection may be used in a trial. Defense counsel often contends, sometimes successfully, that a purported inspection was really a disguised and unwarranted search.

Of still more importance is the soldier's right to express his opinions, especially his political opinions, however half-baked or wrongheaded. Wars arise out of politics, and unanimity of opinion has never been characteristic of American politics. When the Army is filled with civilians and engaged in a war of which many of them deeply disapprove, the problem is sure to arise. In the Civil War, the Army had a large collection of political generals—Butler, Fremont and McClellan, for example—who were far better at fighting Lincoln in the newspapers than Lee and Jackson on the battlefield. Soldiers of all ranks freely denounced the President for subordinating the interests of the slaves to those of the Union or the interests of the Union to those of the slaves. The Vietnam hostilities, though they generated plenty of dissent within and without the armed forces, did not produce the phenomenon of a recently removed commanding general running for President as a Peace Democrat, as McClellan did in 1864. It is remarkable that there is so little hard law—virtually none in the decisions of the Supreme Court—on the First Amendment rights of soldiers, especially when it is considered that there are at least a dozen statutes under which they can be prosecuted for talking too freely.

It is, or should be, reasonably clear that the First Amendment gives soldiers about as much religious freedom as it gives civilians. There is no military reason to establish religion in the armed services. Chapels and chaplains are justified as morale-builders ("see the Chaplain" is the sardonic advice usually given by sergeants to soldiers for whose grievances no remedy exists), but attendance at religious services has not been compulsory for anyone except midshipmen and cadets at service academies, and a federal court of appeals recently held that compulsion unconstitutional.[108] One can imagine cases in which a soldier's exercise of his religious beliefs would collide with reasonable military regulations—*e.g.*, a Sikh's obedience to the command of his faith that he wear a turban and beard and carry a dagger—but such conflicts seem not to have arisen in practice. (One such conflict was avoided when a district court held that a man whose religion prohibited vaccination and inoculation, which are compulsory in the services, could not constitutionally be excluded from the Selective Service Act's exemption of religious objectors to war.[109]) But First Amendment freedom of speech presents tougher problems. It is admitted by even the most zealous civil libertarians that (as the first Justice Harlan put it) "the liberty secured by the Constitution of the United States . . . does not import an absolute right in each person to be, at all times and in all circumstances, wholly freed from restraint."[110] This is true of freedom of speech; even civilians can be muzzled if, in the words of Justice Holmes, "the words used are used in such circumstances and are of such a nature as to create a clear and present danger that they will bring about the substantive evils that Congress has a right to prevent."[111] On many other occasions the Supreme Court has tried to phrase the formula for reconciling the individual's interest in free speech with the government's interest in public safety. One often quoted example is, "In each case [the courts] must ask whether the gravity of the evil, discounted by its improbability, justifies such invasion of free speech as is necessary to avoid the danger."[112] By these criteria, Congress has a right to prevent speech which creates a clear and present danger of military insubordination, indiscipline, or inefficiency.[113]

Under these very general standards, some of the Uniform Code's restriction on speech are unlikely to present serious constitutional problems—for example, Articles 82, 101, and 104, which prohibit such things as soliciting desertion or mutiny; or (in time of war) betrayal of a parole or countersign; or communication or correspondence with the enemy. The same is true of Article 117, whose purpose is to prevent brawling by forbidding "provoking or reproachful words or gestures"; only those which "tend to induce breaches of the peace" are punishable, and even civilian freedom of speech does not extend to "fighting words."[114] I think it equally unlikely that the Court will ever give soldiers a constitutional right to tell the Colonel or the First Sergeant where to get off by striking down Articles 89 and 91, which denounce the use of disrespectful language to military superiors. Nor is there serious doubt about the propriety of forbidding servicemen to disclose genuine military secrets; there is no constitutional privilege to sell to the Russians, or even leak to Dr. Spock or *Ramparts,* the Pentagon's plans in the event of nuclear war.

The swampy area begins where the censorship seems to be based less on military than political considerations, as in the case of Lieutenant Colonel Melvin Voorhees, in which the Court of Military Appeals first tangled with the problem.[115] Voorhees wrote articles and a book about the Korean War which he submitted for clearance as required by Army Regulations. The censors refused to clear some passages, notably one criticizing General Douglas MacArthur for subordinating military security to self-glorification by issuing press releases that "telegraphed Eighth Army's punch" and caused the failure of an offensive. Voorhees went ahead without clearance; thereupon he was court-martialed and convicted of violating an Army Regulation which in terms required deletion not only of matter "classified" (as Top Secret, Secret or Confidential) for "security" reasons, but also of matter objectionable from the standpoints of "policy" and "propriety." The court-martial sentenced him to dismissal, and the Board of Review (as it was then styled), though on various grounds it set aside the convictions on all but one of the specifications, affirmed the sentence.

By a complex, ingenious, and implausible process of construction, Chief Judge Robert E. Quinn, who wrote for COMA, managed to affirm the conviction by holding that the Regulation covered only "matters which may affect the national security and welfare and which are covered by a security classification." He stated categorically that a soldier has "the same constitutional rights, privileges, and guarantees as every other American citizen, except where specifically denied or limited by the Constitution itself," and equally categorically that one of the differences between the military and civilian communities is that members of the former can not only be punished for an "abuse" of their constitutional privilege but can also be prevented from committing it. It is no doubt true that the military has a right to classify and censor information that really does affect national security. The trouble is that Chief Judge Quinn, while he refused to say that the Army has a right to restrict speech or publication that do *not* create such a peril, did not explain in what way Colonel Voorhees' criticisms of General MacArthur could have endangered national security. Indeed, he emphasized that the Colonel's failure to obtain clearance before publishing was only a "technical" violation of the regulation.

Judge George W. Latimer was at least more consistent: Though servicemen are entitled to such constitutional rights as can "reasonably" be given them, he thought it "ill-advised and unwise to apply the civilian concepts of freedom of speech and press to the military service unless they are compressed within limits so narrow they become almost unrecognizable." Since morale and discipline depend on policy and propriety, he concluded that these factors—and not merely security in the narrower sense—justify restriction of the soldier's freedom to say things, however truthful, that tend to destroy the Army's faith in its commanders. But even he stopped short of holding that the Army could arbitrarily forbid statements that bore no reasonable relation to security, or Army policy, or military propriety. He would presumably have been willing to allow that if Colonel Voorhees had written a love story, the Army could not have used the censor's shears on it—unless possibly the protagonist was General MacArthur. If he had written *War and Peace* or *The Charterhouse of Parma* (admittedly a somewhat improbable hypothesis), the Latimer view would permit him to be court-martialed for publishing it without clearance, and it would be an exceptional major or general in the Office of the Chief of Information who would take on himself the responsibility of clearing it. The masterpiece would have had to await the author's retirement or death. This would have been all right for posterity, although hard on the author. But few books dealing with contemporary controversy will keep so long.

Judge Paul W. Brosman dissented. He too believed

that the soldier's freedom to speak and print was less than the civilian's, but not so much less as to permit prior censorship—which the Supreme Court, for reasons which have more to do with history than logic, seems to think more objectionable than subsequent punishment[116]—of speech that offends against nothing more than policy and propriety.[117]

Obviously all three of COMA's judges regarded *Voorhees* as a most important case; the three opinions run to something over 30,000 words. But their mountainous labors produced a mouselike result, for they all agreed that the sentence was too severe for the solitary offense—described by the Chief Judge as a "technical" violation of the regulation—which the Board of Review had left standing, and remanded the case for rehearing.[118] It is not appreciably more significant as precedent; all we can say with assurance is that the judges then sitting on the Court of Military Appeals thought soldiers had First Amendment rights, but fewer of them than civilians.

We learn more from COMA's occasional encounters with the problem in other contexts. "Disloyal statements" are punishable under the general article,[119] and a few servicemen have been court-martialed on such charges, where their bad-mouthing seemed to the authorities to go beyond the legitimate griping and complaining that are the soldier's ancient prerogative. In *Daniels*[120] and *Harvey*,[121] a couple of Black Muslims who had signed up as marines, but washed out of technical training schools and been assigned to the infantry, communicated their disenchantment with the Corps to other Negro marines in fervent language. They were charged with violations of the Smith Act's prohibition of attempts to cause "insubordination, disloyalty, mutiny, or refusal of duty" by members of the armed forces.[122] Daniels was found guilty as charged; Harvey was convicted only of the lesser included offense of making "disloyal statements" to the prejudice of good order and military discipline in violation of the general article. COMA reversed Daniels' conviction because the military judge's instructions failed to make clear to the members of the court that they must be satisfied not only that the accused intended to cause insubordination, disloyalty and so forth, but also that there was a clear and present danger that his inflammatory rhetoric would actually have that effect. In other words, COMA applied to the Smith Act's restriction on freedom of speech (which applies to civilians as well as soldiers) the test originally enunciated by Holmes in the Schenck case.[123] But it found that the evidence supported Daniels' conviction on the lesser included charge of soliciting other marines to commit the military offense of refusing duty, and that he could be convicted of that offense without any showing of a real danger that his advice would be heeded or discipline impaired. Harvey's conviction of making disloyal statements was reversed because the trial judge had failed to make it clear to the court that the statements must show disloyalty to the United States itself, and not merely to the President, or Congress, or the Marine Corps.[124] Thus Harvey, like Daniels, was ultimately convicted only of soliciting other marines to refuse duty—in his case a lesser offense included within the lesser included offense of which the court had convicted him. Since the maximum penalty for the offense to which the convictions were whittled down was less than that awarded, the cases were remanded for reassessment of the sentence. The upshot seems to be that the clear-and-present-danger test is applied to soldiers accused of violating the Smith Act, but not to the military offense of soliciting other soldiers to refuse duty.

The evidence in *Harvey* and *Daniels* probably would have supported a finding that their preachings really did, in the context of racial tension existing at the time and place, create danger of insubordination, mutiny and other substantive evils which Congress had a right to prevent. COMA's most recent, and possibly most important, decision on "disloyal" statements clearly applied that test. It involved one Roger Lee Priest, a "Journalist Seaman" in the Navy. Most of Priest's journalistic talent, such as it was, was devoted to an "underground" newspaper, full of inflammatory and misspelled rhetoric, which he distributed at various naval installations and on newsstands at the Pentagon. Its ominous warning that "Today's Pigs are Tomorrow's Bacon," and its calls for "Guns Baby Guns!" and to "Smash the State," and its frequent editorial encouragement of insubordination and desertion, were undoubtedly intended by their enthusiastic young author to start at least a small mutiny and hopefully a large revolution. COMA, applying the Holmes test, considered that the constitutional question was simply whether Priest's rodomontades did in fact create any measurable risk to naval discipline: "whether the gravity of the effect of accused's publications on good order and discipline in the armed forces, discounted by the improbability of their effectiveness on the audience he sought to reach, justifies his conviction." Considering that not all members of that audience "have the maturity of judgment to resist propaganda," the judges (for once, unanimously) concluded that "the court members were justified in finding that their publication and distribution tended palpably and directly to affect military order and discipline and were punishable under the general article."[125] One may question the conclusion of fact—it is hard to see how any rational person could believe in revolution after reading Priest's effusions—but the criterion seems sound.

The civilian courts have had other doubts about the charge of making "disloyal statements." One upset such a conviction because it found the general articles unconstitutionally vague, laying stress on the fact that they abutted upon "sensitive areas of basic First Amendment freedoms."[126] Another, although it did not doubt that speech "palpably prejudicial to good order and discipline" could constitutionally be forbidden to soldiers and sailors, found the particular specification of making "disloyal statements" unconstitutionally vague and broad, especially because the proscription involved First Amendment rights.[127]

The existence of real danger to military discipline was far from clear in the case of Lieutenant Henry Howe, which marked another milestone in COMA's uncertain progress toward a rational balancing of military need against the soldier's right to tell his political ideas to as much of the world as he can get to listen. Howe, a reserve second lieutenant on active duty, carried a picket sign denouncing President Johnson for "facist aggression."[128] He was off duty, off post, and not in uniform, and there was no substantial evidence that he was recognized as an Army officer by anyone except a military policeman who had been detailed to aid the civilian police if violence should occur. (None did.) Howe was convicted of violating Article 88, which forbids commissioned officers to use "contemptuous words" against the President, and Article 133, "conduct unbecoming an officer and a gentleman." COMA in effect affirmed both convictions.[129] It found no merit in the argument that the Lieutenant had a constitutional right to denounce the war and the President. It recognized the applicability of the clear-and-present-danger test, but in a most peculiar way. It pointed out that in *Schenck* and other World War I cases[130] the Supreme Court had denied the protection of the First Amendment to speech which in fact, however seditiously intended, was very unlikely to have any substantial impact on the nation's war effort. From this premise it drew the conclusion, not that the Supreme Court, in that super-patriotic period of our history, had been too ready to describe as "clear and present" dangers which were neither, but that a very slight risk of impairing military discipline is enough to render constitutional the punishment of overheated language.[131]

Article 88 was justified on still another, and equally

dubious, ground, "the ancient and wise provisions insuring civilian control of the military will restrict the 'man on a white horse.' " Ancient, the provision certainly is; the Articles of War of 1776 denounced any officer or soldier who might "presume to use traitorous or disrespectful words against the authority of the United States in Congress assembled," and the roots of that provision in the British Articles, in the form of prohibiting rude remarks about the King, go back to the time of Henry VIII,[132] who was both vulnerable to rude remarks and easily incensed by them. But its wisdom is debatable. That it is desirable to subordinate the military to civilian authority cannot be doubted; but it can be doubted that a pipsqueak shavetail like Howe was much of a threat to the authority of the President. Indeed, when one considers the thousands of more or less scurrilous diatribes that must have been directed by loud-mouthed soldiers against Abraham Lincoln, Woodrow Wilson, and Franklin Roosevelt, to say nothing of Lyndon Johnson and Richard Nixon, it is remarkable that in nearly two centuries only about a hundred officers and enlisted men[133] have been court-martialed for using such language, most of them in the Civil War and World War I, and a few in World War II. Howe is the only person to have been prosecuted under the article in more than twenty-five years. In none of the reported cases does it appear that the civil government would have been imperiled if the offenders had been allowed to continue to shoot off their mouths; such injury as they inflicted was only to the sense of propriety of better affected soldiers who had to listen. Article 88 seems one of the smallest reasons why the United States has no tradition of military coups. I am not persuaded that it would be constitutional even if it were limited to general and flag officers, and I can see no justification at all for its application to second lieutenants.

In short, the Court of Military Appeals, though it has stated eloquently that servicemen are protected by the First Amendment, has in practice been very ready to find that their utterances are so dangerous as to be removed from that protection, at least where their speech was politically inspired.[134] Though it agrees with Earl Warren that servicemen are protected by the First Amendment, COMA has yet to hold that that armor is proof against even a slight military interest in restraining that speech. The Courts of Military Review have naturally modeled their decisions on COMA's.[135] The question is bound, sooner or later, in one way or another, to come before the civilian courts. I think it probable that those courts will treat it as a more serious problem than the soldier's right to look like Samson before Delilah sheared his locks. But no civilian court has yet laid down clear guidelines on the circumstances in which a soldier can be prevented from speaking or punished for speaking.

A similar conflict between the First Amendment and the alleged needs of the military is presented when (as happened with considerable frequency during the Vietnam war) civilians and soldiers wish to make speeches or distribute propaganda, usually anti-military, on military posts. A federal statute[136] forbids activities on such premises which are "prohibited by law or lawful regulation", and the question is, of course, whether the Post Commander's decision to bar particular people or particular propaganda is "lawful" in the sense of having a reasonable relation to the maintenance of security, order, and discipline on the post. As a general rule, the military authorities cannot bar speech or handbills in areas of the post that are open to the public.[137] Otherwise, the question is whether there is some factual basis for the commander's conclusion that the dissemination of the propaganda in question would in fact present a danger to morale, discipline or order.[138] Such a basis has been found to exist, for example, when previous speeches and assemblies of the same variety had wound up in brawls.[139]

The most interesting decision of a civilian court in the area is probably that of the Court of Appeals for the Second Circuit in the case of Specialist David Cortright, who helped defend his country by blowing the baritone horn in an Army band stationed at Fort Wadsworth, New York, and devoted his leisure hours (which were many, for the bandsmen had an easy schedule) to circulating among the other members of the band anti-war petitions, which were subsequently published. He was not court-martialed; his primary complaint was that he had suddenly been transferred to Fort Bliss, Texas. The district court, finding that the sole reason for the transfer was the command's desire to shut up a "troublemaker" (the Fort Bliss band already had a surplus of baritone hornblowers), held that there was no sufficient military reason to justify what it saw as a curtailment of Cortright's First Amendment rights and ordered the transfer rescinded. But the Second Circuit, balancing the usual reluctance of judges to substitute their judgment for that of military commanders on such matters as promotion or assignment to duty, against whatever infringement there was on Cortright's freedom to express himself, found that the former outweighed the latter and reversed.[140]

When and if the Supreme Court decides such a case, it may apply the clear-and-present-danger test somewhat more strictly than has COMA. Such a stricter application would, I think, produce a different result in the cases of Colonel Voorhees and Lieutenant Howe; it would be less likely to do so in those of Lance Corporal Harvey and Private Daniels, where military commanders might reasonably have found that the tinder was so dry that the defendants' sparks could really have started a fire. The Justices are unlikely to insist that they themselves be satisfied that there was a clear and present danger. They have traditionally been reluctant to upset the decisions of military commanders unless those decisions were clearly unjustified: "Orderly government requires that the judiciary be as scrupulous not to interfere with legitimate Army matters as the Army must be scrupulous not to intervene in judicial matters."[141] What they should insist upon is that there be some substantial basis for the military commander's conclusion that the expression of opinion presented, in the particular circumstances, a clear and present danger to military discipline and efficiency.

Notes to Chapter Four

[1] *Ex parte* Milligan, 71 U.S. 2, 138 (1866).

[2] *See supra*, Ch. 2.

[3] Art. 49, UCMJ.

[4] *E.g.*, SHERRILL, MILITARY JUSTICE IS TO JUSTICE AS MILITARY MUSIC IS TO MUSIC 186 (1970).

[5] Henderson, *Courts-Martial and the Constitution: The Original Understanding*, 71 HARV. L. REV. 293 (1957).

[6] BICKEL, THE LEAST DANGEROUS BRANCH 102 (1962). Colonel Wiener's articles, entitled *Courts-Martial and the Bill of Rights: The Original Practice*, appeared in 72 HARVARD LAW REVIEW 1, 266 (1958).

[7] *See* Wiener, *supra* note 6, at 29–31. The author furnishes many similar examples.

[8] 109 U.S. 336 (1883).

[9] *In re* Carter, 97 Fed. 496 (C.C.S.D.N.Y. 1899), *aff'd sub nom.* Rose *ex rel.* Carter v. Roberts, 99 Fed. 948 (2d Cir. 1900), *cert. denied* 176 U.S. 684, *appeal dismissed* 177 U.S. 496 (1900); Carter v. McClaughry, 105 Fed. 614 (C.C.D. Kan. 1900), *aff'd* 183 U.S. 365 (1902); Carter v. Woodring, 92 F.2d 544 (D.C. Cir. 1937), *cert. denied* 302 U.S. 752 (1937); *see* Burns v. Wilson, 346 U.S. 844

(1953) (separate opinion of Mr. Justice Frankfurter).

[10]It was estimated that the Clemency Board established by the War Department after World War II would examine about 30,000 cases out of a total of 90,000 wartime convictions by general courts-martial of the Army, the remainder of those convicted being restored to duty through the Army's rehabilitation program. *See* Note, 57 YALE L. J. 483, 488, n. 39 (1948).

[11]As of the end of 1945, this prison population numbered over 40,000, more than a thirty-fold increase since 1940. *See* U.S. Bureau of the Census, Prisoners in State and Federal Prisons and Reformatories 103(1946).

[12]64 F. Supp. 238 (M.D. Pa. 1946).

[13]*Id.* at 250. There was no appeal in the *Hicks* case, because the proceedings had been rendered moot by the military authorities' exercise of clemency. *Id.* at 250, n. 28.

[14]Beets v. Hunter, 75 F. Supp. 825, 826 (D. Kan. 1948). The opinion was obviously delivered on the spot, orally, and at white heat.

[15]The subsequent history of the *Beets* case was somewhat anti-climactic. After the writ had been granted and before the appeal was heard, Congress amended the 53d Article of War to permit application to the Judge Advocate General for vacation of sentence or new trial. Selective Service Act of 1948, ch. 625, § 230, 62 Stat. 639. The Court of Appeals reversed on the ground that Beets was required to exhaust his newly granted administrative remedy before seeking collateral review. Hunter v. Beets, 180 F.2d 101 (10th Cir. 1950), *cert. denied* 339 U.S. 963 (1950).

[16]*E.g.*, Hiatt v. Brown, 175 F.2d 273 (5th Cir. 1949), *rev'd* 339 U.S. 103 (1950); United States *ex. rel.* Innes v. Hiatt, 141 F.2d 664, 666 (3d Cir. 1944); see Kuykendall v. Hunter, 187 F.2d 545, 546 (10th Cir. 1951). For an excellent analysis and evaluation of the cases decided immediately after World War II, see Pasley, *The Federal Courts Look at the Court-Martial,* 12 U. PITT. L. REV. 7 (1950).

[17]*Compare* Shapiro v. United States, 69 F. Supp. 205, 207 (Ct. Cl. 1947) ("Flagrant case of military despotism; . . . verdict . . . evidently rendered in spite against a junior officer who had dared to demonstrate the fallibility of the judgment of his superior officers . . . almost complete denial of plaintiff's constitutional rights.")

[18]336 U.S. 695 (1949).

[19] *See Ex parte* Smith, 72 F. Supp. 935, 937 (M.D. Pa. 1947).

[20]Smith v. Hiatt, 170 F.2d 61 (3d Cir. 1948).

[21]336 U.S. at 696. The three dissenting Justices, Murphy, Douglas, and Rutledge, confined their dissent to the pretrial investigation question. *Id.* at 701.

[22]*Id.* at 701.

[23]*Id.* at 696.

[24]336 U.S. 684 (1949). Again Mr. Justice Black wrote for the majority. The three dissenters, who thought Wade *was* put twice in jeopardy, stated flatly, as they had to, that Wade, though a soldier, had rights under the Fifth Amendment, the denial of which was a proper subject of collateral review. *See infra*, p. 127.

[25]Hiatt v. Brown, 175 F.2d 273, 277 (5th Cir. 1949), *rev'd* 339 U.S. 103 (1950).

[26]Mr. Justice Douglas did not participate.

[27]175 F.2d at 277.

[28]340 U.S. 122 (1950), *rehearing denied*, 340 U.S. 923 (1951).

[29] *See* Burns v. Lovett, 202 F.2d 335, 339 (D.C. Cir. 1952), *aff'd sub nom.* Burns v. Wilson, 346 U.S. 137, *rehearing denied* 346 U.S. 844 (1953).

[30]347 U.S. 483 (1954).

[31]Warren, *The Bill of Rights and the Military*, 37 N.Y.U.L. Rev. 181, 187–88 (1962).

[32]346 U.S. 137, *rehearing denied* 346 U.S. 844 (1953).

[33]A petitioner for habeas corpus need not himself be within the territorial jurisdiction of any federal district court. If, for example, he is in a foreign country or aboard a ship at sea, he can bring suit in any court having jurisdiction over an official who can order his release from custody. *See, e.g.,* Kinnell v. Warner, 356 F. Supp. 779 (D. Hawaii 1973).

[34] *See* Burns v. Lovett, 202 F.2d 335, 348, 352–53 (D.C. Cir. 1952) (Bazelon, J., dissenting).

[35]137 U.S. 147 (1890).

[36]Justices Black and Douglas were no strangers to this concept of an adjustable Bill of Rights, for they had earlier suggested in the course of their dissent in Johnson v. Eisentrager, 339 U.S. 763, 791 (1950), that some, but not all, parts of the Bill of Rights applied to the actions of American Military Government in occupied foreign territory.

[37] *See, e.g.,* O'Callahan v. Parker, 395 U.S. 258, 261 (1969); Reid v. Covert, 354 U.S. 1, 37 n. 68 (1957). Even Mr. Henderson, the principal proponent of the idea that the Bill of Rights was intended to apply to servicemen, also conceded that the right to trial by jury was an exception to his general principle. Henderson, *supra* note 5, at 303–4.

[38] *E.g., In re* Yamashita, 327 U.S. 1 (1946); *In re* Vidal, 179 U.S. 126 (1900); *Ex parte* Vallandigham 68 U.S. 243 (1864); Dynes v. Hoover, 61 U.S. 65 (1858); *see* WINTHROP, 50–54.

[39] *See generally* Bishop, *Civilian Judges and Military Justice: Collateral Review of Court-Martial Convictions,* 61 COLUM. L. REV. 40 (1961); Note, *Servicemen in Civilian Courts,* 76 YALE L. J. 380 (1966).

[40] Art. 76, UCMJ.

[41] Gusik v. Schilder, 340 U.S. 128 (1950); *see* Burns v. Wilson, 346 U.S. 137, 142 (1953). The petitioner need not actually be behind bars in order to seek habeas corpus; any restraint on his freedom to come and go is sufficient. *See* Schlanger v. Seamans, 401 U.S. 487 (1971). Indeed, the restrictions which are an inevitable incident of any sort of military status, even membership in the reserve, are sufficient to make habeas corpus the appropriate remedy whenever the serviceman contends that he is entitled to discharge. *E.g.,* Brown v. McNamara, 387 F.2d 150 (3d Cir. 1967), *cert. denied* 390 U.S. 1005 (1968); Schonbrun v. Commanding Officer, 403 F.2d 371 (2d Cir. 1968), *cert. denied* 394 U.S. 929 (1969); Nason v. Secretary of Army, 304 F. Supp. 422 (D. Mass. 1969). Habeas corpus has been held to be an appropriate remedy even when the serviceman seeks not discharge but reassignment to noncombatant duty. Glazier v. Hackel, 440 F.2d 592 (9th Cir. 1971).

[42] Art. I, § 9.

[43] The Supreme Court has held, however, in a civilian case, that a petitioner who had initiated habeas corpus proceedings, but who had finished his sentence and been released from the pen while they were still dragging their tortuous way through the courts, might be treated as still "in custody" for the purposes of the Habeas Corpus Act (28 U.S.C. § 2241), if his conviction entailed other "serious disabilities," such as loss of voting rights and exclusion from jury duty. Carafas v. LaVallee, 391 U.S. 234 (1968). Since a punitive discharge, or even reduction in rank, seems at least as serious a disability as loss of the right to be a juror, a

military convict could well argue that his petition for habeas corpus is not rendered moot by the expiration or remission of his period of confinement.

[44]*E.g.,* Augenblick v. United States, 377 F.2d 586 (Ct. Cl. 1967); Juhl v. United States, 383 F.2d 1009 (Ct. Cl. 1967) (suits to recover pay forfeited pursuant to court-martial sentence). The Supreme Court reversed the Court of Claims in each of these cases, but not on the ground that that court's jurisdiction was barred by the finality clause of article 76. United States v. Augenblick, 393 U.S. 348 (1969). Whether the Court of Claims still believes that it can entertain such suits in not quite clear. It has since awarded back pay in a case in which it found that a dismissed officer had been denied his constitutional rights, but the court-martial in question antedated article 76. Gearinger v. United States, 412 F.2d 862 (Ct. Cl. 1969). In another it denied relief, because it found no denial of constitutional rights, but it seemed to treat as open the question of whether it could have awarded the plaintiff his pay had there been a "flagrant" denial. Gallagher v. United States, 423 F.2d 1371 (1970), *cert. denied* 400 U.S. 849 (1970). Despite this hesitance, I doubt that the Court of Claims would retreat from its holdings in *Juhl* and *Augenblick* if it were faced with a substantial denial of constitutional rights. *Cf.* Shapiro v. United States, 69 F. Supp. 205 (Ct. Cl. 1947); Krivoski v. United States, 145 F. Supp. 239 (Ct. Cl. 1956), *cert. denied* 352 U.S. 954 (1956).

[45]*E.g.,* Ashe v. McNamara 355 F.2d 277 (1st Cir. 1965); Smith v. McNamara, 395 F.2d 896 (10th Cir. 1968), 394 U.S. 934 (1969); Owings v. Secretary of the Air Force, 447 F.2d 1245 (D.C. Cir. 1971), *cert. denied* 406 U.S. 926 (1972). *Contra:* Parrish v. Seamans, 343 F. Supp. 1087 (D.S.C. 1972) (holding that under article 76 of the Code, habeas corpus is the only permissible type of collateral review in a district court). The Secretary of each of the military departments is empowered by statute to "correct any military record of that department [including a record of a punitive discharge] when he considers it necessary to correct an error or remove an injustice." 10 U.S.C. § 1552 (a).

[46]Kauffman v. Secretary of the Air Force, 415 F.2d 991 (D.C. Cir. 1969), *cert. denied* 396 U.S. 1013 (1970); see Stolte v. Laird, 353 F. Supp. 1392, 1395 (D.D.C. 1972).

[47]Matter of Gregory, 219 U.S. 210, 211 (1911); *see* separate

opinion of Mr. Justice Frankfurter in Burns v. Wilson, 346 U.S. 844, 845–46 (1953). *But cf.* Frank v. Mangum, 237 U.S. 309 (1915).

[48]United States v. Hayman, 342 U.S. 205, 210–11 (1952).

[49]*Ex parte* Watkins, 28 U.S. 193, 209 (1830).

[50]Wise v. Withers, 7 U.S. 331, 337 (1806); *Ex parte* Reed, 100 U.S. 13, 23 (1879); *see Ex parte* Watkins, *supra* note 49, at 208–09.

[51]See *Ex parte* Quirin, 317 U.S. 1, 32 n. 10 (1942); Schaffter & Mathews, *The Powers of the President as Commander in Chief of the Army and Navy of the United States,* H.R. Doc. No. 443, 84th Cong., 2d Sess. 4–5 (1956); *cf. Ex parte* Milligan, 71 U.S. 2 (1866); *Ex parte* Mudd, 17 Fed. Cas. 954 (No. 9899) (D.C.S.C. Fla. 1868).

[52]Act of February 5, 1867, ch. 28, 14 Stat. 385; see United States v. Hayman, 342 U.S. 205, 211–12 (1952); HART AND WECHSLER, THE FEDERAL COURTS AND THE FEDERAL SYSTEM 1236–37 (1953).

[53]The present statute provides in pertinent part that "the writ of habeas corpus shall not extend to a prisoner unless—(1) He is in custody under or by color of the authority of the United States or is committed for trial before some court thereof: or . . . (3) He is in custody in violation of the Constitution or laws or treaties of the United States . . ." 28 U.S.C. § 2241(c).

[54]Johnson v. Zerbst, 304 U.S. 458 (1938). The petitioners happened to be marines, but they had been tried and convicted in a civilian court.

[55]*See* Pollak, *Proposals to Curtail Federal Habeas Corpus for State Prisoners: Collateral Attack on the Great Writ,* 66 YALE L.J. 50, 52 (1956); Reitz, *Federal Habeas Corpus: Postconviction Remedy for State Prisoners,* 108 U. PA. L. REV. 461, 462 (1960).

[56]Gideon v. Wainwright, 372 U.S. 335 (1963).

[57]Leyra v. Denno, 347 U.S. 556 (1954).

[58]*Ex parte* Hawk, 321 U.S. 114 (1944).

[59]*See* Brown v. Allen, 344 U.S. 443 (1953); House v. Mayo, 324 U.S. 42 (1945).

[60]The problem of the proper extent of federal intervention in this area—whether the Supreme Court ought to think quite so expansively when defining due process—has naturally provoked an exceedingly hot controversy and a correspondingly voluminous literature, judicial and otherwise, most of it highly polemical. *See, e.g., Report of the Habeas Corpus Committee of the Conference of Chief*

Justices (1954), reprinted in H.R. REP. No. 1293, 85th Cong., 2d Sess. 7–10 (1958); concurring opinion of Mr. Justice Jackson in Brown v. Allen, 344 U.S. 443, 532 (1953); Pollak, *supra* note 55; Reitz, *supra* note 55.

[61]The so-called Jencks Act, passed after the Supreme Court's decision in Jencks v. United States, 353 U.S. 657 (1957), requires the Government to produce "any statement" of the witness which is in its possession and which relates to his testimony at the trial. 18 U.S.C. § 3500.

[62]Augenblick v. United States and Juhl v. United States, *supra* note 44.

[63]United States v. Augenblick, 393 U.S. 348 (1969).

[64]Kauffman v. Secretary of the Air Force, 415 F.2d 991 (D.C. Cir. 1969), *cert. denied* 396 U.S. 1013 (1970).

[65]Kauffman, 14 U.S.C.M.A. 283 (1963).

[66]415 F.2d at pp. 992, 997.

[67]Allen v. Van Cantfort, 436 F.2d 625 (1st Cir. 1971), *cert. denied* 402 U.S. 1008 (1971). It found no error in the particular case.

[68]Arts. 31, 44, 55, UCMJ. There may be some significance in the fact that, whereas the Eighth Amendment prohibits "cruel *and* unusual punishments," the Code bars "cruel *or* unusual punishment." Until the Civil War, some military punishments, such as flogging and branding (the latter of which was not formally prohibited until 1872, although it had not been used for many years before that), were cruel (at least by modern standards) but far from unusual; others, such as shaving the head or causing the offender to wear a barrel, were more unusual than cruel. See WIN-THROP, at 437–42; Wiener, *supra* note 6, at 286–90.

[69]Arts. 10, 30, UCMJ.

[70]Arts. 32(b), 38, 46, UCMJ.

[71]384 U.S. 436 (1966).

[72]Gilbert v. California, 388 U.S. 263 (1967); United States v. Wade, 388 U.S. 218 (1967) (voice identification).

[73]White, 17 U.S.C.M.A. 211 (1967); Penn, 18 U.S.C.M.A. 194 (1969). *Compare* Carroll, 20 U.S.C.M.A. 312 (1971), holding that in a military trial "adverse matter considered in the determination of a sentence at trial must be presented in open court, with the accused having a right to object to its consideration or to rebut it."

The civilian defendant usually has no such right. *See generally* Quinn, *Some Comparisons Between Courts-Martial and Civilian Practice,* 15 U.C.L.A. L. REV. 1240 (1968).

[74]Harris v. New York, 401 U.S. 222 (1971).

[75]Jordan, 20 U.S.C.M.A. 614 (1971).

[76]Clay, 1 U.S.C.M.A. 74 (1951).

[77]Krebs, 20 U.S.C.M.A. 487 (1971).

[78]*See, e.g.,* Smith, 13 U.S.C.M.A. 105 (1962).

[79]Jacoby, 11 U.S.C.M.A. 428 (1960). Another example is Curtin, 9 U.S.C.M.A. 427 (1958), in which COMA held that the Code did not permit conviction of disobeying an order unless it was proved that the accused had actual knowledge of the order. The court considered that a contrary interpretation of the statute would have been in conflict with the Supreme Court's constitutional holding that an ex-con could not be convicted of violating a municipal ordinance requiring him to register with the police, unless it were shown that he was in fact aware of the ordinance. Lambert v. California, 355 U.S. 225 (1957). *See* Note, *Constitutional Rights of Servicemen Before Courts-Martial,* 64 COLUM. L. REV. 127 (1964).

[80]16 U.S.C.M.A. 629 (1967). The decision is discussed in Bellen, *The Revolution in Military Law,* 54 A.B.A.J. 1194 (1968).

[81]384 U.S. 436 (1966).

[82]Wimberley, 16 U.S.C.M.A. 3 (1966).

[83]*E.g.,* Tempia, 16 U.S.C.M.A. 629 (1967); Culp, 14 U.S.C.M.A. 199 (1963); Jacoby, 11 U.S.C.M.A. 428 (1960).

[84]Penn, 18 U.S.C.M.A. 194, 198 (1969).

[85]Justice Black observed some years ago that, "As yet it has not been clearly settled to what extent the Bill of Rights and other protective parts of the Constitution apply to military trials." Reid v. Covert, 354 U.S. 1, 37 (1957). The statement is still accurate.

[86]*See* Gosa v. Mayden, 93 S. Ct. 2926, 2936, n.6 (1973); Moyer, *Procedural Rights of the Military Accused: Advantages over a Civilian Defendant,* 22 MAINE L. REV. 105, 109–14 (1970).

[87]*E.g.,* Levy v. Resor, No. 67-442; D.S.C., July 6, 1967, *aff'd per curiam,* 384 F.2d 689 (4th Cir. 1967), *cert. denied* 389 U.S. 1049 (1968); United States *ex rel.* Watkins v. Vissering, 184 F. Supp. 529 (E.D. Va. 1960); Levy v. Resor, 17 U.S.C.M.A. 135 (1967).

[88]Art. 10, UCMJ; MCM, ¶20c.

[89]Art. 13, UCMJ.

[90]Noyd v. Bond, 395 U.S. 683 (1969). The Court of Military Appeals made the issue moot a few weeks later by affirming his conviction, thus completing the process of direct appellate review. Noyd, 18 U.S.C.M.A. 483 (1969).

[91]Snyder, 18 U.S.C.M.A. 480 (1969). In the few such cases which have come before it COMA has refused to upset the convening authority's decision as to the degree of restraint necessary. *E.g.,* Font v. Seaman, 20 U.S.C.M.A. 387 (1971); Green v. Wylie, 20 U.S.C.M.A. 391 (1971).

[92]The Supreme Court's original holding to this effect is Gusik v. Schilder, 340 U.S. 128 (1950). The similar decisions of the inferior federal courts are too numerous to cite. *See, e.g.,* Allen v. Van Cantfort, 420 F.2d 525 (1st Cir. 1970); Small v. Commanding General, 320 F. Supp. 1044 (S.D. Cal. 1970), *aff'd per curiam* 448 F.2d 1397 (9th Cir. 1971) (holding that exhaustion of military remedies includes the Judge Advocate General's review, under article 69 of the Code, of verdicts, including most of those in special courts-martial, which cannot be appealed to a Court of Military Review).

[93]*See* Noyd v. Bond, *supra* note 90. The Court cited as examples Toth v. Quarles, Reid v. Covert, and the other cases involving attempts to court-martial civilians, discussed in Chapter 3.

[94]*E.g.,* Cole v. Laird, 468 F.2d 829 (5th Cir. 1972); Lyle v. Kincaid, 344 F. Supp. 223 (M.D. Fla. 1972), *modified* 352 F. Supp. 81 (M.D. Fla. 1972); Schroth v. Warner, 353 F. Supp. 1032 (D. Hawaii 1973); Moylan v. Laird, 305 F. Supp. 551 (D.R.I. 1969).

[95]Department of Defense Directive No. 1300.6, May 10, 1968.

[96]Parisi v. Davidson, 405 U.S. 34 (1972).

[97]*Id.* at note 15.

[98]Lenox, 21 U.S.C.M.A. 314 (1972).

[99]An example of "conditions peculiar to military life" was presented by a soldier who made incriminating statements after being confined overnight in a large box known as a "Conex container," in an area of Vietnam where the mosquitoes were as big as bullfrogs and much more pugnacious. COMA, considering that no more comfortable accomodations were available to anyone in the area, held the statements admissible. Mackey, 21 U.S.C.M.A. 254 (1972).

[100] *E.g.*, Richards v. Thurston, 424 F.2d 1281 (1st Cir. 1970); Griffin v. Tatum, 425 F.2d 201 (5th Cir. 1970); Breen v. Kahl, 419 F.2d 1034 (7th Cir. 1969), *cert. denied* 398 U.S. 937 (1970); Lindquist v. City of Coral Gables, 323 F. Supp. 1161 (S.D. Fla. 1971).

[101] HERODOTUS, PERSIAN WARS, Bk. VII, Chs. 208–209.

[102] *See* Wiener, *supra* note 6, at 18–19.

[103] *E.g.*, Gianatasio v. Whyte, 426 F.2d 908 (2d Cir. 1970), *cert. denied* 400 U.S. 941 (1970); Doyle v. Koelbl, 434 F.2d 1014 (5th Cir. 1970), *cert. denied* 402 U.S. 908 (1971); Anderson v. Laird 437 F.2d 912 (7th Cir. 1971), *cert. denied* 404 U.S. 865 (1971); Agrati v. Laird, 440 F.2d 683 (9th Cir. 1971) (regulation valid even as to actor). The lower federal courts have disagreed on the momentous question of the military's right to forbid long-haired reservists, not on active duty, to wear short-hair wigs at reserve drills. Some have found insufficient military justification and held the regulation unlawful. Friedman v. Froehlke, 470 F.2d 1351 (1st Cir. 1972); Hough v. Seaman, 357 F. Supp. 1145 (W.D.N.C. 1973); Harris v. Kaine, 352 F. Supp. 769 (S.D.N.Y. 1972). Others disagree. Cossey v. Seamans, 344 F. Supp. 1368 (W.D. Okla. 1972); Comunale v. Mier, 355 F. Supp. 429 (W.D. Pa. 1973); McWhirter v. Froehlke, 351 F. Supp. 1098 (D.S.C. 1972).

[104] *E.g.*, Kazmierczak, 16 U.S.C.M.A. 594 (1967); United States v. Miller, 261 F. Supp. 442 (D. Del. 1966); Robson v. United States, 279 F. Supp. 631 (E.D. Pa. 1968). *See supra*, Ch. 2.

[105] MCM, ¶ 152.

[106] *E.g.*, Alston, 20 U.S.C.M.A. 581 (1971); Mossbauer, 20 U.S.C.M.A. 584 (1971).

[107] MCM, ¶ 152.

[108] Anderson v. Laird, 466 F.2d 283 (D.C. Cir. 1972), *cert. denied* 409 U.S. 1076 (1972).

[109] United States v. Carson, 282 F. Supp. 261 (E.D. Ark. 1968).

[110] Jacobson v. Massachusetts, 197 U.S. 11, 26 (1905).

[111] Schenck v. United States, 249 U.S. 47, 52 (1919).

[112] Dennis v. United States, 341 U.S. 494, 510 (1951).

[113] This is acknowledged by such vigorous defenders of free speech as Professor Thomas I. Emerson of the Yale Law School. "To a certain extent, at least, the military sector of a society must function outside the realm of democratic principles, including the principle of freedom of expression. . . . [M]embers of the armed

forces, at least when operating in that capacity, can be restricted in their right to open discussion." Emerson, *Toward a General Theory of the First Amendment*, 72 YALE L.J. 877, 935–36 (1963). There are many similar statements by federal judges. *E.g.*, Dash v. Commanding General, 307 F. Supp. 849 (D.S.C. 1969), *aff'd per curiam* 429 F.2d 427 (4th Cir. 1970), *cert. denied* 401 U.S. 981 (1971); Noland v. Irby, 341 F. Supp. 818 (W.D. Ky. 1971).

[114]Chaplinsky v. New Hampshire, 315 U.S. 568, 571 (1942).

[115]Voorhees, 4 U.S.C.M.A. 509 (1954).

[116]Near v. Minnesota, 283 U.S. 697 (1931).

[117]Judge Brosman was clear that Voorhees' writings presented no security problem and that the denial of clearance must have been based on policy and propriety. He was unable to follow Chief Judge Quinn's convenient interpretation of the Regulation.

[118]Colonel Voorhees does not again appear in the reported decisions of either the Boards of Review or COMA, from which it may be inferred that the rehearing resulted in a lesser penalty than dismissal, or no penalty.

[119]MCM, ¶ 213f(5): "Examples are utterances designed to promote disloyalty or disaffection among troops, as praising the enemy, attacking the war aims of the United States, or denouncing our form of government."

[120]19 U.S.C.M.A. 529 (1970).

[121]19 U.S.C.M.A. 539 (1970).

[122]18 U.S.C. § 2387. Like other penal provisions of federal law it can be charged under article 134 as a "crime or offense not capital."

[123]The Supreme Court had applied the principle to the Smith Act's predecessor statute in a case involving a civilian's circulation of allegedly seditious materials to civilians and troops. Hartzel v. United States, 322 U.S. 680 (1944).

[124]To the same effect, see Gray, 20 U.S.C.M.A. 63 (1970).

[125]Priest, 21 U.S.C.M.A. 564 (1972).

[126]Levy v. Parker, 478 F.2d 772 (3rd Cir. 1972).

[127]Stolte v. Laird, 353 F. Supp. 1392 (D.D.C. 1972).

[128]Lieutenant Howe's sympathizers have tended to clean up his spelling in their accounts of the affair. Professor Edward F. Sherman corrects "agression," although he leaves "facist" in its original condition. Sherman, *The Military Courts and Servicemen's*

First Amendment Rights, 22 HASTINGS L.J. 325, 334 (1971). Robert Sherrill, more partisan and less scholarly, represents Howe as completely literate. SHERRILL, *supra* note 4, at 179. It is a depressing thought (at least to a professor) that Howe, whose political analyses seem to have been not much more sophisticated than his spelling, had graduated from the University of Colorado, where he majored in political science.

[129]Howe, 17 U.S.C.M.A. 165 (1967). The court's opinion, though in reality an opinion on the merits, took the odd form of denying Howe's petition for reconsideration of its original refusal to review his case.

[130]Frohwerk v. Unites States, 249 U.S. 204 (1919); Debs v. United States, 249 U.S. 211 (1919).

[131]It must be admitted that the Supreme Court itself has been known to draw the same moral from *Schenck* and its companion cases. Dennis v. United States, *supra* note 112, at 504.

[132] *See generally* Kester, *Soldiers Who Insult the President: An Uneasy Look at Article 88 of the Uniform Code of Military Justice,* 81 HARV. L. REV. 1697 (1968).

[133]Prior to the adoption of the Uniform Code in 1950, the President, the Vice President, Congress, and the rest, were protected from the insults of enlisted men as well as officers.

[134]In two nonpolitical cases involving speech, COMA reversed convictions. In one it held invalid an order to a sergeant, who had been attempting to persuade other soldiers not to give information to officers conducting an investigation, not to talk to anyone about the investigation. Wysong 9 U.S.C.M.A. 249 (1958). In another it held that a soldier who threatened to publish his complaints about the food and the first sergeant to his congressman and the press could not be convicted of wrongful communication of a threat. Schmidt, 16 U.S.C.M.A. 57 (1966).

[135] *E.g.,* Bell, 40 C.M.R. 807 (1969); Amick & Stolte, 40 C.M.R. 720 (1969); Levy, 39 C.M.R. 672 (1968). The latter three were sprung by the civilian courts, although on the ground that the charges against them were unconstitutionally vague. *See supra* notes 46, 126, 127.

[136]18 U.S.C. § 1382. *See generally* Lloyd, *Unlawful Entry and Re-entry into Military Reservations in Violation of 18 U.S.C., §1382,* 53 MIL. L. REV. 137 (1971).

[137]Flower v. United States, 407 U.S. 197 (1972); Spock v. David, 469 F.2d 1047 (3d Cir. 1972); Burnett v. Tolson, 474 F.2d 877 (4th Cir. 1973). They may, however, impose reasonable conditions, such as requiring pamphlet distributors to police up their litter.

[138]*E.g.*, Kiiskila v. Nichols, 433 F.2d 745 (7th Cir. 1970); Bridges v. Davis, 443 F.2d 970 (9th Cir. 1971), *rehearing denied* 445 F.2d 1401 (9th Cir. 1971), *cert. denied* 405 U.S. 919 (1972); Schneider v. Laird, 453 F.2d 345 (10th Cir. 1972), *cert. denied* 407 U.S. 914 (1972).

[139]Dash v. Commanding General, 307 F. Supp. 849 (D.S.C. 1969), *aff'd per curiam*, 429 F.2d 427 (4th Cir. 1970), *cert. denied* 401 U.S. 981 (1971).

[140]Cortright v. Resor, 447 F.2d 245 (2d Cir. 1971), reversing 325 F. Supp. 797 (E.D.N.Y. 1971), *cert. denied* 405 U.S. 965 (1972). The lower court's opinion contains a lengthy survey of the judicial precedents and scholarly articles dealing with the application of the Bill of Rights to servicemen. *See* Comment, *Judicial Review and Military Discipline—Cortright v. Resor: The Case of the Boys in the Band*, 72 COLUM. L. REV. 1048 (1972).

[141]Orloff v. Willoughby, 345 U.S. 83, 94 (1953). Similar expressions are to be found in dozens, or even hundreds, of opinions of the Supreme Court and the lower federal courts. Many of them are collected in Mindes v. Seaman, 453 F.2d 197 (5th Cir. 1971). *See also* Locks v. Laird, 300 F. Supp. 915 (N.D. Cal. 1969), *aff'd on other grounds* 441 F.2d 479 (9th. Cir 1971), *cert. denied* 404 U.S. 986 (1971), which refused to find an unconstitutional interference with free speech in an Air Force Regulation forbidding servicemen to wear their uniforms at anti-war demonstrations.

CHAPTER FIVE

"To Provide for the Common Defence": *The War Power*

CHARLES EVANS HUGHES, one of the greatest among Chief Justices, had a unique ability to strip away the spongy pieties which conceal so much of the law's truth. One famous instance is his statement (made when he was not a Justice) that "We are under a Constitution, but the Constitution is what the judges say it is." Another is the blunt and pithy declaration that "The power to wage war is the power to wage war successfully." While Hughes originally uttered this apophthegm in a speech to the American Bar Association, rather than *ex cathedra*, he later repeated it from the bench and his successor as Chief Justice, Harlan F. Stone, quoted it with approval in a decision that upheld the most drastic exercise of the war power that the nation has yet seen—the first of the

Japanese Exclusion Cases.[1] In the name of the "common defence" the President and the Congress have done many drastic things, some of which would otherwise have been clearly unconstitutional. They have, for instance, deported citizens from their homes for no other reason than that their ancestors were Japanese; caused citizens to be tried and sentenced to death without a jury or the benefit of any other part of the Bill of Rights; conscripted men into the armed services and ordered them to sacrifice their comfort and even their lives for very modest pay; and seized and destroyed private property, with or without compensation. Oftener than not the Supreme Court has found that the Constitution allowed what had been done.[2]

Certainly the framers of the Constitution were much concerned with the security of the new nation against enemies, both foreign and domestic. Alexander Hamilton saw potential enemies wherever he looked. Aside from Great Britain to the North, Spain to the South and Southwest, and warlike tribes of Indians on the Western frontier, "the improvements in the art of navigation have, as to the facility of communication, rendered distant nations, in a great measure, neighbours."[3] Thus, *The Federalist* (which Thomas Jefferson called "the best commentary on the principles of government, which ever was written" and made required reading for the students at the University of Virginia) devoted more space to national security and military matters than to any other problem.[4] Hamilton saw four principal purposes of the union of the States; of these, two—and the first two at that—were "the common defence of the members" and "the preservation of the public peace, as well against internal convulsions as external attacks."[5] He had his way. All of the powers whose grant to the federal government he thought "essential to the common defence" are in fact provided in the Constitution.

A major purpose of the Constitution, as set forth in its preamble, is to "provide for the common defence." It achieves this purpose by granting to the President and Congress powers that are both great and ill-defined. "The President shall be Commander in Chief of the Army and Navy of the United States, and of the Militia of the several States, when called into the actual Service of the United States."[6] Congress can declare war, grant Letters of Marque and Reprisal, and make rules concerning captures on land and water; raise and support armies; provide and maintain a navy; and—as we have already seen—make rules for the government and regulation of the land and naval forces.[7] Congress is also empowered to provide for organizing and training the militia of the States; but it can call them forth only to "execute the Laws of the Union, suppress Insurrections and repel Invasions"—not to engage in foreign wars. (When the State National Guards, the present avatar of the militia, are called into federal service, the militiamen come as members of the National Guard of the United States, which is part of the organized reserve of the Army, Navy or Air Force. About the only role the militia clauses have played in the defense of the United States for the last century and a half is to ground a constitutional argument, several times buried by the courts[8] but regularly resurrected by opponents of the draft, that Congress cannot raise armies by conscription. The other powers are the important ones.)

Hamilton thought "These powers ought to exist without limitation, because it is impossible to foresee or to define the extent and variety of national exigencies, and the correspondent extent and variety of the means which may be necessary to satisfy them."[9] Whatever limits the Constitution places on the power to provide for the common defense must be sought in the Bill of Rights. With two minor exceptions,[10] those amendments make no distinction between war and peace. But the Supreme Court does; many actions have been held lawful in time of war which would assuredly have been unconstitutional in ordinary circumstances.

But what is "war?" No doubt war usually exists when Congress declares it. But there are exceptions even to this seemingly obvious rule: the existence of a declared war, which has not been terminated by a peace treaty or formal action of the Congress, does not always and for all purposes determine the question whether the gates of the temple of Janus are legally open or shut. The old Articles of War, for example, forbade courts-martial to try the capital crime of murder if committed in domestic territory "in time of peace." On June 10, 1949, when a soldier named John Lee was tried for a murder committed in Leavenworth, Kansas, the United States was still in a state of declared war with both Germany and Japan. But the Supreme Court, looking at the realities, held that this was "time of peace."[11]

On the other hand, "war" can certainly exist for many purposes without benefit of formal declaration, as the draftsmen of the Constitution well knew. Hamilton remarked in *The Federalist* that "the ceremony of a formal denunciation [*i.e.*, declaration] of war has of late fallen into disuse."[12] Those who fought in the Civil, Korean, and Vietnam wars did not find that the lack of a formal declaration made the proceedings any less warlike. In fact, all but five of the conflicts to which the United States has committed its armed forces since 1789—and the armed services have been used to back up American policy about 150 times—have been carried on without benefit of a declaration of war, although usually not without the more or less explicit authority of Congress. The courts, sensibly enough, have decided which of them amounted to "war" in the light of the realities and the purpose of the statutes before them. The naval hostilities against France in 1798 and 1799, for instance, were treated as war for the purposes of an Act of Congress rewarding those who recaptured American ships "from the enemy."[13] The Supreme Court held early in the Civil War that the secession of the Confederate States and President Lincoln's countermeasures created a state of war for the purposes of international law; neutral vessels running Mr. Lincoln's blockade of Confederate ports could lawfully be captured and sold as prizes.[14] The American forces in China during the Boxer Rebellion were engaged in war within the meaning of the Article of War that permitted courts-martial to try charges of murder in time of war.[15] COMA held both the Korean and Vietnam conflicts "wars," as that word is used in sections of the Uniform Code attaching stiffer penalties or suspending the statute of limitations as to military offenses committed in wartime,[16] although, as noted in a preceding chapter,[17] it also held that only a Congressional declaration could trigger wartime court-martial jurisdiction over civilians.[18] But the latter decision was something of an aberration, motivated by a prudent disinclination to tackle a tough constitutional question. As a general proposition, courts are inclined to believe that for most legal purposes the difference between war and peace depends largely on the amount of shooting.

The tougher question, still not clearly settled, is the allocation, between the President and the Congress, of power to commit the armed forces to combat.[19] Congressmen—especially those who are deeply convinced that they are far better fitted than the incumbent President to conduct the relations, diplomatic and military, of the United States with other nations— have frequently raised the cry of "usurpation" when Presidents exercised their powers to conduct foreign relations, or command the armed forces, in ways of which the Congressmen disapproved. Occasionally they have attempted to restrict the Executive's power by proposing amendments to the Constitution or introducing legislation to give Congress more say in these matters. The constitutional amendment sponsored by Senator Bricker and like-minded politicians in 1957, which would have required affirmative action by Congress before a treaty obligation could be implemented, was essentially a reaction to Harry Truman's use of the United Nations Charter as a basis for American intervention in the Korean War. The Vietnam War finally produced the War Powers Resolution of November 7, 1973, passed over President Nixon's veto, which provides in essence that, although the President may commit the armed forces to hostilities or put them in places where hostilities are likely to occur, he must first consult with Congress "in every possible instance" and must withdraw them within 90 days unless Congress declares war or provides "specific authorization" for their continued use.[20] Whether the Resolution is constitutional may be doubted. The historical record does not support the bootstrap declaration in Section 2 of the Resolution that its purpose is "to fulfill the intent of the framers of the Constitution." Equally doubtful is its practical effect: History suggests that it will be very difficult for Congress to deny support to the President when the troops are actually fighting. Indeed, some of those who voted against the Resolution, notably Senator Thomas Eagleton, did so on the ground that it gave the President more explicit power than he already had.

Whether such Presidents as Abraham Lincoln and Franklin Roosevelt (to say nothing of Harry Truman, John F. Kennedy, Lyndon Johnson, and Richard Nixon) "usurped" powers which the framers of the Constitution meant to put in the hands of Congress is debatable; a strong case can be made for the proposition that when those framers altered the British model by creating the President, with all his vague but enormous powers, they meant to leave the development of those powers to history and would not have been shocked by their actual historical development.[21] The intent of the Resolution is certainly to alter the historical balance of power between President and Congress, although that may not be its actual effect. "Strong" Presidents have moved far and fast without waiting for Congress. As fate (or the logic of events) would have it, our greatest President coincided with our greatest emergency, and Lincoln made fuller use of the powers of the Commander in Chief than any President before or since. On April 15, 1861, he called a special session of Congress—for July 4. He used the intervening weeks to take, on his own authority, a series of measures that Congress would probably have authorized, but not without controversy, hesitation and delay. On April 15, he called for 75,000 troops. On April 19 and 27, he proclaimed a blockade of the Confederacy. On April 27, he suspended the writ of habeas corpus—and when Chief Justice Roger Taney, sitting alone,[22] held that the Constitution had given this power to Congress alone and ordered the release of a lieutenant of a secessionist company of Maryland militia (whose ambitious plan to blow up railroad bridges between Baltimore and Washington had been frustrated by his confinement in Fort McHenry),[23] the order was simply ignored. On May 3, Lincoln ordered an increase of forty thousand men in the authorized strength of the regular Army and Navy. By the time the Congressmen gathered in Washington, about all they could do was ratify and approve the President's actions—which they did. The breadth and force displayed by Franklin Roosevelt in the use of his powers as Commander in Chief were second only to Lincoln's; that use included, *inter alia,* the destroyers-for-bases swap, the occupations of Greenland and Iceland, the use of the Navy to convoy vessels carrying supplies to England, and the order to the Army and Navy to attack any German submarine that entered American "defensive waters"—all prior to Pearl Harbor and all, of course, without benefit of a declaration of war, or other explicit Congressional sanction.[24] Senator Fulbright and other critics of "Presidential War" have been too preoccupied with the "usurpations" of Presidents Kennedy, Johnson, and Nixon to dwell upon the precedents or to consider whether the national interest would have been better served if Congress could have kept Lincoln and Roosevelt on a shorter leash. Indeed, the theories on the respective roles of President and Congress expounded in some of Senator Fulbright's speeches would lead to the conclusion that Abraham Lincoln was the worst President the United States ever had, and Calvin Coolidge the best.

As a practical matter, of course, it is harder for Congress to exercise its constitutional powers over the use of the armed forces than it is for the President to exercise his, and not merely because the President is one man and the Congress several hundred. Congress cannot well take the lead in initiating or conducting hostilities: when powerful Congressmen proposed in 1896 to liberate Cuba by declaring war on Spain, Grover Cleveland, motivated more by reasons of economy than love of peace, scotched the project by telling them that so long as he was Commander in Chief no declaration of war could force him to use the Army in any such expensive adventure.[25] The power of Congress is thus essentially negative. And even its veto—the power to withhold or withdraw the sinews of war—is often hard to exercise for the President can put the country in a posture from which Congress cannot easily back away, as Lincoln and Franklin Roosevelt did. Theodore Roosevelt, that improbable recipient of the Nobel Peace Prize, supplied what is still the most perfect, if not the most important, illustration of this political truth: when he showed the flag on a colossal scale by sending the fleet around the world, he was not at all deterred by the consideration that appropriated funds were only sufficient to take it half-way, for he knew that Congress would hardly be able to refuse a supplemental appropriation to bring it home.

But as a general thing, of course, Presidents have acted with the authority, express or tacit, of the legislature, for the Constitution clearly entrusts to Congress alone not only the power to impeach the President but the less drastic and more usable power to furnish or deny the men and money without which hostilities cannot be long conducted. In the last analysis, Congress could always say the last word—as it did, for example, when it denied funds for operations in Laos and Cambodia.[26] All of the armed hostilities to which American Presidents have committed the armed forces, from John Adams' undeclared war with France, to Vietnam, have had some form of Congressional backing. The lower federal courts consistently held that Congress, by supplying the money and men to carry on the fighting in Vietnam, made constitutional the actions of the President, and the Supreme Court refused to review their decisions.[27]

The third branch, too, has a role to play, for only the courts and the Court (when they cannot evade the issue) can decide whether the President and/or Congress have exceeded the powers that the Constitution allows them. And on hundreds of occasions in our history, sometimes when fighting was going on and sometimes when it had ceased or not yet begun, federal judges and Justices have had to decide whether civilians could be placed in detention camps or excluded from certain employment or tried by military courts; whether private property could be seized, with or without compensation; whether reluctant soldiers could be forced to fight in wars that Congress had not declared; whether the needs of national security justified restrictions on freedom of speech and publication. The ultimate questions are usually whether the President needed, or had, the sanction of the legislature, and whether the exercise of power was a greater interference with the liberties of individuals than the Bill of Rights can tolerate—whether, as the Supreme Court has often phrased, and sometimes applied, the basic rule, that it was more than "the least possible power adequate to the end proposed."[28]

The leading decision, at least in modern times, on the power of the President to act by himself is the famous "Steel Case," *Youngstown Sheet & Tube Co.* v. *Sawyer.*[29] Harry Truman, in the midst of the Korean War, acted to avert a nationwide strike in the steel industry by ordering Secretary of Commerce Sawyer to seize and operate the steel mills. This method of resolving labor disputes in defense industry had regularly been resorted to by Wilson and Roosevelt in both World Wars. But this time no act of Congress authorized such a seizure; indeed, Congress had four years before rejected an amendment to the Taft-Hartley Act which would have given the President just such power. Truman had thus to rely on "the authority vested in me by the Constitution and laws of the United States, and as President of the United States and Commander in Chief of the armed forces of the United States." At the suit of the steel companies, the Supreme Court, moving with unaccustomed celerity, heard arguments by as eminent and expensive a crowd of lawyers as ever appeared before it and, pausing only to compose seven separate opinions, affirmed a district court's order enjoining the seizure. The President, said Justice Black, had arrogated to himself a power which the Constitution gave only to Congress. Black's opinion, as was often the case with his constructions of the Constitution, was more emphatic than enlightening; as Justice Frankfurter delicately phrased it, "the legal enforcement of the principle of separation of powers seems to me more complicated and flexible than may appear from what Mr. Justice Black has written." But Justice Jackson did what is probably the best job to date, and as good a job as could be done today, of mapping this *terra* nearly *incognita* of constitutional law:

1. When the President acts pursuant to an express or implied authorization of Congress, his authority is at its maximum, for it includes all that he possesses in his own right plus all that Congress can delegate. In these circumstances, and in these only, may he be said (for what it may be worth), to personify the federal sovereignty. If his act is held unconstitutional under these circumstances, it usually means that the Federal Government as an undivided whole lacks power. A seizure executed by the President pursuant to an Act of Congress would be supported by the strongest of presumptions and the widest latitude of judicial interpretation, and the burden of persuasion would rest heavily upon any who might attack it.

2. When the President acts in absence of either a congressional grant or denial of authority, he can only rely upon his own independent powers, but there is a zone of twilight in which he and Congress may have concurrent authority, or in which its distribution is uncertain. Therefore, congressional inertia, indifference or quiescence may sometimes, at least as a practical matter, enable, if not invite, measures on independent presidential responsibility. In this area, any actual test of power is likely to depend on the imperatives of events and contemporary imponderables, rather than on abstract theories of law.

3. When the President takes measures incompatible with the expressed or implied will of Congress, his power is at its lowest ebb, for then he can rely only

upon his own constitutional powers, minus any constitutional powers of Congress, over the matter. Courts can sustain exclusive presidential control in such a case only by disabling the Congress from acting upon the subject. Presidential claim to a power at once so conclusive and preclusive must be scrutinized with caution, for what is at stake is the equilibrium established by our constitutional system."[30]

But, despite Jackson's lucid logic, the decision can best be explained by two practical considerations, not mentioned in any of the seven opinions. First: If the steel strike had really threatened to deprive the troops in Korea of tanks, trucks, artillery, and ammunition, Congress would have given the President the authority he needed. Second: If Congress had not done so, the Supreme Court would have.

The plain fact is that the Supreme Court's willingness to apply constitutional brakes varies in exact proportion to the degree of the emergency in which the Commander in Chief acted and the distance of the decision from that emergency. Its conduct in the Civil War is a paradigm of this political truth. Lincoln, as has been noted, resorted freely to arrest and detention without trial and to military trials of Copperheads and other Northern friends of the rebels. His proclamation of September 24, 1862, ordered first, that "during the existing insurrection, and as a necessary measure for suppressing the same, all rebels and insurgents, their aiders and abettors, within the United States, and all persons discouraging volunteer enlistments, resisting militia drafts, or guilty of any disloyal practice afford-

ing aid and comfort to rebels against the authority of
the United States, shall be subject to martial law and
liable to trial and punishment by courts-martial or
military commissions;" second, that "the writ of *habeas
corpus* is suspended in respect to all persons arrested,
or who are now or hereafter during the rebellion shall
be imprisoned in any fort, camp, arsenal, military
prison, or other place of confinement by any military
authority or by the sentence of any court-martial or
military commission." There was no legislative sanction for this order, nor was there any indication of
Congressional disapproval.

The Supreme Court might have decided the issue in
1864. Clement Vallandigham was a "Peace Democrat"
whose smug self-righteousness and talent for intemperate invective have had few parallels until very recent times.[31] Defeated for re-election to the House of
Representatives in 1862, he became Supreme Commander of the Sons of Liberty, a sort of military
branch of the extremist wing of the Peace Democrats,
which devoted itself to violent anti-Lincoln rhetoric
and the hatching of more or less fantastic plots to raise
pro-Confederate insurrections in the Middle West. In
the summer of 1863 the newly appointed commander
of the Department of the Ohio was General Ambrose
Burnside, remembered chiefly for the luxuriant side-
whiskers to which he gave his name and secondarily
for his crushing defeat at Fredericksburg. Burnside
seems to have been hardly less self-righteous and zealous than Vallandigham. Finding himself in an area
infested with Copperheads, he promptly issued Gen-

eral Order No. 38, which provided, *inter alia*, that "All [persons], found within our lines, who commit acts for the benefit of the enemies of our country, will be tried as spies or traitors, and, if convicted, will suffer death. . . . The habit of declaring sympathies for the enemy will not be allowed in this department. Persons committing such offences will be at once arrested, with a view to being tried as above stated, or sent beyond our lines into the lines of their friends. It must be distinctly understood that treason, expressed or implied, will not be tolerated in this department." Thereupon Vallandigham naturally staged a rally of the Peace Democrats, spat and stamped upon a copy of General Order No. 38 (flag-burning having not yet come into fashion), and declared that "Lincoln and his minions," having refused to negotiate an end to the war, were waging it for the purpose of crushing liberty, "for the freedom of the blacks and the enslavement of the whites." General Burnside, equally naturally, had him arrested and clapped into what Vallandigham, whose rhetoric was better than his spelling, described as a "military bastile." Two days later, he was tried by a military commission, found guilty, and sentenced to be closely confined in a United States fortress for the duration of the rebellion. A federal judge in Cincinnati denied his petition for a writ of habeas corpus,[32] thus leaving to Chief Justice Taney the distinction of being the only federal judge to attempt to interfere with military jurisdiction during the Civil War. The denial might have been appealed to the Supreme Court. But at this point Lincoln, who had not been consulted about the arrest and trial and seems to have been embarrassed by them, took astute steps to avoid such a confrontation. He commuted the sentence to deportation within the Confederate lines, and Vallandigham was turned over to a surprised Confederate picket at Murfreesboro, Tennessee. He proceeded to Richmond, where he assured Jefferson Davis and Judah Benjamin that, if the Confederacy could only hold out until November of the next year, the peace movement would sweep the tyrant Lincoln out of office. Thence, by way of a blockade runner to Bermuda, he went to Canada, where he waged a lively, if remote, campaign for the governorship of Ohio, with predictably small success. He returned to the United States in June, 1864, but Lincoln (presumably judging that he was much less dangerous at liberty than in a martyr's cell) ignored his presence.

Lincoln had, of course, made moot any appeal from the lower court's denial of the writ, for Vallandigham was no longer confined. When his lawyer petitioned the Supreme Court for a writ of certiorari, directed to the Judge Advocate General, to review the verdict of the military commission, the Justices fell back on the proposition, even then well settled,[33] that there can be no direct appeal (as distinct from collateral review of jurisdiction via habeas corpus) to a civilian court from the verdict of a military tribunal.[34] It has been suggested that they might, if so disposed, have elected to treat the petition as one for a writ of habeas corpus.[35] The Supreme Court can, of course, do anything it really wants to do, but it would not have been easy to

grant Vallandigham a writ of habeas corpus when he
was at liberty and in Canada. In any case, the Justices
had no more eagerness for such a confrontation than
Lincoln had. When, in May, 1865, Lincoln's assassins
were tried and sentenced to death by a military commission, there was no interference by the Supreme
Court or any other court.

But if the Court displayed prodigious prudence
while the great rebellion was in progress, its attitude
was very different after it had ended. At the end of
1866 it decided *Ex parte Milligan*,[36] which is a Landmark of the Law, less because of any effect it ever had
or is ever likely to have on the war powers of the
President or Congress than because of the spread-
eagle rhetoric with which Justice David Davis embel-
lished his opinion and which has ever since been copi-
ously quoted by libertarian lawyers.[37] Lambdin P. Milligan was a "Major General" in the Sons of Liberty,
and his case differed from Vallandigham's chiefly in
that a military commission found him guilty of conduct far more dangerous than the rabble-rousing with
which Vallandigham was charged. Milligan had
planned to start a Copperhead insurrection in Indiana
and Illinois, to free and arm Confederate prisoners of
war, and generally to raise holy hell. Like Vallandigham and the Lincoln conspirators, he could have
been tried in a civilian court though it would not have
been easy to impanel an Indiana jury which did not
include even one secessionist sympathizer. Sentenced
to death (although Andrew Johnson commuted the
sentence to life imprisonment), he sought habeas cor-

pus and got it, with ruffles and flourishes, drums and trumpets. Justice David Davis said the case involved "the very framework of the government and the fundamental principles of American liberty"; he declared that "No doctrine involving more pernicious consequences was ever invented by the wit of man than that any of [the Constitution's] provisions can be suspended during any of the great exigencies of government." He held, four other Justices concurring, that neither the President nor Congress could ever authorize the trial of a civilian by a military court at a time and in a place where the civilian courts were open. Chief Justice Chase and three other Justices refused to go so far; they concurred, but only on the ground that Congress, although it could have done so, had not in fact authorized such trials as Milligan's.

The actual effect, or lack of it, of the grand vindication of constitutional liberty is best shown by *Ex parte Quirin*,[38] decided seventy-six years later. On June 13, 1942, Richard Quirin, Ernest Peter Burger, and Heinrich Heinck landed in the dead of night from a German submarine on Amagansett Beach, Long Island. Four nights later, Herbert Hans Haupt, Edward Kerling, Werner Thiel, and Hermann Otto Neubauer landed from another submarine at Ponte Vedra Beach in Florida. All were Germans who had lived in the United States and spoke fluent American; one, Haupt, we may assume to have been a citizen of the United States. All had attended a sabotage school near Berlin. They came ashore amply supplied with explosives, fuses, and incendiary devices, as well as large sums of

American currency, their mission being to do as much injury as possible to American war production. The FBI arrested all of them in New York and Chicago within two weeks of their landing, and before they had blown up or burned down anything; it has been supposed that at least one of the saboteurs made it his first order of business to communicate with Mr. Hoover's G-Men.[39]

The civilian courts in New York and Florida were, of course, open and functioning, and the saboteurs might have been tried in those courts for violations of the Espionage Act of 1917. But President Roosevelt, not unmindful of the parallels between himself and Lincoln, immediately issued two proclamations. One provided, in very sweeping terms, that "all persons who are subjects, citizens or residents of any nation at war with the United States or who give obedience to or act under the direction of any such nation, and who during time of war enter or attempt to enter the United States . . . through coastal or boundary defenses, and are charged with committing or attempting to commit sabotage, espionage, hostile or warlike acts, or violations of the law of war, shall be subject to the law of war and to the jurisdiction of military tribunals." Moreover, such persons were denied access to the civil courts—which is to say that the President suspended the writ of habeas corpus in the case of these persons. The second proclamation created a military commission, prescribed its procedure (which gave defendants substantially less protection than they would have had in a civil court or court-martial),[40] and directed it to try the saboteurs for offenses against the law of war. They were convicted: six were sentenced to death, one to life imprisonment, and one to thirty years. Their military counsel[41] promptly sought habeas corpus on behalf of all save the saboteur who had gotten off with thirty years. The case reached the Supreme Court in record time; although the Justices had scattered across the country for the summer recess, they hurried back to Washington and heard argument on July 29 and 30. The very next day they announced their unanimous decision[42] that the military commission had jurisdiction in a cryptic *per curiam* opinion that gave no reasons but promised a full opinion at a later date. With equal promptitude, the sentences were executed. The full opinion followed three months later.

The Court could have followed *Milligan,* which predictably was the mainstay of the petitioners' argument. There were, of course, differences, which the Court stressed, and some of them were arguably important. There *was* legislative authority for the military commission of 1942, for the Articles of War (like the present Uniform Code) gave military commissions "jurisdiction in respect of offenders or offenses that . . . by the law of war may be triable by such military commissions," and the Espionage Act provided in terms that it should not be deemed to limit the jurisdiction of military tribunals. But the majority had held in *Milligan* that Congress could not constitutionally authorize the trial of civilians in military courts when the civilian courts were open. Milligan was a citizen and resident of Indiana and had never been a resident of any of the Confederate States. But if Haupt was an American citizen, as the Court assumed, it is hard to see why his constitutional rights were lessened by his sojourn in Germany. Milligan, said the Court, "not being a part of or associated with the armed forces of the enemy, was a nonbelligerent, not subject to the law of war," whereas Quirin and the others clearly violated that law when, acting under the orders of the German government, they came behind the lines of the United States in disguise and with hostile intent.[43] Here is the most convincing distinction. Milligan had in fact been charged, *inter alia,* with violation of the law of war, but there was no evidence that he and his fellow Sons of Liberty had any authority from the Confederate government or formed any part of its military or paramilitary forces. They were doubtless guilty of treason and many other offenses, but they were not "belligerents", lawful or unlawful, as that term is understood today[44] or as it was understood in 1864. But, as a practical matter, it seems to me that the decisive difference between *Milligan* and *Quirin* is that the former was decided after the last army of the Confederacy had surrendered, and the latter when the nation was waging war with enemies who seemed uncomfortably near to winning. The point is further illustrated by the Court's apparent reaffirmation of *Milligan* in *Duncan* v. *Kahanamoku,*[45] decided after Japan had surrendered. That case is discussed in the next chapter.

The Court's pragmatic approach to the war power is even better demonstrated by the Japanese Exclusion

Cases. On February 19, 1942, President Roosevelt issued an Executive Order that empowered the Secretary of War and subordinate military commanders to designate "military areas" from which any or all persons might be excluded and within which they were to be subject to whatever restrictions the Secretary or his subordinates might in their absolute discretion impose. Under the authority of this Order the entire West Coast was made a "military area," and all persons of Japanese ancestry, regardless of their citizenship or loyalty to the United States, were first required to register for evacuation and subjected to an 8 P.M. curfew, and then removed to "relocation centers." On March 21 Congress in effect ratified Roosevelt's action by making it a misdemeanor, punishable by fine and imprisonment, to violate any restriction imposed under the Executive Order. The first case to reach the Supreme Court, in May, 1943, was that of a young man who, though of Japanese descent, had been born and raised in Seattle, had never been in Japan, and was an American citizen. He was convicted in federal court of having violated the curfew and sentenced to three months confinement. The Court held unanimously that the curfew was constitutional: though "distinctions between citizens solely because of their ancestry are by their very nature odious," the Justices said the President and the military might reasonably have concluded that such a measure was necessary to reduce the danger of invasion, sabotage, and espionage in an area full of shipyards, aircraft factories, and other vital installations.[46] It may be observed that a curfew is a relatively minor restriction on personal liberty, and that the Japanese Empire in early 1943 still looked extremely formidable.

Two more cases reached the Court in the fall of 1944 and were decided on the same day, December 18. One held constitutional an order excluding from his home in California an American citizen of Japanese descent, although "no question was raised as to petitioner's loyalty to the United States."[47] But this time Justices Owen Roberts, Frank Murphy, and Jackson (although not Justice Black, who wrote the opinion, or Justice Douglas) dissented. And in the other case, the Court finally held—unanimously—that what was being done to a citizen of Japanese descent, concededly loyal, could not be justified by the needs of the common defense.[48] Mrs. Mitsuye Endo was confined in a "relocation center" for no other reason than that she had not succeeded in finding a place to go where "community sentiment" was not unfavorable to banished Japanese-Americans. None of the Justices could see any connection between such community sentiment and the national defense. Technically, the holding was only that neither the Executive Order nor the Act of Congress authorized confinement for any such reason; but the opinion left little doubt that if they had, they would to that extent have been unconstitutional.

The treatment of Japanese-Americans by the President, the Congress, and the Court (in its first two decisions) was subjected to severe criticism even during World War II,[49] and no commentator has had a kind word since then. But the condemnation is not based on error in the Court's construction of the Constitution, but on the simple fact that we know, in the light of hindsight, that the vast majority of Japanese-Americans were loyal to the United States and that there was in fact no need to remove them from their homes, much less to confine them in "relocation centers." If they had really posed the same threat as did, for example, the Nazified "Sudetendeutsch" who populated the part of Czechoslovakia which bordered on Nazi Germany, neither the actions of the President nor the Supreme Court's upholding of those actions could have been denounced. As it was, Roosevelt, his generals, and Congress should bear most of the blame. The Supreme Court would have taken a very heavy burden on itself if it had held, in the midst of war, that there was no justification for a military decision made by those to whom the conduct of the war was entrusted.

When no great crisis exists, the Court is naturally more inclined to scrutinize sharply the actions of President and Congress in the name of national security, and to deny them the benefit of the doubt. Two recent examples will make the point. The Subversive Activities Control Act, passed in 1950 over the veto of President Truman, in effect made it criminal for a member of the Communist Party to work in a "defense facility"—regardless of whether there was any evidence that he was himself likely to commit espionage or sabotage, or whether his particular job gave him any opportunity to do so. A majority of the Court, seventeen years later, held the Act "an unconstitutional abridgment of the right of association protected by the First Amendment."[50] "The phrase 'war power' cannot be invoked," said Chief Justice Warren, "as a talismanic incantation to support any exercise of congressional power which can be brought within its ambit." Real security risks could be barred from "sensitive" positions, but only under "narrowly drawn" legislation, providing for accurate separation of sheep and goats. The case seems to be distinguishable from the Japanese Exclusion Cases, which upheld a mass expulsion without effort to determine whether any particular Japanese-American was actually disloyal, only on the pragmatic ground that a great war was in progress in 1943, while there was no comparable crisis in 1967.

The other example is the celebrated case of the Pentagon Papers,[51] in which the Court, holding that the Government had not carried its "heavy burden" of showing justification for prior restraint of publication, refused to enjoin the New York *Times* and the Washington *Post* from publishing an assortment of top-secret documents that had been stolen by Daniel Ellsberg, that curious combination of exhibitionist and sneak, and given to the *Times*. (Whether Ellsberg or the newspapers could be tried and punished for their roles in the affair is a different question, depending on the construction of various statutes, such as the Espionage Act of 1917, as well as the First Amendment. Unfortunately, the inept and illegal attempt of some people in the Executive Branch to get some dirt on

Ellsberg by burglarizing his psychiatrist's office, led to the dismissal of the charges against him without any resolution of these questions.) As the event has proved, it would have been difficult to show that publication by the *Times* and *Post* would endanger the national security, if only because, in the age of Xerox, so many copies were already in other unauthorized hands. (By the time the case reached the Supreme Court, the Government had made a hasty screening of the documents and sought to bar publication of only a few of them.) All of the Justices except Hugo Black were willing to concede that there might be circumstances in which publication could constitutionally be prevented. (Justice Douglas said that the "war power" was not involved, although he mentioned it only to make his points [which no one else on the Court seemed to share] that the war power belongs exclusively to Congress and that Congress can exercise it only by declaring war. He managed to overlook the Civil War, along with many lesser precedents.) I think it reasonably safe to guess that if a newspaper proposed to publish information which really might endanger national security and which would not otherwise get into unfriendly hands—if, for example, a newspaper had proposed to publish the Allies' plans for the invasion of France on June 6, 1944—the Court, including Justice Black, would have talked much less about the First Amendment and much more about national security.

No aspect of the common defense stimulates more polemics and emotion than the draft, for the simple reason that none affects so many citizens so directly and painfully. Though conscription has occasionally been loosely described as an exercise of the "war power,"[52] it has bases entirely independent of the Congressional power to "declare war"; it rests on the authority to raise and support armies, and to provide and maintain a navy. Except in time of actual war, it is an exercise of the power in time of peace to prepare for war.

All ancient societies seem to have accepted the principle that every able-bodied male could be required to bear arms.[53] The Saxon "fyrd" was a force of this sort. The Norman monarchs, of course, relied primarily upon feudal levies, but they claimed the same power as the Saxon kings and used it once or twice to put down insurrections by the feudal nobility. In the wars of the eighteenth century and the Napoleonic wars, Parliament passed many acts providing for conscription into the militia.[54] But these acts did not allow the conscripted militiamen to be sent outside the realm.[55] For foreign service, His Britannic Majesty had to rely on those who volunteered for service in the regular forces, supplemented occasionally by vagrants, idlers, smugglers, deserters from the militia, and incorrigible rogues, whom Parliament permitted to be sentenced to service in the regular forces.[56] But not even the lash and the rest of the apparatus of eighteenth century military discipline could make useful soldiers out of such unlikely prospects—they usually deserted at the first opportunity—and the experiment was abandoned before the Napoleonic wars. England was not to resort

to all-out conscription for foreign service until 1916.
The Royal Navy, whose use could hardly be limited
to home waters and whose service was harder to de-
sert, was another story. The right to impress seamen
was an ancient prerogative of the crown, going back at
least to the thirteenth century and probably to the
time of Alfred; it reached its peak in the Napoleonic
wars.[57] It never had any affirmative parliamentary
sanction, although many acts of Parliament implicitly
recognized its existence, by granting exemptions.[58]
The administrative technique was simple and efficient:
if the press gang spotted a likely-looking man, he was
tendered the King's shilling. ("Press" came from Nor-
man-French "prêt," the ready money which was thrust
into the recruit's hand to bind the "contract".) If he
had the temerity to refuse the King's shilling, he was
promptly knocked down and then ordered to stand in
the King's name. In theory, the press gangs were limited to seamen and seaports, but in their great days
they roved far inland and embraced within their jurisdiction any man who looked as if, by the liberal use of
a rope's end, he might be made into a sailor. The press
had never been very popular, and by 1815 it was so
detested that the King has never since asserted his
prerogative.

The draftsmen of the Constitution were thus familiar with the idea of compulsory military service, at
least in the militia. (It is extremely unlikely that they
intended to write into the Constitution the royal
prerogative of pressing seamen. Indeed, the British
Navy's custom of halting American merchantmen on

the high seas and pressing members of the crew who sounded like Englishmen was a major cause of the War of 1812.) Conscription for militia duty was practiced in the colonies, and the constitutions of at least nine of the original thirteen States explicitly allowed it.[59]

Whether the framers of the Constitution intended to include in the power to raise and support armies the power to do so by conscription is a question of history that can never be quite settled. It seems to me intrinsically unlikely that, having once made the great decision to have a standing federal army, they meant Congress to have less power than the States. This conclusion is reinforced by the fact that they rejected in 1790 an amendment, proposed by Rhode Island, that "no person shall be compelled to do military duty otherwise than by voluntary enlistment, except in cases of general invasion";[60] both those who proposed and those who rejected the amendment must have supposed that without it Congress would have the power to raise armies by conscription.

Congress did not in fact resort to a draft until March 3, 1863.[61] (The Confederate Congress, acting under a similar constitutional provision, had done so a year earlier.) The constitutionality of the Civil War draft, which seems to have operated principally as a stimulus to voluntary enlistment,[62] seems not to have been tested in any federal court. The only important decision was rendered by the Supreme Court of Pennsylvania which, by a 3–2 majority, first held the federal draft unconstitutional on the ground that such a Congressional power was inconsistent with the militia clauses (reasoning that the States would be left with no militia if Congress could conscript the militiamen) and then, a new Justice having replaced one of the Justices who had comprised the majority and whose term had expired, reversed itself, 3–2.[63] The constitutionality of the Confederate draft was similarly challenged in a number of cases and invariably upheld.[64]

Although the constitutionality of conscription has been disputed on all imaginable, and some nearly unimaginable, grounds, neither the Supreme Court nor any other federal court has ever been persuaded. The World War I draft was unanimously held constitutional, as was the peacetime draft of 1940.[65] Chief Justice Warren said flatly in 1968 that "the power of Congress to classify and conscript manpower for military service is 'beyond question.' "[66] But opponents of the draft never give up, and their incessant litigation has produced literally hundreds of decisions of the federal courts rejecting their claims that Congress can raise Armies only by voluntary enlistment, that the draft violates the First Amendment, that it deprives them of liberty without due process, that it constitutes involuntary servitude in violation of the Thirteenth Amendment, that limiting its operation to males is a denial of Equal Protection, and so forth and so on, *ad infinitum, ad nauseam.*[67] The anti-draft lawyers have always been full of moral outrage and red-hot rhetoric; in 1918 Chief Justice Edward White (like Holmes, an old soldier of the Civil War, although on the other side) reluctantly decided not to strike one of their briefs from the record as "impertinent and scandalous," but only because "we think the passages on their face are so obviously intemperate and so patently unwarranted that if, as a result of permitting the passages to remain on the files, they should come under future observation, they would but serve to indicate to what intemperance of statement an absence of self-restraint or forgetfulness of decorum will lead."[68]

The latest Selective Service Act did, however, present one very substantial constitutional question, which the Supreme Court avoided only by devices which do no credit to the Justices who resorted to them. The old English statutes providing for the conscription of militiamen had generally exempted clergymen and "the People called Quakers," although, in some of them, Parliament required a drafted Quaker to pay the reasonable hire of a substitute.[69] Ministers, like schoolmasters and practicing medical men, were presumably exempted on the theory that they were essential to the welfare of the community; the Quakers (and, in some cases, other religious pacifists, such as United Brethren),[70] in recognition of their conscientious scruples. This pattern was continued in the Civil War drafts, both Union and Confederate, and in all subsequent American conscription laws. The Selective Service Act[71] exempted ministers of religion and theological students (a factor that for several years did much to arrest the steady decline in enrollment in the nation's divinity schools) and went on to exempt

Any person . . . who, by reason of religious training and belief, is conscientiously opposed to participation in war in any form. As used in this subsection, the term 'religious training and belief' does not include essentially political, sociological, or philosophical views, or a merely personal moral code.[72]

Congress' preference of religious objectors to military service had obvious reasons, both historical and practical. Historically, pacifism had almost always taken a religious form, as did most political, ethical, or philosophical convictions in the seventeenth and eighteenth centuries. Practically, membership in a pacifist sect like the Quakers was fairly good evidence that the claimed scruples were honest and not an *ad hoc* belief inspired by nothing more sincere than a desire to avoid the inconvenience and danger of military service. But whatever the justification for imposing a religious test for conscientious objectors, obvious difficulties are posed by the First Amendment's command that "Congress shall make no law respecting an establishment of religion." If the price of exemption from the draft is attending divinity school or professing some sort of religious faith, Congress is obviously doing a good deal to promote piety (*i.e.*, to establish religion) —much more than is done, for example, by laws requiring schoolchildren to mumble a nondenominational prayer or listen to a verse or so from the Bible.

The World War I Selective Draft Law, although it exempted ministers and theological students of all faiths, exempted members only of enumerated religious sects, like Quakers, whose tenets forbade participation in war. Unlike the later act, it would not have benefited a member of a non-pacifist sect whose personal expansion of the dogmas of his faith led him to conscientious objection to war. It favored not merely religion in general, but some religions over others. But the Court gave short shrift to the argument that it violated the First Amendment: "We pass without anything but statement the proposition that an establishment of a religion or an interference with the free exercise thereof repugnant to the First Amendment resulted from the exemption clauses . . . because we think its unsoundness is too apparent to require us to do more."[73]

But in the sixties the Court raised high the wall between church and state. It held unconstitutional, as establishments of religion, school-prayer and Bible-reading laws.[74] By such standards as these, the Court would have had great trouble with a statute that required military service from agnostics and atheists, no matter how strong their objection to war, while exempting those who traced their convictions to religious belief. But to hold the provision unconstitutional might have meant subjecting ministers, Quakers, and all of the other beneficiaries of Congressional piety to the draft—unless and until Congress did what it had always refused to do and extended its grace to everyone who sincerely professed total aversion to war. A majority of the Court resolved the dilemma by resorting to a statutory construction of unique implausibility. The first case, *United States* v. *Seeger*,[75] was decided at a time when the Act defined "religious training and belief" as "belief in a relation to a Supreme Being involving duties superior to those arising from any human relationship, but [not including] essentially political, sociological, or philosophical views or a merely personal moral code." Daniel See-ger, a splendid specimen of a rather common modern mentality, whose mooncalf metaphysics almost per-suade me to become an orthodox Christian, said he believed in "goodness and virtue," and expressed "skepticism or disbelief in the existence of God." The closest he came to a belief in a "Supreme Being" was to concede that "the cosmic order does, perhaps, sug-gest a creative intelligence." The Court unanimously concluded that Seeger was religious; "the test of belief 'in a relation to a Supreme Being' is whether a given belief that is sincere and meaningful occupies a place in the life of its possessor parallel to that filled by the orthodox belief in God of one who clearly qualifies for the exemption." Justice Douglas wrote a concurring opinion in which he outdid Seeger, the rest of the Court, and even himself. Quoting the Rig Veda and various works on Buddhism, and crediting Congress with his own "tolerance and sophistication," he con-strued "Supreme Being" to include "the cosmos as well as an anthropomorphic entity." It is difficult, if not impossible, not to believe in the cosmos. I doubt that Voltaire himself could have achieved it; certainly no garden-variety agnostic or atheist could, under this definition of "Supreme Being," disqualify himself. The general flavor of the tolerance and sophistication, the adeptness in the mysterious wisdom of the East that Justice Douglas attributed to Congress is illus-trated by an entirely typical extract from his opinion:

Philosophically, the Supreme Being is the transcendental Reality which is Truth, Knowledge and Bliss. It is the source of the entire universe. In this aspect Brahman is Isvara, a personal Lord and Creator of the universe, an object of worship. But, in the view of one school of thought, that of Sankara, even this is an imperfect and limited conception of Brahman which must be transcended: to think of Brahman as the Creator of the material world is necessarily to form a concept infected with illusion, or *maya*—which is what the world really is, in highest truth. Ultimately, mystically, Brahman must be understood as without attributes, as *neti neti* (not this, not that).[76]

Even this transcendental silliness, which stood without peer or rival in the nearly four hundred volumes of reported decisions of the Supreme Court, was shortly to be transcended. After reading *Seeger* on the nature of the Supreme Being, Congress recast the exemption provision, omitting all mention of a Supreme Being, whether Brahman, Isvara, Buddha, or Jehovah. But the Court was not to be forced into a confrontation with the Constitution. Next came one Elliott Ashton Welsh, II, claiming exemption as a conscientious objector. Welsh very honestly denied that his beliefs had anything to do with religion and refused to say that he believed in a Supreme Being. But a plurality of the Court (Black, Douglas, Brennan, and Marshall, JJ.) knew better.[77] They reversed the Ninth Circuit for placing "undue emphasis on the registrant's interpretation of his own beliefs." "Very few registrants," they added, "are fully aware of the broad scope of the word 'religious' as used in [the Act]." It is likely that very few Congressmen were aware of it either. The four Justices wasted no time explaining what Congress meant when it said that religion did not include "essentially political, sociological, or philosophical views or a purely personal moral code." In its way, it was quite as remarkable a demonstration of how to dodge the First Amendment question as that given by the 1918 Court. Three Justices could not swallow the opinion and dissented. Justice Harlan made a majority by concurring in the result but not the reasoning. Repenting of his own concurrence in *Seeger,* he concluded that the statute meant what it said and that it was unconstitutional. It followed that all conscientious objectors or none must be exempted until Congress made its choice, and he thought it preferable to exempt the non-religious objectors, including Welsh.

And there the matter was left; any objector to war who could convince the Selective Service System or the courts of his sincerity (which was fairly easy for an articulate registrant with a knowledgeable lawyer) was free of obligation to serve in the armed forces. A sappy young man who "regards himself as a god and feels at one with a flower," who could testify that "I found myself inside the soap bubbles I was blowing," and "Each time a bubble broke I trembled," was, for the purposes of the Selective Service Act, exactly as religious as a devout Quaker or Mennonite.[78] But the Court refused to apply such loose canons of construction to Congress' requirement that the claimant must be conscientiously opposed to war in any form; one who objected only to a particular war was not exempt.[79] Yet, here too, there lurks a constitutional question, which the Court chose to slide over, for some religions, such as Roman Catholicism, condemn participation in "unjust" wars (leaving it to the individual communicant to distinguish the just from the unjust); Catholics might complain that the Act violated the First Amendment by favoring indiscriminately pacifist sects over their own.[80]

Property, of course, is no less subject to conscription than men. "Congress can draft men for battle service. . . . Its power to draft business organizations to support the fighting men who risk their lives can be no less."[81] In all wars the Government has both seized it for military use and required its owners to use it in particular (and sometimes unprofitable) ways.[82] Lincoln in 1861 seized railroads that had military importance and caused the Army to operate them.[83] He was not, of course, deterred by the fact that he had no Congressional authority, but the seizure was not challenged, and Congress shortly remedied the deficiency by enacting the Railroad and Telegraph Act of 1862, under which the railroads were run by the Army until August, 1865.[84] Since 1916, when Congress gave the President power "in time of war" to seize and control any "system of transportation," the railroads have been seized no fewer than eight times (by Wilson, Roosevelt, and Truman), in each case in order to head off a strike.[85] Congressional authority to take over and operate industries essential to the war effort is not, of course, limited to transportation; the Selective Service Act, which is not restricted to wartime, permits the

President to place mandatory orders for articles he deems necessary, and to seize and operate the business if its management fails to produce and deliver them.[86] In both World Wars the power was frequently exercised, usually because of labor trouble, but sometimes because management was in financial difficulty, or just plain incompetent.[87]

If there is no Congressional authority for a seizure, it can be justified only by an emergency. When, during the Mexican War, one Colonel David Mitchell compelled an American trader named Manuel X. Harmony, with his wagons and his mules, to accompany the Army on an expedition to Chihuahua, where Harmony's property was abandoned and lost, the Supreme Court held that the public need for the mules was not so urgent as to justify Colonel Mitchell's action: "It is the emergency that gives the right, and the emergency must be shown to exist before the taking can be justified." The Court held the Colonel personally liable for the value of Harmony's property.[88] When Congress has explicitly denied the authority, the Commander in Chief's power to seize property for military reasons is still more questionable, as Harry Truman found out in the Steel Case, discussed above.[89]

Nothing in the Constitution requires Congress to pay the soldiers it drafts, and until recent times it paid them very little indeed. Property, on the other hand, has explicit constitutional rights, although the courts have never dealt very satisfactorily with the problem of compensation for conscripted property. The Fifth

Amendment, of course, provides that no one shall be deprived of property without due process of law, and more explicitly that private property shall not be taken for public use without just compensation. The Supreme Court has tended to draw a rather technical line between the government's "taking" of property in the literal sense, and governmental action that effectively strips the property of most of its value—perhaps because the Court feared to open up a Pandora's box of litigation and enormous expense by holding that someone who shows that wartime regulations interfered with his use of his property in the most profitable way, has a constitutional claim to compensation. The decisions do not form a very coherent pattern, but three of them exemplify their general tenor. In 1943 the United States, in order to avoid a strike, seized the nation's coal mines, including one belonging to Pewee Coal Co. Pewee's management ran the mine as agents of the Government; the stars and stripes flew over it; and placards reading "United States Property" were tacked on every wall. This, said the Court, was plainly a "taking" of private property for public use, for which the Constitution required compensation.[90] In 1942 the War Production Board, concluding that gold was less useful than other metals in the conduct of the war, ordered gold mines to suspend operations, in order, it was hoped, to divert their machinery and miners into the production of other minerals. The Court, stressing that the Government had never had physical possession of the mines, held that there was no "taking" and no right to compensation.[91] In the third case the Army, immediately after the Japanese invasion of the Philippines, "requisitioned" American-owned oil storage depots. Some of the petroleum products it used; the rest, and the storage facilities themselves, were destroyed to keep them from falling into enemy hands. The Army paid for what it had taken, but not for the facilities it destroyed. Again the Court denied compensation: "The terse language of the Fifth Amendment is no comprehensive promise that the United States will make whole all who suffer from every ravage and burden of war."[92]

Notes to Chapter Five

[1]Hirabayashi v. United States, 320 U.S. 81, 93 (1943). Chief Justice Hughes' reiteration of the phrase occurred in Home Building & Loan Ass'n v. Blaisdell, 290 U.S. 398 (1934).

[2] *See generally Developments in the Law—The National Security Interest and Civil Liberties*, 85 HARV. L. REV. 1130 (1972).

[3]THE FEDERALIST, No. 24 (Hamilton).

[4] *See especially* Nos. 23, 24, 25, 26, and 28, all by Hamilton.

[5]THE FEDERALIST, No. 23 (Hamilton).

[6]Art. II, § 2.

[7]Art. I, § 8.

[8] *E.g.*, Selective Draft Law Cases, 245 U.S. 366 (1918). See *infra*, p. 204–5.

[9]THE FEDERALIST, No. 23 (Hamilton).

[10]The Third Amendment permits soldiers to be quartered in houses without the owner's consent in time of war, but not in peacetime. The Fifth Amendment allows members of the militia to be tried without a grand jury indictment only "when in actual service in time of War or public danger."

[11]Lee v. Madigan, 358 U.S. 228 (1959). The decision effectively overruled an earlier holding that the conclusion of the Ar-

mistice did not end World War I for the purposes of the Article, since peace meant "peace in the complete sense, officially declared." Kahn v. Anderson, 255 U.S. 1 (1921). The Lee case is to be contrasted with holdings that the existence of a technical state of war with Germany and Japan was enough to empower the President to seize and operate railroads under a statute which gave him such power "in time of war." United States v. Brotherhood of Locomotive Engineers, 79 F. Supp. 485 (D.D.C. 1948), *cert. denied* 335 U.S. 867 (1948) *vacated as moot* 174 F.2d 160 (D.C. Cir. 1949), *cert. denied* 338 U.S. 872 (1949); United States v. Switchmen's Union, 97 F. Supp. 97 (W.D.N.Y. 1950).

[12]THE FEDERALIST, No. 25 (Hamilton). *See* Lofgren, *War-Making Under the Constitution: The Original Understanding*, 81 YALE L. J. 672 (1972).

[13]Bas v. Tingy, 4 U.S. 37 (1800). But many years later the Court of Claims opined that during the same conflict the United States remained "at peace" with France for the purposes of the Franco-American Treaty of 1778. Gray v. United States, 21 Ct. Cl. 340 (1886).

[14]The Prize Cases, 67 U.S. 635 (1863).

[15]Hamilton v. McClaughry, 136 Fed. 445 (C.C.D. Kans. 1905).

[16]Bancroft, 3 U.S.C.M.A. 3 (1953); Anderson, 17 U.S.C.M.A. 588 (1968). Accord: Broussard v. Patton, 466 F.2d 816 (9th Cir. 1972), *cert. denied* 410 U.S. 942 (1973).

[17]*Supra*, Chap. 3.

[18]Averette, 19 U.S.C.M.A. 363 (1970).

[19]*See generally* Rostow, *Great Cases Make Bad Law: The War Powers Act*, 50 TEX. L. REV. 833 (1972); Ratner, *The Coordinated Warmaking Power—Legislative, Executive and Judicial Roles*, 44 SOUTHERN CALIF. L. REV. 461 (1971); Note, *Congress, the President, and the Power to Commit Forces to Combat*, 81 HARV. L. REV. 1771 (1968); Schaffter & Mathews, The Powers of the President as Commander in Chief of the Army and Navy of the United States, H. R. DOC. No. 443, 84th Cong., 2d Sess. (1956).

[20]*See* N.Y. Times, Nov. 8, 1973, p. 20.

[21]*See* Rostow, *supra* note 19.

[22]The Judiciary Act of 1789 empowered any Justice of the Supreme Court to grant the writ.

[23] *Ex parte* Merryman, 17 Fed. Cas. 144 (No. 9487) (C.C.D. Md. 1861).

[24] The presidential actions here summarized are described and documented in Schaffter & Mathews, *supra* note 19.

[25] 2 McElroy, Grover Cleveland, The Man and the Statesman 249–250 (1923).

[26] *See* Ratner, *supra* note 19, at 471–72.

[27] Commonwealth of Massachusetts v. Laird, 451 F.2d 26 (1st Cir. 1971); Orlando v. Laird, 443 F.2d 1039 (2d Cir. 1971), *cert. denied* 404 U.S. 869 (1971); United States v. Kroncke, 459 F.2d 697 (8th Cir. 1972). Other courts held the question "political" and therefore non–justiciable. *E.g.,* Mitchell v. Laird, 476 F.2d 533 (D.C.Cir. 1973); Atlee v. Laird, 347 F. Supp. 689 (E.D. Pa. 1972).

[28] *E.g.,* Anderson v. Dunn, 19 U.S. 204, 230–31 (1821); Toth v. Quarles, 350 U.S. 11, 23 (1955).

[29] 343 U.S. 579 (1952).

[30] 343 U.S. at 635–638 (footnotes omitted).

[31] Accounts of Vallandigham are contained in VII Nicolay & Hay, Abraham Lincoln: A History, Ch. XII, at 328 *ff.* (1890), and in Fairman, Reconstruction and Reunion 1864–88 (Vol. VI The History of the Supreme Court of the United States) at 192–94, 491, (1971).

[32] *Ex parte* Vallandigham, 28 Fed. Cas. 874 (No. 16,816) (C.C.S.D. Ohio 1863).

[33] Dynes v. Hoover, 61 U.S. 65 (1858); *see* Winthrop at 50–54.

[34] *Ex parte* Vallandigham, 68 U.S. 243 (1864).

[35] *See* Rossiter, The Supreme Court and the Commander in Chief at 37 (1951).

[36] 71 U.S. 2 (1866).

[37] By far the best account of Milligan and his case is contained in Fairman, *supra* note 31, Ch. V.

[38] 317 U.S. 1 (1942).

[39] One of the four who landed at Amagansett, a man named George Dasch, was sentenced to thirty years imprisonment, the lightest sentence awarded by the military commission, and was not among those who petitioned the Supreme Court for habeas corpus. *See* Mason, Harlan Fiske Stone: Pillar of the Law 657 (1956).

[40] The defendants were not allowed to challenge members of

the commission peremptorily: the commission was not bound by the usual rules of evidence: the acquiesence of only two-thirds of the members was required for a death sentence.

[41]Among them was Colonel Kenneth C. Royall, later Secretary of the Army. Major Lausan H. Stone, the son of the Chief Justice, had assisted in the defense before the military commission, but not in the proceedings before the Supreme Court. All counsel urged the Chief Justice not to disqualify himself, and he did not.

[42]Justice Murphy, who was on active duty in the Army, did not participate.

[43]On the advice of the German officer who dispatched them on their mission, the saboteurs wore German uniforms, or parts thereof, when they landed, but they immediately discarded and buried them, proceeding inland in civilian clothes, and thus became unlawful belligerents.

[44]*See* Article 4 of the Geneva Convention of 1949 Relative to the Treatment of Prisoners of War, which defines lawful belligerents in such a way as to exclude persons who have no connection with an enemy country other than sympathy with its aims.

[45]327 U.S. 304 (1946).

[46]Hirabayashi v. United States, 320 U.S. 81 (1943).

[47]Korematsu v. United States, 323 U.S. 214 (1944).

[48]*Ex parte* Endo, 323 U.S. 283 (1944).

[49]*E.g.*, Rostow, *The Japanese-American Cases—A Disaster,* 54 YALE L. J. 489 (1945).

[50]United States v. Robel, 389 U.S. 258 (1967).

[51]New York Times Co. v. United States, 403 U.S. 713 (1971).

[52]*See, e.g.*, United States v. Nugent, 346 U.S. 1, 9 (1953).

[53]*E.g.*, Numbers 1:1–3. *See* Shaw, *Selective Service: A Source of Military Manpower,* MIL. L. REV., July 1961, at 35.

[54]*E.g.*, 30 GEO. II, Ch. XXV (1757); 43 GEO. III, Ch. LXXXII (1803).

[55]Compare clause (15) of article I, section 8 of the Constitution, which empowers Congress to call forth the Militia only "to execute the Laws of the Union, suppress Insurrections and repel Invasions."

[56]*E.g.*, 29 GEO. II, Ch. IV (1756) ("such able-bodied Men as do not follow or exercise any lawful Calling or Employment, or have not some other lawful and sufficient Support and Mainte-

nance"); 30 GEO. II, Ch. VIII (1757) ("all able-bodied, idle and disorderly Persons"); 19 GEO. III, Ch. X (1779) (adding to the categories already mentioned "all able-bodied Persons . . . guilty of illegal landing, running, unshipping, concealing, receiving, or carrying, prohibited Goods . . . or any foreign Goods liable to the Payment of the Duties of Customs or Excise, the same Duties not having been paid" and "Persons convicted of running away and leaving their Families chargeable upon the Parish").

[57] *See generally* HUTCHINSON, THE PRESS-GANG AFLOAT AND ASHORE (1913); LEWIS, A SOCIAL HISTORY OF THE NAVY 1793–1815, 95–116 (1960); DUGAN, THE GREAT MUTINY, 61–62 (1965).

[58] *See* BLACKSTONE, COMMENTARIES ON THE LAWS OF ENGLAND Bk. I, Ch. 13 at 419–420 (Chitty ed. 1827).

[59] *See* Marcus, *Some Aspects of Military Service,* 39 MICH. L. REV. 913, 932 (1941).

[60] 1 ELLIOT, DEBATES ON THE FEDERAL CONSTITUTION 336 (1836).

[61] *See* VII NICOLAY & HAY, ABRAHAM LINCOLN: A HISTORY, Ch. I (1890).

[62] Nicolay and Hay state that "a comparatively small number of men" were obtained directly by the draft. But some $26,000,-000 was raised under the provision which permitted drafted men to purchase exemption by paying $300. A man who could not or would not purchase exemption was financially well advised to volunteer before he was drafted, for volunteers usually received a substantial bounty.

[63] Kneedler v. Lane, 45 Pa. St. 238 (1863).

[64] *E.g.,* Barber v. Irwin, 34 Ga. 27 (1864); Burroughs v. Peyton, 57 Va. 470 (1864); *Ex parte* Coupland, 26 Tex. 386 (1862).

[65] Selective Draft Law Cases, 245 U.S. 366 (1918); Cox v. Wood, 247 U.S. 3 (1918). Decisions upholding the 1940 draft include United States v. Herling, 120 F.2d 236 (2d Cir. 1941) and United States v. Lambert, 123 F.2d 395 (3d Cir. 1941).

[66] United States v. O'Brien, 391 U.S. 367 (1968).

[67] A collection of the leading decisions is contained in Rowland v. Tarr, 341 F. Supp. 339 (E.D. Pa. 1972).

[68] Cox v. Wood, 247 U.S. 3, 6–7 (1918).

[69] *E.g.,* 30 GEO. II, Ch. XXV, § XXVI (1757); 42 GEO. III, Ch. XC, § XXVII (1802): 46 GEO. III, Ch. XC, § VI, XX (1806).

[70] *E.g.,* 46 GEO. III, Ch. XC, § VI, XX (1806).

[71]For a description of the Act *see* Comment, *Selective Service and the 1967 Statute*, 40 MIL. L. REV. 33 (1968).

[72]The Department of Defense, although it is not required by law to do so, as a matter of policy allows discharges to persons already in the armed services who develop conscientious objections meeting the same standards which the Act prescribes for draftees seeking exemption. There has, of course, been a huge volume of litigation, often successful, by applicants who contended that the service secretaries' determinations that they were not genuine conscientious objectors were "without basis in fact." *See, e.g.,* DeWalt v. Commanding Officer, 476 F.2d 440 (5th Cir. 1973); Note, *Habeas Corpus and the In-Service Conscientious Objector*, 1969 UTAH L. REV. 328.

[73]Selective Draft Law Cases, 245 U.S. 366, 389–90 (1918).

[74]Engel v. Vitale, 370 U.S. 421 (1962); School District v. Schempp, 374 U.S. 203 (1963).

[75]380 U.S. 163 (1965).

[76]380 U.S. at 189–90.

[77]Welsh v. United States, 398 U.S. 333 (1970).

[78]Confield v. Tillson, 312 F. Supp. 831 (S.D.Ga. 1970).

[79]Gillette v. United States and Negre v. Larsen, 401 U.S. 437 (1971).

[80]A District Court had so held prior to the Supreme Court's decisions in *Gillette* and *Negre*. United States v. McFadden, 309 F. Supp. 502 (N.D. Cal. 1970), *vacated and remanded* 401 U.S. 1006 (1971). In one other curious case a District Court held that the First Amendment required Congress to exempt those whose religious objection to military service was that it would force them to submit to vaccination, inoculation, and medical treatment, if it exempted religious pacifists. United States v. Carson, 282 F. Supp. 261 (E.D. Ark. 1968).

[81]United States v. Bethlehem Steel Corp., 315 U.S. 289, 305 (1942). To similar effect *see* Lichter v. United States, 334 U.S. 742, 754 (1948). Somewhat ironically, the ringing declaration in the Bethlehem case was used to refute a Government contention that the urgency of its needs in World War I had "coerced" it into making contracts which were excessively generous to Bethlehem and that it should therefore be relieved of its contractual obligation to pay enormous bonuses to that corporation. Congress can

(and before World War II did) constitutionally provide for the renegotiation of contracts which result in excessive profits. Baltimore Contractors, Inc. v. Renegotiation Board, 383 F.2d 690 (4th Cir. 1967).

[82]Congress may also forbid the use of property for a purpose which it thinks harmful to the war effort. In World War I the Supreme Court held constitutional, as a reasonable incident of the power to raise and support armies, the Secretary of War's authority to padlock bawdy houses within five miles of a military post. McKinley v. United States, 249 U.S. 397 (1919).

[83]*See* RANDALL, CONSTITUTIONAL PROBLEMS UNDER LINCOLN (rev. ed. 1951); Aitchison, *War Time Control of American Railways*, 26 VA. L. REV. 847, 856 (1940).

[84]Act of January 31, 1862, Ch. 15, 12 Stat. 334. The Act expired by its own terms upon "the suppression of this rebellion." *See* VIII RICHARDSON, MESSAGES AND PAPERS OF THE PRESIDENTS 3314 [Lincoln, Order of May 25, 1862] (1897).

[85]*See* 10 U.S.C. §§ 4742, 9742. On the rare occasions when seizures under the statute were challenged, they were upheld, even when the "time of war" was technical, resulting merely from failure to sign a peace treaty after the end of hostilities. United States v. Brotherhood of Locomotive Engineers, 79 F. Supp. 485 (D.D.C. 1948), *cert. denied* 335 U.S. 867 (1948), *vacated as moot* 174 F.2d 160 (D.C. Cir. 1949), *cert. denied* 338 U.S. 872 (1949); United States v. Switchmen's Union, 97 F. Supp. 97 (W.D.N.Y. 1950).

[86]50 U.S.C. (App.) § 468.

[87]An exhaustive survey of the numerous statutes authorizing seizure of various types of industrial property and of the many instances in which such seizures were effected during the two World Wars is contained in Appendices I and II to Justice Frankfurter's concurring opinion in Youngstown Sheet & Tube Co. v. Sawyer, 343 U.S. 579 (1952).

[88]Mitchell v. Harmony, 54 U.S. 115, 134 (1852). Whether Congress appropriated funds to indemnify Colonel Mitchell, I do not know.

[89]*See supra*, pp. 186–88.

[90]United States v. Pewee Coal Co., 341 U.S. 114 (1951).

[91]United States v. Central Eureka Mining Co., 357 U.S. 155 (1958). Justice Harlan could not see the distinction; "Making the

respondents' right to compensation turn on whether the Government took the ceremonial step of planting the American flag on the mining premises . . . is surely to permit technicalities of form to dictate consequences of substance." *Id.* at 181.

[92]United States v. Caltex, Inc., 344 U.S. 149, 155 (1952). To similar effect, *see* National Board of Y.M.C.A. v. United States, 395 U.S. 85 (1969), holding that damage suffered by the Y.M.C.A.'s property, which was temporarily occupied and defended by American troops during rioting in the Canal Zone, was not compensable because there was no "taking." In the curious old case of United States v. Pacific R. Co., 120 U.S. 227 (1887), the Army attempted unsuccessfully to carry the principle to its logical conclusion by requiring a railroad to reimburse the Army for the cost of rebuilding bridges which the Army had first destroyed in order to hinder a Confederate advance and then rebuilt to permit the passage of its own forces.

CHAPTER SIX

———

"To Insure Domestic Tranquillity": Martial Law

WAR IS NOT THE ONLY CRI-
sis that may require the use of military force and even
military intervention in the process of government.
Upheavals and disasters, human and natural, can create emergencies with which the police and the rest of
the civilian magistracy cannot deal unaided. Every
government has, on occasion, resorted to the use of
military force in its own territory, and against its own
citizens. Indeed, in many parts of the world, rule by
the armed forces is so common as to be practically a
part of the normal constitutional process. But the soldiers have never ruled England since Cromwell's day,
and, as I have noted, except for a few who took off
their uniforms and got elected in the usual way, such
as Washington, Jackson, Grant, and Eisenhower, they

have never played much of a direct role in the government of the United States. Of course, the generals and admirals may exert considerable influence on both the President and Congress, for both must usually rely on them for military information and advice. They are a powerful—though not always successful—lobby,[1] but some such role is probably inevitable in any form of government. Certainly, the armed forces play a great role in both Russia and China. (But no government ever reduced its military commanders to such complete subservience as Nazi Germany.) The military "governs" the United States no more than does any other powerful bureaucratic or private lobby. Even as a lobby, it has had hard sledding of late.

There have, however, been many occasions in which the President, with or without authority from Congress, has resorted to the ultimate sanction of military force, and many more in which the governors of the States have done so. That this power has not yet, on the whole, been seriously abused is due partly to our political habits, and partly to the fact that the courts, when forced to it, have generally been willing and able to place some constitutional bounds on the use of the armed forces as a tool of government.

The framers of the Constitution were very familiar with the lesson of Roman history—that the legions could make and unmake Emperors—and they took care both to make the Army dependent on Congress for its very existence and to make the chief civilian magistrate the Commander in Chief of the Army and Navy. But they also knew something of riots and mobs, and they never confused mob rule with democracy. So the Constitution, though it does not contain the words "martial law," gives Congress power "to provide for calling forth the Militia to execute the Laws of the Union [and to] suppress Insurrections," as well as to repel invasions.[2] The President "shall take Care that the Laws be faithfully executed."[3] The privilege of habeas corpus may be suspended "when in Cases of Rebellion or Invasion the public Safety may require it"[4]—whether by Congress alone, or also by the President, being a question never yet settled. Finally, considering that state governments might be faced with rebellion and riots too formidable for their own militia, they provided in unusually explicit language that "The United States shall guarantee to every State in this Union a Republican Form of Government, and shall protect each of them against Invasion; and on Application of the Legislature, or of the Executive (when the Legislature cannot be convened) against domestic Violence."[5] (The bit about "Republican government" was applied with peculiar literalness in the Reconstruction era.)

There are three principal acts of Congress, sections 331, 332, and 333 of Title 10 of the United States Code, which implement these provisions of the Constitution. They merit description.

The militia of the Commonwealth of Massachusetts had had its hands full in suppressing Shay's rebellion in 1786, and the Congress of 1792 undoubtedly had that uprising in mind when it enacted the original version of section 331. That section today provides that, "Whenever there is an insurrection in any State against its government, the President may, upon the request of its legislature or of its governor if the legislature cannot be convened, call into Federal service such of the militia of the other States, in the number requested by that State, and use such of the armed forces as he considers necessary to suppress the insurrection." Federal forces were employed with some frequency in the riots, bombing, and assassinations that characterized labor disputes in the latter decades of the nineteenth century and the early part of the twentieth.[6] In 1967 and 1968 the statute was invoked in the riots that devastated substantial areas of Detroit and other cities.[7] It is reasonably safe to predict that we have not seen the last occasion in which a State is compelled to appeal to the President for regulars to suppress disturbances that are too much for its own police and national guardsmen. The statute, unlike its constitutional base, which speaks only of "domestic Violence," is limited to "insurrection" against the State government. "Insurrection" might be thought of as something closer to a revolution than mere "domestic violence," an uprising intended to overthrow the government,[8] rather than a disorganized spree of looting and arson. Webster gives "rebellion" as a synonym for "insurrection." But, for the purposes of section 331, "domestic violence" so serious that the forces available to the State cannot control it, has always been treated as "insurrection," most recently by then Attorney General Ramsey Clark, in a letter to State governors dated August 7, 1967.[9]

But on many occasions the States have needed no outside help to deal with what their governors chose to treat as crises requiring some form of military force, or even martial law. Virtually all States have in their constitutions provisions similar to those of the federal Constitution, allowing the use of the militia to suppress insurrections and requiring the governor to see to the enforcement of the law. A few State constitutions forbid, or restrict, the subjection of the citizens to "martial law," but the wording of these provisions shows that what the draughtsmen had in mind was the trial of civilians by military courts.[10] The constitution of Rhode Island (the scene of one of the most ridiculous abuses of martial law in the nation's history, when its governor, embroiled in a political row with the proprietor of a racetrack and having been told by the State Supreme Court that he had no power to deny it a license to operate, declared a "state of insurrection" and called out the State Guard to close the track)[11] piously provides that "the law martial shall be used and exercised in such cases only as occasion shall necessarily require." A number of State constitutions explicitly authorize the governor to declare "martial law," and that of West Virginia (which has had more than its share of bloody labor-management relations) actually allows him to declare "a state of war" if he finds "insurrection, rebellion or riot" to exist in any town or county.[12] On literally hundreds of occasions State governors have used these powers, with and without justification—far oftener than federal troops have been employed. State authorities used the militia (in its modern form of the National Guard) to quell civil disturbances on more than four hundred occasions between 1957 and 1970.[13]

The other two acts of Congress mentioned above, sections 332 and 333 of Title 10, deal with situations in which the States cannot—or will not—enforce the federal Constitution and laws. Section 332, which stems from an Act of Congress of May 2, 1792, and which was employed in 1794 to suppress the Whiskey Rebellion in Western Pennsylvania, was revised and reenacted for obvious and urgent reasons in 1861. It now provides that

> Whenever the President considers that unlawful obstructions, combinations, or assemblages, or rebellion against the authority of the United States, make it impracticable to enforce the laws of the United States in any State or Territory by the ordinary course of judicial proceedings, he may call into Federal service such of the militia of any State, and use such of the armed forces, as he considers necessary to enforce those laws or to suppress the rebellion.

Section 333, dating from 1871 and sometimes known as the "Ku Klux Klan Act," is still more sweeping in its grant of discretion and power to the President. In its present form, it reads:

> The President, by using the militia or the armed forces, or both, or by any other means, shall take such measures as he considers necessary to suppress, in a State, any insurrection, domestic violence, unlawful combination, or conspiracy, if it—
>
> (1) so hinders the execution of the laws of that State,

and of the United States within the State, that any
part or class of its people is deprived of a right,
privilege, immunity, or protection named in the
Constitution and secured by law, and the constituted authorities of that State are unable, fail,
or refuse to protect that right, privilege, or immunity, or to give that protection; or

(2) opposes or obstructs the execution of the laws of
the United States or impedes the course of justice
under those laws.

In any situation covered by clause (1), the State shall be
considered to have denied the equal protection of the
laws secured by the Constitution.

These sections, it goes without saying, require no
call for help by the State authorities, nor even their
consent. They are intended for use when those authorities cannot, or will not, enforce the law, especially
federal law, or go so far as to use state force to prevent
the enforcement of federal law. Their most notable
use in modern times was, of course, to frustrate the
efforts of some of the former Confederate States to
block the enforcement of orders of federal courts to
desegregate public schools, notably in Arkansas in
1957. Governor Faubus did not merely refuse to use
the Arkansas National Guard—*i.e.,* the State militia—
to control a mob that gathered to prevent the entrance
of Negro students into Little Rock's Central High
School; he actually used the Guard to achieve the
mob's purpose. President Eisenhower, as everybody
knows, made full use of both the statutes and his own
constitutional powers to handle the situation: he took

away the Governor's army by calling the Arkansas National Guard into federal service, and he ordered it, and units of the Regular Army, to enforce the desegregation orders. The events are chronicled and the law expounded in a lengthy opinion of the Attorney General, written for the record and after the fact.[14] Attorney General Herbert Brownell, although citing the authority conferred by sections 332 and 333, added that "there are . . . grave doubts as to the authority of the Congress to limit the constitutional powers of the President to enforce the laws and preserve the peace under circumstances which he deems appropriate." The Supreme Court has, indeed, more than once upheld, in the strongest terms, the inherent power of the President to use whatever degree of military force was needed to enforce federal law. When, during the Pullman strike of 1894, federal marshals were unable to enforce the orders of the federal courts, Grover Cleveland sent in units of the Regular Army to do the job. The Supreme Court unanimously, and in the most emphatic terms, endorsed his action: "The strong arm of the national government may be put forth to brush away all obstructions to the freedom of interstate commerce or the transportation of the mails. If the emergency arises, the army of the Nation, and all its militia, are at the service of the Nation to compel obedience to its laws."[15]

There are one or two additional statutory complications. Section 334 requires the President, whenever he decides to use the troops under one of the three preceding sections, "by proclamation, immediately

[to] order the insurgents to disperse and retire peaceably to their abodes within a limited time." When rioters are obviously unlikely to pay much attention to the proclamation, the time may be very limited indeed. Thus, President Johnson during the 1968 riots following the assassination of Martin Luther King signed the proclamation commanding the rioters to disperse at 4:02 P.M.[16] and the Executive Order to the troops to suppress the riot at 4:03 P.M.[17] Of not much more practical significance is the Posse Comitatus Act of 1879,[18] which, in its present form, in substance forbids the use of the Army or Air Force "to execute the laws . . . except in cases and under circumstances expressly authorized by the Constitution or Act of Congress." (There has been some debate, largely academic, as to whether it bars use of the Marine Corps, which is legally a part of the Navy.) The purpose of the Act, of course, was to end the use of the Army to enforce the Reconstruction Acts (especially by policing elections) in the states of the late Confederacy,[19] and its importance in modern times has not been great; Presidents who wanted to use the troops have had no trouble in finding the necessary authority either in sections 331–333 of Title 10 or in the Constitution, or both. It does, however, keep local military commanders from aiding the police in ordinary criminal matters.

If there were no check on the freedom of presidents and governors to do by military force what they cannot do by lawful political means, no doctorate in political science is needed to perceive that democracy and constitutional liberty in the United States would fare no

better than they have in banana republics. But, of
course, such checks do exist. Perhaps the strongest
restraint lies in our political tradition. A would-be
Caesar could not count on the obedience of the centu-
rions and legionaries. (This is, I think, an argument
against an all-volunteer army.) No American general
has ever attempted a *coup d'état,* and most of our Presidents and governors have, to do them justice, been
fairly resistant to the temptation to rule by military
force. But when a politician does yield to that temptation, in circumstances in which he can count on the
indifference, if not the support, of most of the voters,
the ultimate power to enforce the Constitution lies in
the courts, especially the Supreme Court.

At the outset, it ought to be noted that not every use
of the military in domestic emergencies raises a substantial constitutional problem. The situations which
too many journalists, civil libertarians, and politicians
loosely lump together as "martial law" cover a very
broad spectrum, ranging from the use of troops as, in
effect, auxiliary police, subject to the control of the
civilian authorities, to the complete supersession of
civilian by military authority. At one end of the spectrum, for example, was the action of the Army's local
commander during the San Francisco earthquake and
fire of 1906. Realizing that the municipal authorities
could not cope with the complete breakdown of communications, the raging fires, the thousands of home-
less people, and the huge criminal population for
which the city's Barbary Coast was justly famed, General Frederick Funston turned out the garrisons of the

Presidio and Fort Mason and placed them at the disposal of the chief of police and the rest of the city government.[20] His action probably violated the Posse Comitatus Act, but nobody complained. At the other end is virtually total martial rule, including the promulgation of ordinances by the military commander and the establishment of military courts to try civilian offenders, such as was instituted in Hawaii after Pearl Harbor. When soldiers set up tents, chowlines, and field hospitals for the victims of an earthquake, and help the police to establish firelines and guard abandoned property from looters, not even the most zealous civil libertarian is likely to go to court about it. But when civilians are arrested, confined, tried, and punished by the military, there are real and difficult problems for the courts.

Unfortunately, it cannot be said that the decisions of the Supreme Court have been clear and consistent. It follows that the decisions of the inferior federal courts and of the state courts are equally unclear and inconsistent. There are decisions that seem to say the executive can do whatever he, in his unfettered discretion, decides is necessary to cope with what he regards as a crisis; others that seem to say there are certain things he can never do, even with the explicit authority of the legislature and in the greatest emergencies; and still others—which I think are right—that say he can do whatever is reasonably necessary to deal with a real emergency, and that the existence of the emergency and the reasonableness of his action are questions for the courts.

The Supreme Court's major decisions start with *Luther* v. *Borden.*[21] In 1842 Rhode Island was convulsed by violence, incident to the efforts of one Thomas Dorr and his followers to reform its antiquated constitution—essentially the same charter that Charles II had granted 180 years earlier—by establishing a rival government. The "Charter" government (which was recognized as the lawful government by the President of the United States) declared martial law and ordered the militia to suppress the insurrection. Luther Borden, a militiaman, carried out the order of his superior officer to arrest Martin Luther, a member of the Dorr faction, by breaking into Luther's house. After the insurrection had ended (and the old Charter had been reformed), Luther brought a civil action of trespass against Borden for breaking and entering. Borden pleaded military justification and got a verdict. The Supreme Court affirmed. Chief Justice Taney's opinion is full of language which can only be reconciled with his abortive ruling, thirteen years later, that the President of the United States could not constitutionally arrest the rebel Merryman,[22] on the assumption that Taney had far more sympathy for the Southern rebels of 1861 than he had for the Rhode Island rebels of 1842. Some of it suggests that the government's discretion is almost unchecked:

> A State may use its military power to put down an armed insurrection, too strong to be controlled by the civil authority. . . . The State itself must determine what degree of force the crisis demands. And if the government of Rhode Island deemed the armed opposition so

formidable, and so ramified throughout the State, as to require the use of its military force and the declaration of martial law, we see no ground upon which this court can question its authority. . . . And in that state of things the officers engaged in its military service might lawfully arrest any one, who, from the information before them, they had reasonable grounds to believe was engaged in the insurrection; and might order a house to be forcibly entered and searched, when there were reasonable grounds for supposing he might be there concealed.

But Taney's passions were not engaged on either side in the mini-crisis of 1842, and it will be observed that he inserted certain cautious hedges. The military had to have "reasonable grounds" for their action, and he added the significant qualification that "No more force, however, can be used than is necessary to accomplish the object." (The suggestion that the federal courts could place any limits at all on the State government's discretion must have been based on federal common law, for the Fourteenth Amendment, which forbids the States to deprive any person of life, liberty, or property without due process of law, was still twenty years in the future.)

In the *Milligan* case, as we have seen,[23] a majority of the Court, once the crisis was safely past, and Lincoln's assassins safely hanged by the sentence of a military commission, declared in ringing terms that neither Congress nor the President could authorize the military trial of a civilian in domestic territory, provided only that the civilian courts were open. That case, it is true, dealt with perhaps the most extreme form of martial rule—the trial and sentencing to death of a civilian by a military commission. The Court did not again face the problem in the Reconstruction period, although plenty of civilians in the former Confederacy were tried by military courts under the Reconstruction Act of March 2, 1867, which had been passed over Andrew Johnson's veto.[24] The Attorney General ruled such trials constitutional, distinguishing *Milligan* on the ground that the states of the Confederacy, until such time as they should create constitutions and governments acceptable to Congress, were still occupied enemy territory in which *Milligan* had allowed that military government courts could try civilians.[25] The Supreme Court might have disagreed. But when such a case reached the Court, Congress, acting under the constitutional provision[26] that "the supreme Court shall have appellate jurisdiction . . . with such Exceptions, and under such Regulations as the Congress shall make," removed this class of cases from its jurisdiction, and the Court thought it prudent to acquiesce.[27] No major test of the executive's power to suspend ordinary civil rights in an emergency was to reach the Court until 1909.

In 1904 Colorado was convulsed by one of the labor disputes so typical of the period, marked by the free use of firearms and explosives by all parties to the argument. Governor James H. Peabody declared the county to be in a state of insurrection, called out the militia, and ordered them, *inter alia,* to arrest and confine Charles H. Moyer, the President of the Western Federation of Miners. Moyer was not tried by a

military court, nor even charged with any offense, but
he stayed in the clink for nearly three months.
Released, he brought an action for wrongful imprisonment against the Governor, the Adjutant General of
the Colorado National Guard, and the company commander who had arrested him. The Supreme Court
found no deprivation of Moyer's constitutional rights
—put another way, that the Governor's actions were
permissible under the Constitution.[28] In fact, the
Governor's action was probably reasonable in the circumstances; there was more violence than could be
controlled by the State's ordinary procedure, and
removing Moyer from the scene might well be deemed
an efficient palliative. But Oliver Wendell Holmes, Jr.,
speaking for a unanimous Court, went far beyond that,
and beyond what Taney had said in *Luther* v. *Borden.*
"The Governor's declaration," said the old fighter of
the Civil War, "that a state of insurrection existed is
conclusive of that fact." It mattered not that there
might in fact have been no sufficient reason for the
Governor's act; so long as he believed in good faith
that it was necessary in order to suppress the insurrection, the courts would not interfere. The case is another of those which make one wonder how Holmes
ever came to be canonized by civil libertarians.

His language in *Moyer* was, of course, simply an
invitation to governors—and inferentially to presidents as well—to use military force, *ad libitum*, whenever they could claim an honest belief in the necessity
for a suspension of civil liberties, and in all too many
cases in the ensuing years, the invitation was gladly

accepted by governors, if not Presidents.[29] Some sort
of climax of absurdity was reached in 1931, when Governor Ross S. Sterling of Texas, attempting to keep up
the price of Texas crude by enforcing state restrictions
on oil production and impeded by a federal court's
temporary injunction of those restrictions, declared
that the oil-producing counties were in "a state of
insurrection, tumult, riot, and a breach of the peace"
—all of which, as the federal courts presently found,
was imaginative fiction, for there was, in truth, no
violence, nor any substantial threat thereof. He ordered Brigadier General Jacob F. Wolters of the Texas
National Guard to take such steps as he might deem
necessary "to enforce and uphold the majesty of the
law"—*i.e.,* to enforce the rigging of oil prices which
the federal court had just enjoined.

This was too much for Chief Justice Charles Evans
Hughes, a strong-minded man, and the rest of the
Supreme Court. The sweeping language of *Moyer* v.
Peabody was then and there abandoned. That case was
not actually overruled, for Hughes pointed out that in
fact Governor Peabody's arrest of Moyer *did* have a
reasonable relation to the suppression of an actual
insurrection; but, as Hughes put it, "the general language of the opinion must be taken in connection with
the point actually decided." What *Sterling* v. *Constantin*[30]
did was put to rest the idea that governors (or, presumably, presidents) could suspend the Constitution
by the simple expedient of declaring martial law. The
core of the opinion is worth quoting:

What are the allowable limits of military discretion, and whether or not they have been overstepped in a particular case, are judicial questions.

And, quoting from another of Taney's opinions,[31]

Every case must depend on its own circumstances. It is the emergency that gives the right, and the emergency must be shown to exist before the taking can be justified.

In short, there must be a real emergency, and the measures taken by the executive and his troops must bear some reasonable relation to the demands of that emergency. In the last analysis, it is for the courts to decide those questions. The injunction was enforced —though it should be noted that since the Court was dealing with a State governor, and not the President, there was no problem of power to enforce its order. If necessary, as in Arkansas a quarter of a century later, the Texas National Guard could simply have been ordered into federal service and told to enforce the orders of the federal courts.

But *Moyer* v. *Peabody* dies hard. Two recent decisions suggest that it is alive and well in some of the inferior federal courts—and, incidentally, these decisions are paradigms of the sort of situation in which such problems arise. The first involved the insurrectionary activities of Reies Tijerina's "Alianza Federal de Mercedes," an organization whose aims, while never very clearly specified, seem to have included the assertion of the right of Mexican-Americans to govern large tracts of land in the Southwest. In 1967 members of the Alianza met to plan the "takeover" of local government in Tierra Amarilla, the county seat of Rio Arriba county, New Mexico. Three weeks later, members of the Alianza, and their friends and relations, assembled at a nearby ranch, armed themselves with knives, guns, and explosives, and marched on Tierra Amarilla, where they seized the courthouse. There was a good deal of shooting, and various public officials were wounded or held prisoner. A state judge, a captive in his own chambers, managed to call the acting Governor, who promptly declared Rio Arriba county to be in a "state of extreme emergency." He ordered the National Guard to assist the state police in restoring peace and order. The raiders, apparently tired but happy after a long day's labor, went home to the ranch at 5 P.M. There, the police and the National Guard arrested some and temporarily detained others for questioning. All were permitted to leave on the following morning.

Juan Valdez and others who had been detained or arrested brought suit under the Civil Rights Act against the police and the Commander and various members of the National Guard, alleging a violation of their constitutional rights. On the evidence, it would have been easy enough to find that there was in truth a real emergency and that the Governor's military measures, which were not very drastic, were reasonable under the test of *Sterling* v. *Constantin*. But the trial court charged the jury in the language of Holmes: "If you find . . . that such detention was made in good faith and in the honest belief that it was necessary under the circumstances to preserve peace, then you should find for the defendant," the Commander of the National Guard. The Court of Appeals affirmed a verdict for the defendants, pointing out that the trial court's instruction was based on the language of *Moyer* v. *Peabody.*[32]

The second recent case arose out of the campus disturbances that followed President Nixon's Cambodian "incursion" in the spring of 1970. Governor James Rhodes of Ohio, finding that there were "disorders and threatened disorders" on the campuses of Ohio State University and Kent State University, called out the National Guard and ordered them "to take action necessary for the restoration of order . . . on the campuses." This time the consequences were more serious. A company of guardsmen, attempting to keep order on the Kent State campus, thought themselves menaced by a mob, some of whose members were throwing rocks and bottles, as well as epithets, at the troops. The guardsmen opened fire and killed four students who may or may not have been among the rioters. Thereafter the victims' parents brought suit, under both the Civil Rights Act and Ohio's wrongful death act, against (among other people) the Governor and the commanders of the Ohio National Guard. They sought damages of $11,000,-000. The district court dismissed the complaints on several grounds, and a majority of the Sixth Circuit affirmed the dismissal.[33] The majority quoted *Moyer* v. *Peabody* with approval; it also quoted Hughes' opinion in *Sterling* v. *Constantin*, although not the passages about judicial review of the Governor's discretion, and seemed to believe that the latter case had reinforced rather than modified *Moyer*.[34] The dissenting judge, who had read *Sterling* v. *Constantin* more carefully than his associates, rejected the idea that *Moyer* gives "a governor and National Guardsmen total immunity from any form of judicial review of their actions." "The trier of the fact," he said, "would be required to determine whether those actions fell within the permitted range of discretionary measures which were justified by the exigencies of the situation."[35] A trier of the fact might find that the emergency and the violence were great enough to place the firing on the mob within the rather broad range of permissible discretion; but that issue should have been determined. I think he was right, and I think it probable that the Supreme Court, which granted certiorari on June 25, 1973, will agree with him.

In all of these cases the troops were acting in aid and under the orders of the civilian authorities. However unconstitutional the actions of the governors may have been, there was nothing properly describable as "martial rule." In particular, no civilians were tried by military courts. The Supreme Court has always seemed to regard this particular kind of supersession of civilian by military power as the gravest of all. It went so far as to hold in *Ex parte Milligan*[36] that neither Congress nor the President could, under any circumstances, authorize the military trial of a civilian in domestic territory, not a theatre of actual warfare, "where the courts are open." There may be some doubt as to whether courts are "open" when the bias of prosecutors, judges, and jurors in a state is such that it is a practical impossibility to have a fair trial in certain classes of cases—when, for example, as was the case in the deep South for many years, whites accused of crimes against Negroes who took the Thirteenth Amendment too seriously were very rarely prosecuted and virtually never convicted. Charles Evans Hughes (speaking off the bench) did not believe that the "open court" language of *Milligan* should be taken literally: "Certainly, the test should not be a mere physical one, nor should substance be sacrificed to form."[37] In fairness, too, it should be noted that in *Milligan* Justice Davis himself added the ambiguous qualification that the courts must be "in the proper and unobstructed exercise of their jurisdiction." But, apparently, not even this qualification applied if the civilian courts were not in "the locality of actual war."[38] It could well have been argued that in Southern Indiana in 1864 it would have been impossible to have a fair trial of a Copperhead in any court except a military court: half the jurors would have voted to convict without regard to the evidence and the other half to acquit, also without regard to the evidence. Unfortunately, the Government's case was badly overargued: Attorney General James Speed and Ben Butler (a shrewd trial lawyer and politician, but a rash and intemperate partisan) urged on the Court the proposition that the Constitution was virtually suspended in time of war—and got the reaction they might have expected.

These mistakes were repeated in two cases decided

a few months after the end of World War II.[39] On December 7, 1941, immediately after the Japanese attack on Pearl Harbor, Governor Joseph B. Poindexter of the then Territory of Hawaii, acting under the Hawaiian Organic Act, declared martial law. That Act of Congress empowered him "in case of rebellion or invasion, or imminent danger thereof, when the public safety requires it, [to] suspend the privilege of the writ of habeas corpus, or place the Territory, or any part thereof, under martial law until communication can be had with the President and his decision thereon made known." The Governor virtually turned the Territory over to the Commanding General; he suspended the writ of habeas corpus and authorized the military to exercise not only his own powers, but those of the judicial branch. President Roosevelt approved the Governor's action two days later. Military tribunals were established and proceeded to try civilians, according to their own rules, for a broad spectrum of offenses.

In August, 1942, Harry White, a civilian stockbroker, was convicted by a military "Provost Court" of embezzling his clients' securities and sentenced to five years. Lloyd Duncan, a civilian employee of the Honolulu Navy Yard, was convicted by a military court of assaulting a couple of Marine sentries on February 24, 1944, and given 6 months. Both sought habeas corpus.[40] A majority of the Supreme Court, headed by Justice Black, held in each case that the military court lacked jurisdiction. Technically, the decision involved merely an interpretation of the Organic Act, finding

that when Congress used the term "martial law" it had
not intended to include the power to try civilians in
military courts: as Justice Black rightly observed, "the
term 'martial law' carries no precise meaning. The
Constitution does not refer to 'martial law' at all and
no Act of Congress has defined the term." But the
majority's language and its frequent references to *Milligan* left small doubt that if Congress had explicitly
authorized military trial of civilians in Hawaii (which,
of course, was never a theatre of actual war after
December 7, 1941), the provision would have been
held unconstitutional.

Why the Government chose to carry these cases to
the Supreme Court is something of a mystery. Two
weaker sets of facts on which to argue the necessity of
military trial could hardly have been found, or imag-
ined. Eight months after Pearl Harbor, with the
American fleet still very much at a disadvantage in the
Pacific, it might reasonably have been thought that
Hawaii was still threatened with invasion—but White's
offense had precisely nothing to do with military
security. Duncan's brawl with the sentries might, with
some stretching, have been said to affect military
security—but by 1944, neither the Chiefs of Staff nor
anyone else thought there was any danger of the ban-
ner of the rising sun being raised over Honolulu.
Chief Justice Stone concurred, but without the loose
rhetoric, loose reasoning, and sweeping generaliza-
tions of Justice Black, on grounds which correctly applied the principles of *Sterling* v. *Constantin:* "I assume
. . . that there could be circumstances in which the

public safety requires, and the Constitution permits, substitution of trials by military tribunals for trials in the civil courts. But the record here discloses no such conditions in Hawaii."[41] Justices Burton and Frankfurter, also applying the tests of *Sterling* v. *Constantin,* dissented: they thought the Court should not use quite so much hindsight in reviewing the exercise of discretion by those responsible for Hawaii's safety at the time the decisions were made. They suggested, probably correctly, that the Court would not have decided the cases in the same way if it had reached them "with the war against Japan in full swing."[42]

Like Chief Justice Stone, I can imagine circumstances in which the Constitution would permit the substitution of military for civilian trials, and in which the Court would manage to distinguish the *Milligan* and *Duncan* cases. Suppose that the situation that existed in Mississippi and Alabama a few years ago had been a little worse than it was, that not a hundred or so, but a thousand Negroes and civil rights workers had been murdered without any of the murderers being convicted by a local jury. Suppose a situation, like that in Ulster, where Catholics can murder Protestants and Protestants Catholics, each secure in the knowledge that the odds against the impaneling of twelve jurors who will vote to convict are astronomical. Such suppositions are, unfortunately, not fantastic, and they may arise in new contexts; in states where any jury trying a Black Panther is pretty sure to include some Negroes and perhaps an ardent New Leftist or so, the Panthers may well share the sort of immunity so long accorded to Ku Kluxers. The doubts of Yale's President Kingman Brewster that a black revolutionary could get a fair trial in the United States may indeed have been justified, although not in the way he meant. If people were really murdering other people in large numbers, and with perfect impunity, in Mississippi or Connecticut or California, would the Supreme Court really forbid the use of the kind of court in which such charges of murder could be fairly and impartially tried? I doubt it. Remember that here the powers of the President and Congress would be conjoined, for section 333 of Title 10 of the United States Code empowers the President, if he finds that any part or class of the people are being deprived of a right or protection named in the Constitution (such as the right not to be deprived of life without due process of law), and that the constituted authorities are unable or unwilling to protect that right, to use the armed forces to take such measures as he considers necessary.

The Court has never questioned the Government's right, in situations of domestic violence, to empower the military to arrest and confine, without charges, people likely to contribute to the violence. Justice Davis said in *Milligan,* "Unquestionably there [may be] an exigency which demands that the government, if it should see fit in the exercise of a proper discretion to make arrests, should not be required to produce the persons arrested in answer to a writ of *habeas corpus.*"[43] Justice Black emphasized in *Duncan* that the Court was not considering "the power of the military simply to arrest and detain civilians interfering with a necessary military function at a time of turbulence and danger from insurrection or war."[44] If, for example, the police or armed forces had simply arrested and detained for the duration of the emergency the violent peace demonstrators who were entertaining themselves by trying to block traffic and generally disrupt the normal life of the city of Washington in the spring of 1971, instead of attempting the impossible task of putting thousands of them through the normal criminal process, the Court (despite the indignant squeals of the American Civil Liberties Union and the *New York Times*) might well have held the action a permissible method of coping with the emergency. For similar reasons, I think the Court, had the occasion arisen, would have held constitutional the Emergency Detention Act of 1950, which in case of invasion, war declared by Congress, or insurrection in aid of a foreign enemy, permitted the arrest and detention of persons whom there was reasonable ground to believe would probably engage in espionage or sabotage—especially in view of the fact that the Act explicitly preserved the rights of people so detained to seek habeas corpus.[45] (It will be recalled that the Court has never yet passed on the President's power unilaterally to suspend the writ of habeas corpus in cases of rebellion or invasion.) In short, I think that the decision of the Nixon administration, not to oppose its repeal, was a function of its lawyers' belief that the President's powers would be greater without it than with it.

There is, of course, a considerable difference between hanging a man and placing him in preventive

detention for an indefinite period; there is less difference between such detention and imprisonment upon
conviction by a military court. But the difference is, in
any case, only one of degree. If some emergencies
justify detention, other and greater emergencies may
justify stronger measures of martial rule, including the
use of military courts to try crimes committed by civilians. Such power is drastic and dangerous. In the last
analysis, only the Court can ensure that it is not
abused.

Notes to Chapter Six

[1] *See* Halperin, The President and the Military (Brookings Institution, 1972).

[2] Art. I, § 8, cl. 15.

[3] Art. II, § 3.

[4] Art. I, § 9, cl. 2.

[5] Art. IV, § 4.

[6] *See* FAIRMAN, THE LAW OF MARTIAL RULE 80–93 (2d ed. 1943); Federal Aid in Domestic Disturbances 1903–1922, S. Doc. No. 263, 67th Cong., 2d Sess. (1922).

[7] *See* Wiener, *Helping to Cool the Long Hot Summers*, 53 A.B.A.J. 713 (1967); Poe, *The Use of Federal Troops to Suppress Domestic Violence*, 54 A.B.A.J. 168 (1968).

[8] *See* Univ. of Colo. Law Revision Center, *A Comprehensive Study of the Use of Military Troops in Civil Disorders with Proposals for Legislative Reform*, 43 U. COLO. L. REV. 399, 413 (1972).

[9] Mr. Clark's letter is quoted in full in footnote 2 to the opinion of the Supreme Court in Laird v. Tatum, 408 U.S. 1 (1972), in which the Court in effect upheld the Army's right to collect information on radicals and radical organizations who

might be involved in riots that the Army might be called upon to quell. As the Circuit Court of Appeals said in the same case, "No logical argument can be made for compelling the military to use *blind* force." 444 F.2d 947, 952 (D.C. Cir. 1971). Apparently most or all of the information collected came from the news media and other public sources.

[10]These States include Maryland, Massachusetts, New Hampshire, South Carolina, Tennessee, and Vermont. *See* Fairman, *supra* note 6, at 96–99.

[11]*See* CHAFEE, STATE HOUSE VERSUS PENT HOUSE (1937); Leach, *The Law at Harvard: A Quasi-Review with Personalia,* 19 Harv. Law School Bull. 4, 12–13 (1968).

[12]Fairman, *supra* note 6, at 99.

[13]*See* Univ. of Colo. Law Revision Center, *supra* note 8, at 399–400.

[14]41 OPS. ATTY. GEN. 313 (1957).

[15]*In re* Debs, 158 U.S. 564, 582 (1895). *See also,* for example, *Ex parte* Siebold, 100 U.S. 371, 395 (1880).

[16]Proclamation No. 3840, April 5, 1968, 3 C.F.R. 35 (1968).

[17]Executive Order No. 11403, April 5, 1968, 3 C.F.R. 107 (1968).

[18]18 U.S.C. § 1385. "Posse Comitatus" is an ancient term describing a sheriff's power to summon the citizenry (including those who happen to be soldiers) to help him enforce the law.

[19]For a history and discussion of the statute, *see* Furman, *Restrictions Upon Use of the Army Imposed by the Posse Comitatus Act,* 7 MIL. L. REV. 85 (1960).

[20]Annual Report of the Secretary of War for 1906, quoted in MILITARY JURISPRUDENCE: CASES AND MATERIALS (Lawyers Cooperative Publishing Co. [1951]) at 1076.

[21]48 U.S. 1 (1849).

[22]*See supra,* Ch. 5.

[23]*See supra,* Ch. 5.

[24]Ch. 153, 14 Stat. 428.

[25]Case of James Weaver, 13 OPS. ATTY. GEN. 59 (1869). Weaver, a citizen of Texas, was accused of the murder of a freedman. The Commanding General of the Military District in which Texas was included removed the case from a state court upon the representation of the state judge that the civil courts were "so

badly situated and managed that . . . no trial could probably be had." It is reasonable to infer that it would have been well-nigh impossible to impanel a jury of twelve Texans willing to hang a white man for murdering a former slave, who had not only asked for higher wages but threatened to seek other employment if he didn't get them.

[26]Art. III, § 2.

[27]*Ex parte* McCardle, 74 U.S. 506 (1869).

[28]Moyer v. Peabody, 212 U.S. 78 (1909). The Colorado Supreme Court, denying Moyer's petition for habeas corpus, had already held that there was no violation of the State constitution. *In re* Moyer, 35 Colo. 159, 85 Pac. 190 (1905). Moyer was later accused of causing a bomb to be planted in the home of Governor Steunenberg of Idaho, with fatal results, but after the acquittal of his colleague in the Federation, Big Bill Haywood, the charges against him were dropped.

[29]For a parade of horrible examples of "bogus martial law," *see* Wiener, *Helping to Cool the Long Hot Summers*, 53 A.B.A.J. 713, 715 (1967).

[30]287 U.S. 378 (1932). *See* Fairman, *Martial Rule, in the Light of Sterling v. Constantin*, 19 CORN. L. Q. 20 (1933).

[31]Mitchell v. Harmony, 54 U.S. 115 (1852). *See supra*, Ch. 5.

[32]Valdez v. Black, 446 F.2d 1071 (10th Cir. 1971), *cert. denied*, 405 U.S. 963 (1972). The Circuit Court, however, also found that "the undisputed evidence establishes that there was a very real insurrection." *Id.* at 1077.

[33]Krause v. Rhodes, 471 F.2d 430 (6th Cir. 1972), *cert. granted* 93 S. Ct. 3065 (1973). *Cf.* Bright v. Nunn, 448 F.2d 245 (6th Cir. 1971), in which the same court denied injunctive relief against the Governor of Kentucky in somewhat similar circumstances.

[34]There is some suggestion that the pleadings and arguments, which were in large part the work of the American and Ohio Civil Liberties Unions, were so overstated and intemperate as to cause a corresponding reaction by the court. See especially the concurring opinion of Judge O'Sullivan at 471 F. 2d 445–47. If so, the case is one, like *Ex parte* Milligan, in which the intemperance of counsel helped to produce bad law.

[35]471 F.2d at 448, 464.

[36]71 U.S. 2 (1866). *See supra*, Ch. 5.

[37]Hughes, *War Powers Under the Constitution*, 42 A.B.A. Rep. 232, 245 (1917).

[38]71 U.S. at 127.

[39]Duncan v. Kahanamoku and its companion case, White v. Steer, 327 U.S. 304 (1946). Excellent accounts of these cases and their background are contained in Fairman, *The Supreme Court on Military Jurisdiction: Martial Rule in Hawaii and the Yamashita Case*, 59 HARV. L. REV. 833 (1946) and Wiener, *Martial Law Today*, 55 A.B.A.J. 723 (1969).

[40]By the time the case reached the Supreme Court, the issue of the validity of the suspension of the writ had become moot, since a Presidential Proclamation of October 24, 1944, had restored the privilege of the writ and ended the state of martial law in the Territory.

[41]327 U.S. at 336.

[42]*Id.* at 337, 357.

[43]71 U.S. at 125–26.

[44]327 U.S. at 314.

[45]The Act was not, as the American Civil Liberties Union and its other zealous opponents seemed to believe, a creature of Senators McCarran and McCarthy. It was sponsored by a group of liberals, including Senators Kilgore, Douglas, Benton, Lehman, Kefauver, and Humphrey.

CHAPTER SEVEN

The International Law of War

*A*COUPLE OF YEARS AGO THE
Yale Law School gave a luncheon in honor of Cyrus
Vance, an alumnus who had served successively as
General Counsel of the Department of Defense,
Secretary of the Army, and Deputy Secretary of Defense under the Kennedy and Johnson administrations. The proceedings were about as lively as they
generally are on such occasions until, coincidentally
with the serving of the Jello parfait, a door opened,
and a couple of dozen representatives of the counterculture filed into the dining hall, where they stood at
ease while their leader, a young man, clad principally
in hair, granny glasses, and a sort of hand-knit lavender poncho, declaimed the text of a prepared statement. The acoustics in Yale's Freshman Commons are·

poor, and the *Gruppenführer* had a slight tendency to gobble his words, but the burden of his manifesto was that Mr. Vance was a "war criminal." The allegation was, as lawyers say, conclusory, and the specifications of the charge were not distinctly set forth, but these words were several times repeated with obvious relish.

It is reasonable to surmise that Mr. Vance's accuser and his supporting cast knew approximately as much about the international law of war as I know about the pathology of the human kidney. Ignorance *is* strength, in the sense that it is usually easier to make strong, confident, and dogmatic assertions when one's knowledge of the subject matter consists of a few easily memorized slogans. I doubt that the protesters were, in any case, inclined to place undue emphasis on precise information and rigorous analysis. But in this instance, they had some excuse for ignorance. In the last few years the American public has been buried by a Vesuvian eruption of intellectual sludge on the subject of war crimes. Much of it has been produced by scholars like Jane Fonda and the Brothers Berrigan, but some of it comes from people whose legal credentials are fairly imposing. According to Professor Richard A. Falk of Princeton, "the United States Government [was] waging an illegal war of aggression by criminal means in Vietnam."[1] Ramsey Clark, making the Haj to Hanoi under the auspices of an organization whose point of view and purpose are sufficiently described by its name, the "International Commission of Inquiry into United States War Crimes," strongly implied first, that the United States was engaged in a deliberate effort to destroy the system of dikes in North Vietnam, and second, that all persons responsible for such bombing were war criminals. Mr. Clark, who is said by many people to be a better lawyer than Miss Fonda, did not, so far as I know, use the words "war crime." But he accused the United States of "inhuman behavior" in Vietnam and said that the bombing was "without justification." Bombing without military justification is in my opinion, and presumably in Mr. Clark's, a violation of the law of war—*i.e.*, a war crime. When such language and opinions are put forth by the Milbank Professor of International Law at Princeton and a former Attorney General of the United States, I think that it is in order to examine the law of war and try to explain what a war crime is, and also what it is not.

The subject is complex and sometimes obscure. Certainly I cannot cover, in a chapter of moderate length, details—some of them important details—to which eminent scholars have devoted weighty tomes.[2] But I think its essentials can be expounded with tolerable clarity and brevity, and that is the purpose of this chapter. In trying to do so, I shall make no attempt to say what is immoral—not because I think morality unimportant, but because my views on it are entitled to no more weight than Jane Fonda's or Richard M. Nixon's or yours. Professor Falk and other thinkers of his school frequently seem to use "illegal" and "immoral" interchangeably. A casebook specimen of this sort of reasoning is contained in a review of Telford Taylor's *Nuremberg and Vietnam*.[3] The writer, starting with a declaration that the war in Vietnam "is a horrendous moral evil, a criminal undertaking of the most serious sort," proceeds to denounce Professor Taylor because "like almost all lawyers, he is most at ease when reasonably precise, reasonably well-established rules and conventions happen to be available . . . Taylor embraces a very limited and morally unattractive notion of what constitutes a war crime."

I plead guilty to sharing the Taylor point of view. I am, in fact, in general agreement with his limited and morally unattractive version of the law of war, though I do not share all of his conclusions. He seems, for example, to believe that massive firepower, which necessarily inflicts great suffering on noncombatants, should not be used to resist guerrillas, though he stops short of saying that such use violates the law of war.[4] Certainly the defender has a duty, to say nothing of strong practical reasons, to search for weapons and tactics that can discriminate between enemy combatants and people whose deepest desire is to stay as far as possible from the fighting. But suppose no such weapons and tactics are to be found? The logical end of this reasoning would be that no resistance should be made to an aggressive power, or a terrorist group, determined to subject other people to its rule by force, if only it is ruthless enough to create conditions in which effective resistance endangers the innocent. The dilemma is essentially that of the airplane hijacking, or of Eichmann's offer to trade Jews for trucks.

Law and morality are not, and (in the present imperfect state of man) cannot be, coextensive. Law means, or should mean, a standard on which there is general (although rarely, if ever, universal) agreement and, more than that, a standard whose violation may subject the violator to known or knowable sanctions. Justice Holmes defined law as "a statement of the circumstances in which the public force will be brought to bear upon men through the courts."[5] In the criminal context, this means that an act is not illegal unless the actor knew, or should have known, that he might be punished for it. Only in despotisms are people tried, executed, or imprisoned for violating the moral (as distinct from legal) code of those in power. *Nulla poena sine lege.* Our Constitution permits no *ex post facto* law, and neither should international law. If a man takes advantage of a weasel clause in a contract, or orders the bombing of enemy cities, or turns himself into a communications satellite for relaying the propaganda of a totalitarian regime, you are free to denounce him as immoral and to refuse to do business with him or to vote for him at the next election, but you cannot demand that he be punished or call him a criminal. I emphasize again that what I propose to do in this chapter is not to make moral judgments, and still less to make judgments on what sort of military conduct is wise. What I propose to describe is international *law* —those rules which most nations have agreed, whether by treaty or as a matter of custom, to obey and enforce.

The Constitution gives Congress power "to define and punish . . . Offences against the Law of Nations."[6] Congress has never attempted to codify the law of war;

it has chosen to define it simply by incorporating that law as it may from time to time exist by reference in the Uniform Code of Military Justice. Article 18 provides that "General courts-martial shall also have jurisdiction to try any person who by the law of war is subject to trial by a military tribunal and may adjudge any punishment permitted by the law of war." Article 21 adds that "The provisions of this Chapter conferring jurisdiction upon courts-martial do not deprive military commissions, provost courts, or other military tribunals of concurrent jurisdiction with respect to offenders or offenses that by statute or by the law of war may be tried by military commissions, provost courts, or other military tribunals." The Supreme Court has, thus far, held that this technique of incorporating treaties and customary law by reference is a permissible way of exercising the power to define and punish offenses against the law of nations.[7] In practice, of course, the common types of war crime, such as mistreating or killing prisoners of war, or noncombatants, are also violations of domestic law and can be tried as such by whatever ordinary courts have jurisdiction. Lieutenant William Calley, for example, was not tried by a military commission for a war crime, but by a general court-martial for premeditated murder in violation of the Uniform Code. But when an act must be charged and tried as a violation of the law of war —because, for example, the perpetrator (like the Germans who were tried after World War II) is an enemy whose offense was committed outside the territorial jurisdiction of any American civil court—where are the prosecution, the defense, and the court to find that law?

The law of war has two sources: treaties and custom. Both, of course, have historical roots, but the law of war, even in its customary form, is far from coeval with warfare. The idea that some methods of warfare are illegal is, in fact, comparatively modern. As any reader of the Old Testament, Thucydides, Caesar, or Livy knows, ancient history is full of appalling chronicles of rapine, pillage, and massacre—some of it not merely permitted, but practically mandatory under contemporary notions of morality. There was, of course, much philosophical discussion of "natural law" and condemnation of unnecessary barbarity, but the actual, effective law on the subject was tersely summed up by the famous aphorism quoted in Chapter 1, of that eminent jurist, Marcus Tullius Cicero: *"Silent leges inter arma."* When Marcus Crassus put a definitive end to Spartacus' revolt by crucifying six thousand captive slaves along the road from Capua to Rome, it would not have occurred to Cicero or anyone else to call him a criminal; the Senate decreed him a triumph.[8] The Romans were probably the cruelest of ancient peoples, but even the Athenians and Spartans saw nothing immoral, much less illegal, in killing or enslaving the population of a conquered city.[9]

The savagery of medieval warfare was not restrained by anything properly describable as law, though there was a certain deference to ideas of chivalry and Christian duty. But chivalry operated principally for the benefit of the well-born and rich; nobles

264 / *JUSTICE UNDER FIRE*

and knights could be held for ransom and thus were far more valuable alive than dead. Two passages in the *Chronicles* of Jean Froissart illustrate the point that the mercy of the Middle Ages was based more on prudential than humanitarian considerations; after that terrible new weapon, the longbow, had destroyed the French army at Crécy:

> among the English there were pillagers and irregulars, Welsh and Cornishmen armed with long knives, who went out after the French . . . and, when they found any in difficulty, whether they were counts, barons, knights or squires, they killed them without mercy. Because of this, many were slaughtered that evening, regardless of their rank. It was a great misfortune and the King of England was afterwards very angry that none had been taken for ransom, for the number of dead lords was very great.[10]

In other words, the royal outrage was largely economic. Other considerations were also at work. When Calais, after a long and stubborn siege, surrendered, the same king, Edward III, was so enraged that he proposed to give the citizens no quarter. Sir Walter Manny (who seems really to have been a very gentle, as well as a very gallant, knight) talked him out of it with an argument which to this day underlies much of the international law of war:

> 'My lord, you may well be mistaken, and you are setting a bad example for us. Suppose one day you sent us to defend one of your fortresses, we should go less cheerfully if you have these people put to death, for then they would do the same to us if they had the

chance.' This argument did much to soften the King's heart, especially when most of his barons supported it.[11]

The concept of *law* which limits the freedom of belligerents is usually traced to seventeenth and eighteenth century jurists like Grotius and Pufendorf. By the time of the American revolution both British and American military courts were trying violators (usually, of course, belonging to the other side) of what had by then become the customary law of war, the "practice of civilized nations." Grotius and the other fathers of international law had based their arguments in large part on moral, and even theological, considerations, but Gibbon, an eighteenth century rationalist if not a cynic (and no very good friend of Christianity), still saw the law of war as founded on convenience:

> The laws of war, that restrain the exercise of national rapine and murder, are founded on two principles of substantial interest: the knowledge of the permanent benefits which may be obtained by a moderate use of conquest and a just apprehension lest the desolation which we inflict on the enemy's country may be retaliated on our own.[12]

Whatever its impulse, codification of the customary law of war began in the nineteenth century. A landmark was General Order 100 of April 24, 1863, "Instructions for the Government of Armies of the United States in the Field," drafted by Professor Francis Lieber of Columbia (himself a soldier in the Napoleonic wars, with sons in both the Union and Confederate armies) and put into effect by Abraham Lincoln.[13] Lieber's Code, of course, had no binding effect on other nations, but it summarized, clarified, and improved the rules that most of the countries of Europe at least professed to respect and is a direct ancestor of the treaties now in force.

The major treaties are the Hague Regulations of 1907 and the Geneva Conventions of 1949, especially those relating to prisoners of war, the wounded and sick, and the protection of civilians.[14]

The Hague Regulations, which were fairly well observed by both the Allies and the Central Powers in World War I and are still in effect, deal principally with prisoners of war, the conduct of hostilities, and the government of territory which has been conquered and occupied by an enemy. The 1949 Geneva Conventions, on prisoners of war and the protection of civilians in time of war, expand and "complement" the Hague Regulations, but add very little to the old treaty's provisions on the conduct of hostilities. In this respect, the most important of that treaty's articles are those which prohibit the employment of "arms, projectiles, or material calculated to cause unnecessary suffering,"[15] and "attack or bombardment, by whatever means, of towns, villages, dwellings, or buildings which are undefended."[16]

Both of these provisions, of course, raise problems of interpretation and application. The latter, for example, has been cited to support the assertion that most of the American bombing in South Vietnam, and some of the bombing in North Vietnam (such places as Hanoi and Haiphong, of course, could hardly be called "undefended") violated the law of war. But none of the signatories to the Hague Treaty has ever construed Article 25 as prohibiting the bombardment of a military target in the enemy's rear (*e.g.*, an arms factory, a supply depot, or a railroad) simply because it was defended only by the presence of his armed forces between it and the attacker, and was neither fortified nor supplied with anti-aircraft weapons.[17]

Article 23*e* obviously raises exceedingly difficult questions of fact. All or almost all governments, scholars, and soldiers accept the principle that the amount of force employed by a belligerent against the enemy should not exceed that which it reasonably believes necessary to the achievement of some legitimate military goal.[18] But the achievement of such a goal, especially when aerial bombing and long-range rockets are employed, necessarily endangers noncombatants and their property, and religious edifices and hospitals in the vicinity of the target. Bombing is still far from pinpoint accuracy, and the hotter the defense, the harder it is for pilots to bomb from low altitudes and take time for precision.

The massive bombings of Hamburg and Frankfurt, though they necessarily inflicted enormous suffering on civilians, were, in my opinion, not war crimes, for the RAF had no other way to knock out such legitimate targets as arms factories, submarine pens, and transportation networks. But many people, including myself, think that the bombing of Dresden fell into a different category because the German armies had by that time virtually collapsed, and it did little or nothing to hasten the end of the war. The bombings in Vietnam undoubtedly had the military purpose of destroying enemy troops and supplies and interfering with their movement. Whether they were an excessive or "disproportionate" use of force, and therefore illegal, depends on whether those goals could have been achieved by less and more discriminating force—a military question which I am no more competent to decide than is Professor Falk or Mr. Clark. The fact that the bombing did not produce victory (except in the sense that North Vietnam and the Viet Cong did not conquer South Vietnam) does not, of course, demonstrate that it was an unjustifiable use of force. A general does not become a war criminal because he loses a bloody battle, even if he had small hope of winning it.

There have been many loud and eloquent assertions that American bombing in Vietnam was a war crime on a gigantic scale. But no treaty forbids aerial bombing; as noted, the law of war condemns only bombing (or any other type of force) unrelated or disproportionate to the achievement of a military purpose. A bombardment (by airplanes, artillery, rockets, or mortars) whose sole, or principal, purpose was to kill noncombatants would be a war crime, precisely as My Lai was. But there is very little hard evidence against, and a good deal of evidence to support, the United States' contention that much effort was expended, and some peril incurred, to limit the risk that bombs would kill noncombatants or destroy nonmilitary property. A military target cannot be protected from attack by the simple expedient of placing it in the middle of a civilian community,[19] and I am profoundly skeptical of the claims by North Vietnam and its friends that American bombs usually hit hospitals, schools, and homes for the aged.[20] The evidence does not persuade me that the bombing in Vietnam was any more illegal than was the bombing of Germany, when bombs were dumber than they are now. I noted with some interest that during the presidential campaign of 1972, Senator McGovern while denouncing the bombing in Vietnam as "immoral" and "probably one of the worst crimes in the history of the world" made a good deal of his own excellent record as a bomber pilot over Germany.

Article 23a of the Hague Regulations forbids "poison or poisoned weapons," words on whose precise meaning there has been much disagreement.[21] All the belligerents of World War I followed the German lead and employed a variety of toxic gases. The Geneva Protocol of 1925 forbids poison gas and "analogous liquids, materials or devices" and also "bacteriological methods of warfare." All of the great powers except the United States (where the Senate failed to ratify) are parties. In declarations in 1969 and 1970, President Nixon reaffirmed the already existing policy of the United States not to use lethal chemicals except in retaliation for their prior use by another country (a reservation made by most of the major signatories to the Protocol), renounced the use of bacteriological weapons in any circumstances, and urged the Senate to ratify the 1925 Protocol.[22] The use of nuclear weapons is limited only by fear of retaliation and, perhaps, considerations of humanity; no treaty speaks to the subject. It is pretty generally agreed that the 1925 Protocol does not forbid the use of fire in such forms as napalm and white phosphorus,[23] and certainly no other treaty does. The use of fire in warfare is, of course, very ancient: it is found in the Old Testament,[24] and Greek fire, which goes back to the seventh century, saved the Byzantine Empire from more than one barbarian invasion.[25] In short, about the only weapons which are more or less categorically banned are lethal chemicals and bacteria. Many weapons, whose employment is restricted only by the general rule that it must bear a reasonable relation to the achievement of some military goal, are quite as capable of mass destruction. For that matter, as the Royal Navy showed in World Wars I and II, an old-fashioned naval blockade can cause malnutrition, and even starvation, on a fearful scale. The simple and obvious fact is that nations if willing to resort to violence at all are reluctant to place limits on the kinds of violence they may employ—especially on weapons that cause them to think that they have an advantage over potential foes. Germany before and after World War I, for obvious reasons, opposed any rules that would have forbidden submarines to sink merchant ships without warning, and Great Britain, for reasons equally obvious, would accept no restrictions on blockade by surface vessels. Cobras would advocate the banning of hooves, claws, and cutting teeth but would denounce in the strongest terms a proposal to outlaw venom.

The treaties, particularly the Geneva POW Convention of 1949, are considerably more explicit as to the treatment of prisoners of war. That Convention provides in some detail for adequate food, quarters, clothing, and medical attention. It regulates the conditions of their confinement, the types and conditions of the labor they may be required to perform, and the compensation for such labor. It requires prompt notification of the names of captives and that they be allowed to send and receive mail, and to receive relief packages. They are to be allowed to receive small advances on their pay (in addition to the wages, which may be as low as a quarter of a Swiss franc, or about seven cents per day, for their labor), and to be furnished canteens in which to spend it. They can be tried and punished for offenses, whether committed before or during capture, only in the same manner as members of the detaining power's own forces and are, in any case, entitled to such fundamentals of due process as counsel, an interpreter, and service of charges. Attempts to escape may be punished only by comparatively minor "disciplinary" measures. The killing or mistreatment of prisoners, and reprisals against them, are categorically forbidden. They must at all times be "humanely treated" and "protected, particularly against acts of violence or intimidation, and against insults and public curiosity." Finally, representatives of the Protecting Power (a neutral nation designated by the POW's own government) and the International Committee of the Red Cross are to be allowed free access to POWs, and the installations in which they are confined, in order to ensure compliance with the Convention.

The sad fact is that these provisions have done less to minimize the suffering of captives than the 1929 Convention did in World War II. Practically none of them was observed by North Vietnam in its treatment of American prisoners of war. Originally that government took the position that the Convention was inapplicable because there was no armed conflict between signatories—the war was purely a civil war within South Vietnam in which North Vietnam was in no way engaged. When this contention became too plainly preposterous to be believed, even by Ramsey Clark, it fell back on the argument that all of the American prisoners of war were war criminals and, therefore, not entitled to POW status.[26] This had, in fact, been a debatable issue under the Geneva Convention of 1929, and the Supreme Court in General Yamashita's case[27] upheld the United States Government's contention that the General, being accused of war crimes, was an unlawful belligerent and, therefore, not entitled to the protection of the Convention —specifically, that he could be tried by a military commission which did not provide the same protection (particularly in respect to the rules of evidence and the right of appeal) to which a member of the United States armed forces would have been entitled in a court-martial. Article 85 of the 1949 Convention dealt with the problem by providing that "Prisoners of war prosecuted under the laws of the Detaining Power for acts committed prior to capture shall retain, even if convicted, the benefits of the present Convention." North Vietnam, like Soviet Russia and other Communist signatories, declared that it would not be bound by this provision:

> The Democratic Republic of North Vietnam declares that prisoners of war prosecuted for and convicted of war crimes and crimes against humanity, in accordance with the principles established by the Nuremberg Tribunal, will not enjoy the benefits of the provisions of the present Convention as provided in Article 85.

But this excuse for non-compliance was scarcely more convincing than the first, for none of the American POWs was prosecuted for, or convicted of, war crimes. The simple fact seems to be that North Vietnam, discerning an advantage in creating American concern for the POWs, and thus increasing the pressure on the United States to accept its terms for their release, simply resorted to such legal arguments as it could get to justify disregard of the treaty. The United States and South Vietnam took the position that there was an armed conflict between signatories, as plainly there was, and that the Convention was applicable in its entirety, and both permitted the International Red Cross to inspect their POW installations. Both, especially South Vietnam, were guilty of some mistreatment of POWs, and the United States has properly been criticized for its practice of turning captives over to the South Vietnamese without very strict insistence that that government comply with the Convention. But the fact that Red Cross inspection was allowed justifies skepticism about the Hanoi government's charges (made after returning American POWs had given detailed accounts of torture and other mistreatment, and probably in more or less automatic reaction to those accounts) that the United States systematically subjected North Vietnamese POWs to torture, medical experimentation, and poisoning with various chemicals. The accusation of medical experimentation, suggested by actual Nazi crimes, has been a staple of Communist propaganda. The poison charge is more original. But even the *New York Times* buried the story on an inside page.

The most serious inadequacy of the POW Convention (and of the other Geneva Conventions) lies in their general inapplicability to a kind of warfare which, while far from novel, has since 1945 been much commoner than the sort of large-scale hostilities between organized, disciplined national armies with which the Conventions were intended to deal. The protective provisions that are summarized above are applicable only to armed conflicts between signatory powers,[28] and the only persons entitled to them are members of the regular armed forces of such powers, and such members of their irregular forces as meet the Convention's criteria of lawful belligerency—specifically, that they be commanded by a person responsible for his subordinates; that they wear, if not a uniform, at least "a fixed distinctive sign recognizable at a distance;" that they carry arms openly; and that they conduct their operations in accordance with the laws of war. The Viet Cong, Al Fatah, the Irish Republican Army, and all the rest naturally do not, and could not, meet any of these tests.

Guerrilla warfare, which the Communist powers describe as a "war of national liberation" (unless, as in

Hungary and Yugoslavia, it happens to occur in their own territory), in its modern form usually means an insurrection or campaign of terrorism within the territory of one country, often more or less openly supported (by the furnishing of troops, arms, and sanctuary) by a second power friendly to the insurgents but ostensibly not at war with the first sovereign. The insurgents do not wear uniforms or carry arms openly; their object is so far as possible to make themselves indistinguishable from the civilian population, so that it is difficult to resist or attack them without endangering noncombatants. Likewise, they typically resort to assassination and other acts of terror against noncombatants. Such a tactical doctrine violates the first, and most basic, principle of the Hague and Geneva Conventions, which is that noncombatants are not legitimate military targets and that combatants are so far as possible to be distinguished from them. It must be conceded that the guerrillas would have small chance of success if they followed the rules of those treaties. None of the signatory governments, whether totalitarian or democratic, had any desire to facilitate domestic insurrections, at least in its own country.

Thus, the law of war, as it now exists, makes criminal most of the tactics which offer to guerrillas their only chance of success. If there are no legal or political means by which the insurgents can pursue their ends —that is, when there are no honest elections, no honest courts, and no constitutional safeguards against oppression—they cannot fairly be expected to obey the rules prescribed by those in power. In their case, the law of war, to the extent that it applies to them, is in part unjust. It does not follow that the law should be changed to permit them deliberately to kill the innocent in order to create terror or to kidnap innocent hostages in order to extract concessions. But here I find myself straying into a moral question and had better desist, if only because the international law of war has little to do with most of the terrorists.

The activities of organizations like the I.R.A. or the various Palestinian terrorist groups are neither protected nor condemned by the law of war; it does not apply to them at all, even if they are receiving support from an outside government, or even if they are agents of that government. They are simply violators of the criminal law of the country in which they act, to be tried and punished in whatever way that law prescribes. If they can raise the violence to a level at which it can be called "an armed conflict not of an international character occurring in the territory of one of the High Contracting Parties," as the Viet Cong did and the I.R.A. has very nearly done, the Geneva Conventions give them some basic protection—if they surrender or are placed *hors de combat* by wounds, they may not be subjected to "murder, . . . mutilation, cruel treatment and torture" or executed "without previous judgment pronounced by a regularly constituted court affording all the judicial guarantees which are recognized as indispensable by civilized peoples"[29]—although it is not easy to think of any guarantee which is not dispensed with by some arguably civilized peoples. They are certainly not entitled to be treated as prisoners of war, and they can be tried for violating the local law. Even if there is an armed conflict between nations party to the treaties, the irregulars are entitled to no more protection than this unless they wear some sort of insignia recognizable at a distance, carry arms openly, and themselves obey the laws of war—which, of course, they almost never do. During Dr. Sukarno's "confrontation" with Malaysia, Osman Bin Haji Mohamed Ali and another member of the Indonesian army, wearing sports shirts and slacks, planted a satchel charge in a Singapore bank and killed a couple of tellers. The Privy Council, assuming that there was an "armed conflict" between the two countries, and that the Prisoner of War Convention was applicable, held them outside its protection; they could be, and were, tried for murder and sentenced to death by an ordinary Malaysian criminal court.[30] (I have a doubt, which may seem rather technical, about the rightness of the British judges' holding; as I read the treaty, if the defendants were members of Indonesia's regular armed forces, they were entitled to treatment as POWs, although they could still have been tried for a war crime.)

So far as domestic insurgents are concerned, the Hague Regulations and the Geneva Convention Relative to the Protection of Civilian Persons in Time of War add nothing, for they apply only to civilians who are under the control of an *enemy* nation—citizens of belligerent A who are resident in the territory of belligerent B, like the Germans and Italians who were interned in England in World War II—and inhabitants of territory which has been conquered and occupied by an enemy's army. Beyond the very rudimentary protection conferred by the provision applicable to "armed conflict not of an international character occurring in the territory of one of the High Contracting Parties," the international law of war does not restrict the freedom of sovereigns to treat, or mistreat, their own subjects in any way they want.

The assertions by polemicists like Leonard Boudin (who is a lawyer) that "the forced 'relocation' of rural populations [in South Vietnam is], in all contexts [a] war crime"[31] seem to be based, at least in part, on ignorance of the scope of the Convention. Article 26 of the Hague Regulations and Article 49 of the Geneva Convention, in fact, encourage the evacuation of civilians from areas of combat, and the Secretary General of the United Nations in 1970 urged all belligerents "to ensure that civilians are removed from, or kept out of areas . . . likely to place them in jeopardy or to expose them to the hazards of warfare."[32]

The law of belligerent occupation does not at the present time pose serious problems. Since the return of Okinawa to Japan, the only part of the world that is in theory (but not in practice) governed by victorious military occupants is West Berlin, and the only reason that occupation has not been formally terminated is that it forms the legal basis of the Western Allies' right of access to West Berlin.[33] The territories conquered by Israel in the Six-Day War of 1967, on the other hand, are occupied in practice, but not in theory, although Israel's *policy* is to comply with the provisions of the 1949 Geneva Convention on the Protection of Civilian Persons.[34] The Geneva Convention when applicable does clearly forbid the more outrageous practices resorted to by the Third Reich in World War II and (to a lesser extent) by the Second Reich in World War I. Vicarious and collective punishments are banned, as is the taking of hostages. The civilian population must not be massacred or tortured and cannot be deported. If they are tried in the occupant's courts, they must be accorded such fundamental rights as the assistance of counsel and the opportunity to call witnesses and present evidence. But both the Geneva Convention and the Hague Regulations contain plenty of ambiguities. The Hague Regulations forbid confiscation of private property and the Geneva Convention, "pillage," but both permit the requisitioning of property for the use of the occupying forces, and neither is very clear as to who is to pay for it. (In practice, it has usually been the government of the occupied territory.) Perhaps the greatest ambiguity is contained in Article 43 of the Hague Regulations, which requires the occupant to respect, "unless absolutely prevented, the laws in force in the [occupied] country." This presented the Western Allies, at least, with difficult problems after the defeat of Nazi Germany. It could fairly be argued, of course, that they were "absolutely prevented" from respecting such characteristically Nazi laws as the Nuremberg racial code. But it was not so easy to square the decartelization program (which, for instance, broke I. G. Farben into several independent companies) with the rule; it stretched the ordinary meaning of English (or French) to say that they were "absolutely prevented" from respecting the German law's tolerance (which was matched in France and other European countries) of monopolies and cartels. One way out of the dilemma was to argue that after the cessation of hostilities and Germany's unconditional surrender, the Hague Regulations' limits on the occupant's powers lost their status as binding international law and became, at most, a code of humanitarian ethics. A number of American scholars took this position.[35] German scholars thought otherwise.[36] It cannot be said that the controversy has yet been resolved; all that is clear is that the Hague Regulations cease to be applicable when an occupation is terminated by the return of the territory to its former sovereign or by a peace treaty under which it becomes independent, or is annexed by the victor.

The 1949 Geneva Convention specifically provides that it shall remain in force for a year after "the general close of military operations"—whatever that means—and that certain of its more fundamental protections shall apply until the occupation is ended. That Convention places some limits on the occupant's power to change the criminal law of the occupied territory; it can, for example, change that law to authorize death sentences only for "espionage" or "serious acts of sabotage." But, aside from the fact that a number of signatories, including the United States, reserved the right to impose the death penalty for murder and other serious offenses against the occupying forces,

the Convention permits the suspension or repeal of
penal laws which constitute a threat to the occupant's
security and the enactment of whatever new penal
laws it thinks necessary to that security. These are the
sort of provisions that nations at war have generally
construed to suit their convenience. Moreover, the
Convention does not seem to hamper an occupant's
freedom to change the political and economic structure of occupied territory to suit its own ideology.
None of these subtle legal problems, it may be remarked, troubled the Soviet Union after World War
II. It simply installed Communist governments in the
conquered territories (except Austria) and signed
treaties with them. The Red Army ceased to be an
occupant and became a visiting friendly force, like the
American troops in NATO countries. The example
has probably not escaped the observation of other
nations. For this and other reasons, it is very likely that
the law governing belligerent occupation will create
fewer problems than it has in the past.

So much has been said in recent years about the
Nuremberg Charter and Judgment, mostly by politicians and journalists who do not appear to have read
either document, that they require explanation. Contrary to the popular impression, they added very little
to the law of war. All but three of those who were
sentenced at Nuremberg (and all but one, Streicher, of
those executed) were found guilty of acts which in
1939 were recognized as war crimes—as the Charter
described them: "murder, ill-treatment, or deportation to slave labor or for any other purpose of civilian

population of or in occupied territory, murder or ill-treatment of prisoners of war or persons on the seas, killing of hostages, plunder of public or private property, wanton destruction of cities, towns, or villages, or devastation not justified by military necessity." Likewise, practically all of the "crimes against humanity" of which the defendants were convicted, could just as well have been charged as violations of the law of war—or, when German nationals were the victims, as violations of German law, for the Nazis, not being much concerned about the rule of law, did not bother to change the German Penal Code to legalize the extermination of German Jews and other minorities.

"Crimes against peace" are a different matter. The Charter and Judgment are undoubtedly precedent for the proposition that the "initiation or waging of a war of aggression" violates the law of nations. (The Charter of the United Nations requires the members to refrain from the threat, or use, of force against other states, but it also recognizes the right of self-defense, including collective self-defense.) What is not so clear is whether it has any practical effect or serves any useful purpose. Its history since 1945 suggests that it does not.[37]

In August of that year the great powers who had triumphed in World War II proclaimed that the initiation, or waging, of a war of aggression was a crime. In Nuremberg an international court, with judges appointed by the victors, convicted a dozen civilian and military leaders of Nazi Germany of "crimes against peace" and sentenced them to death or long prison terms. (But perhaps it ought to be noted that Rudolf Hess, who got life and is still in Spandau, was the only one who was not also convicted of conventional war crimes or "crimes against humanity.") Many wise and famous men compared the Nuremberg Charter and Judgment to the Magna Carta and the Bill of Rights. Justice Robert H. Jackson, the American prosecutor, thought it the crowning achievement of his career. Mankind had at last brought down the first of the Four Horsemen.

Making aggressive war a crime did seem to be a new and higher stage in the development of the law of nations. The philosophers and jurists of an earlier day had allowed the initiation of "just" wars; the launching of an "unjust" war was universally condemned by civilized nations.[38] But the general acceptance of the principle did not seem to reduce the incidence of war, for "justice" could be, and generally was, found in the enemy's refusal to recognize a legitimate claim, such as a claim to the territory invaded, or in his being an international pest (like the pirate states of Algiers and Tripoli), or in his barbarous mistreatment of his own subjects, or simply in the civilizing mission of the conqueror. Frederick the Great was as unique in his own day as he would be in ours when he candidly stated his reasons for wresting Silesia from the Hapsburg Empire: "Ambition, interest, the desire of making people talk about me, carried the day; and I decided for war." Few statesmen, then or now, would even think such thoughts, much less publish them.

But "justice" long continued to be the test of war's propriety. When the Allies after World War I proposed to give Kaiser Wilhelm a fair trial and hang him, he was to be arraigned not for aggression, but for "a supreme offense against international morality." The Kellogg-Briand Pact of 1928 did indeed outlaw war (except defensive war), but it provided neither means of enforcement nor any penalty for violation. So far as "crimes against peace" were concerned, Nuremberg was something new under the sun.

What, then, has the Magna Carta of international law done for the welfare of humanity since its promulgation? The answer is clear and simple: nothing. Since Nuremberg, there have been at least eighty or ninety wars (some calculators exclude armed invasions of neighbors too weak to attempt resistance), some of them on a very large scale.[39] The list includes the Korean war, the Suez invasion of 1956, the Algerian rebellion, the four Arab-Israeli wars, the Vietnam wars (including the accompanying fighting in Laos and Cambodia), and the invasion of Czechoslovakia by the Soviet Union and its myrmidons. In none of these cases, nor in any other, was an aggressor arrested and brought to the bar of international justice, and none is likely to be. For all the good it has done, the doctrine that aggressive war is a crime might as well be relegated to the divinity schools.

In virtually every case, each side denounced the other as an aggressor or, at the very least, claimed to be defending itself and its allies against the aggressive plots of Imperialists or Communists. "Aggressive" wars, like "just" wars, turned out to be definable only in terms of the definer's politics. In very few cases can a disinterested historian say with much assurance which side, if either, was the "aggressor." Such clear cases of aggression as the North Korean invasion of the South were highly exceptional. (Even North Korea advanced some sort of contention that it had acted in order to forestall an attack by South Korea and the United States. This explanation was accepted by all the Communist countries.) It is probable that in all cases all the parties were convinced of the purity of their intentions and the justice of their causes. One can be quite certain that not even the sensitive conscience of the sanctified Mrs. Gandhi nor the still more sensitive conscience of her still more sanctified father were in the least troubled by their respective decisions to invade East Pakistan (as it then was) and Goa. It was not, to be sure, easy to argue that these invasions were undertaken in self-defense; but the old reliable concept of justice could be invoked, and was.

Still more discouraging is the fact that in many of these conflicts, the parties have paid even less attention to the conventional law of war than was paid by the belligerents in World War I and by some of them, at least, in World War II. In all wars, of course, the forces of all belligerents will violate the law of war to a greater or lesser extent. The difference, which is important, is one of degree and government policy. War crimes will only be wiped out when war itself is wiped out. Few, if any, nations seem to be prepared to take that step, and I am not much impressed by the argument that the law of war is hypocritical and immoral, and ought to be abolished because it seen.s to legitimize war. I very much doubt that any of the wars of the present century, great or little, would have been avoided if the Hague and Geneva Conventions had never been signed. But the fighting in Vietnam was unusually dirty, and the record of the American forces seems to me much worse than it was in World War II or the Korean war. The My Lai massacre was the worst atrocity to be charged against American troops since the Fort Pillow and Sand Creek massacres of 1864 (the former committed by Confederates against Union soldiers and the latter by a regiment of Colorado volunteers against Indians) and the Wounded Knee massacre of 1890. As the court-martial records show, and other evidence suggests, there were many other incidents in which American soldiers deliberately killed noncombatants and captive combatants, although I know of no substantial evidence that any of these episodes was on a scale remotely approaching that of My Lai. The United States was also guilty of some mistreatment of prisoners of war and of some degree of complicity in their mistreatment by the South Vietnamese. There was certainly some degree of command failure to take adequate measures to prevent and punish violations, although, on the evidence so far available, I am doubtful that such guilt was widespread, or that it extended to commands above the brigade or division level.

This bad record is not palliated by the fact that, on the very substantial evidence which is now available, the record of North Vietnam and the Viet Cong is much worse. *The New York Times,* which cannot be accused of chauvinist bias against them, has (to its credit) printed many eyewitness accounts of such incidents as the massacres of civilians at Hué (which seems to have involved about three thousand victims), Duc Duc, and, still later, An Loc. There were countless similar episodes on a smaller scale, such as the attacks on the refugee camps at Da Nang. It has been estimated that by 1969, North Vietnamese and Viet Cong forces had deliberately killed twenty-five thousand to thirty thousand noncombatants in order to spread terror, deter cooperation with the government, and encourage cooperation with themselves.[40] The number must have greatly increased, especially after the start of North Vietnam's 1972 offensives.

Some of this dirtiness resulted from the fact, above noted, that guerrillas cannot, and do not, obey the laws of war, and that conventional forces employed against them have far too often yielded to the temptation to ignore those laws themselves in dealing with such enemies. But the guerrillas' supporters have been astute to devise legal excuses for their atrocities. One of them seems to be that since aggression is a crime, its victims are free to employ any kind, and degree, of force which serves their purpose. Although Professor Falk, like Professor Noam Chomsky and the other champions of the Viet Cong and North Vietnam, never clearly concedes that anyone except the Americans and South Vietnamese committed any war crimes in Vietnam,[41] he makes a gingerly approach to this indelicate topic by saying: "Some may say that war crimes have been committed by both sides in Vietnam. ... Such a contention needs to be evaluated, however, in the overall context of the the war, especially in relation to the identification of which side is the victim of aggression and which side is the aggressor."[42] If this means anything at all, it means that it is all right for belligerents whom Professor Falk believes to be the victims of aggression to commit war crimes. Elsewhere he reinforces this reasoning by arguing that guerrillas, like the Viet Cong (or, presumably, Al Fatah or the Irish Republican Army), have "no alternative other than terror to mobilize an effective operation."[43] Professor Chomsky, a subtler casuist, says that if the international law of war permits the tactics employed by the United States and other governments but not those of the guerrillas, then that law is of "no moral force or validity."[44] It follows that if the North Vietnamese or the Viet Cong directed artillery, mortar, or machine gun fire at columns of refugees, the act was legal, and moral, since it served the Good Cause by creating confusion and traffic blocks behind the lines of the South Vietnamese and American aggressors.

Thus, as perverted by Professor Falk and like-minded pundits, the Nuremberg doctrine itself has actually contributed something to the decline in the observance of the laws of war. Even when a belligerent, like North Vietnam, could reasonably be expected to obey at least some of those laws, such as the Geneva Prisoner of War Convention, its partisans argue that a victim of aggression—which their side always is—is not bound to respect the treaties; it is free to commit whatever assassinations or massacres may further its military goals. Since all parties to a conflict are commonly victims of aggression, this is dangerous doctrine.

As with all law, and especially international law, enforcement is the toughest problem. Protest, the "appeal to world opinion," though constantly resorted to by all belligerents, and possibly useful as propaganda, has never proved very effective in forcing the enemy to stop doing whatever it is that the protester is protesting about. Reprisal—an act that would itself be illegal if it were not in retaliation for a prior violation by the other side—is a two-edged weapon, with a tendency to invite counter-reprisals, and has not been much used in modern times. (But the fear of reprisal may operate as a deterrent; it probably accounts for the fact that nobody used gas in World War II.) The Geneva Conventions forbid reprisals against prisoners of war or noncombatants.

The remaining method of enforcement is trial and punishment of those who violate the laws of war. Such trials have usually taken place in the courts of the victors. (The commentators agree that a war criminal can be tried by any sovereign that has physical custody of him, but nations have rarely shown much interest in trying crimes of which they were not the victims.)[45] Many such trials were held after World War II, some before International Tribunals composed of judges appointed by the victors in Nuremberg and Tokyo, and some in the courts, usually military, of the United States, Great Britain, France, Russia, and many other nations.

Although I think that the great majority of the resulting convictions were just, the fairness of a trial in such a court must necessarily be suspect. Moreover, this method of enforcement is available only when there *is* a victor. When a war ends inconclusively, as the Korean war ended, and the Vietnam war appears to be ending, neither side is likely to try war criminals in its custody for fear that the other will retaliate—by fabricating charges if necessary—against its own prisoners. Ideally, of course, war crimes would be tried in an impartial international tribunal. But no such tribunal exists, and I find it extremely difficult to imagine one whose impartiality the United States and North Vietnam, Israel and Egypt, Pakistan and Bangladesh, Russia and China, would all be willing to trust.

Thus, at the present time, it seems to me that the most realistic prospect for punishing war criminals is by trial in the courts of the accused's own country. All of the Geneva Conventions obligate each signatory power to search for persons alleged to have committed "grave breaches" of those Conventions and to "bring such persons, regardless of their nationality, before its own courts." There is still too little precedent for such enforcement of the law of war. I know of no instance in which North Vietnam or any other totalitarian government has ever accused a member of its own forces of a violation of the Geneva Conventions or any other war crime. But the most recent available figures show that, as of April, 1971, American courts-martial had tried 117 servicemen and convicted 60 on charges of murdering civilians in Vietnam; an unknown, but probably larger, number had been tried for lesser offenses, such as rape and robbery, against civilians.[46] Murder and other violence against the persons of noncombatants or captured enemies violate the Geneva Conventions, but they are also, of course, violations of the Uniform Code of Military Justice and have been charged as such. The main practical difference is that trial by court-martial for a violation of the Code guarantees the accused procedural protections and appellate review to which he might not be entitled if he were tried by a military commission for a war crime.

Some of the acquittals were probably unjustified, and in at least one case, that of Captain Ernest Medina, the acquittal may have been based on the military judge's erroneous instruction that Medina had no responsibility for the My Lai massacre unless he had "actual knowledge" of it: as laid down by the Supreme Court in General Yamashita's case, the law is that a commander is responsible for war crimes committed by his subordinates if he knew, *or should have known,* that they were going on and failed to do what he could to prevent or punish them.[47] It is also safe to assume that many war crimes committed by Americans have never been investigated, tried, or punished. The Pentagon has not shown much enthusiasm for investigating the possible failures of commanders at divisional and higher levels to take adequate measures to prevent and punish war crimes. Moreover, the Department of Justice seems to take the position that an honorably discharged serviceman cannot be tried for a war crime committed prior to his discharge. The Supreme Court did hold some years ago that such a discharged soldier could not be tried for an ordinary offense—*i.e.*, one that was not a war crime—committed prior to his discharge.[48] But it had earlier held, in World War II, that a Nazi saboteur who was an American civilian could constitutionally be tried by a military commission for a war crime,[49] and it did not overrule that decision. I am myself of the opinion (though I seem to be in the minority) that a discharged serviceman *can* be tried by a military court on a charge of violating the law of war. In any case, Congress could and should give the federal courts jurisdiction to try such cases: under the Geneva Conventions, in fact, the United States is obligated to "enact any legislation necessary to provide effective penal sanctions" for persons committing "grave breaches."

The record is thus very far from perfect. All that can be said is that it is a better record than that of any other nation in the world and that it lends a degree of credibility to the Pentagon's numerous orders and regulations that aim to prevent and punish war crimes by requiring a report and an investigation of such incidents, and the training and indoctrination of the troops on the subject.

It should go without saying that a war crime, like any other crime, requires *personal* dereliction. A military commander, whether General Westmoreland or Captain Medina, is responsible for crimes committed by his subordinates if he ordered them, or if he failed to do what he reasonably could to prevent and punish them, and not otherwise. Likewise, a soldier is under no duty to obey an unlawful order: he has (as the Court of Military Appeals has several times held) a duty to *disobey* one which an ordinary man would realize was unlawful, such as an order to kill a noncombatant or a captured enemy.[50] In all of the reported convictions for such offenses, it was pretty plain both that the accused knew that his act was illegal, and that he could have refrained from committing it. The fuzzy notion that every citizen of the United States (except the saints and martyrs of the anti-war movement) is guilty of the war crime at My Lai—that the unfortunate Lieutenant Calley was merely a scapegoat—is, to a lawyer, nonsense, and pernicious nonsense at that.

The international law of war, as it now exists, is undoubtedly very imperfect. Its most fundamental rule, which is that combatants are so far as possible to be distinguished from noncombatants, in effect outlaws the sort of guerrilla warfare that has become common in many parts of the world and makes unlawful belligerents of those who engage in it. By the same token, it permits the use of modern weapons that can reach military targets far in the enemy's rear but necessarily endanger the innocent. It has never restricted the freedom of sovereigns to mistreat their own citizens. Such as it is, its enforcement depends largely on the willingness of governments to discipline and punish their own forces—a willingness that has only begun to develop in some countries and of which there is no discernible trace in others. All that can be said is that it is better than no law; I think it probable that much suffering has been prevented in the last sixty years by the existence of a body of law which nearly all governments profess to respect, and which most are reluctant to violate openly and on a large scale.

The prospects are not bright for changes in the conventional law of war that would mitigate the savagery of "wars of national liberation." It is nearly impossible to imagine even rudimentary rules by which guerrillas and terrorists would feel themselves bound, and equally difficult to imagine governments conceding them any greater rights than they have now. Some improvement may come from better technology— more accurate weapons, such as "smart" bombs, that can attack military targets with less danger to nearby civilians. Above all, much more can and should be done, especially by countries, like the United States, which have a free press and a relatively enlightened public conscience, to prevent and punish war crimes by their own forces—regardless of whether there is any hope of reciprocity.

Notes to Chapter Seven

[1]Falk, *The Question of War Crimes: A Statement of Perspective*, in CRIMES OF WAR (Falk, Kolko and Lifton ed.), at 3 (1971).

[2]*E.g.*, MCDOUGAL AND FELICIANO, LAW AND MINIMUM WORLD PUBLIC ORDER (1961); OPPENHEIM, INTERNATIONAL LAW (8th ed. 1955).

[3]Wasserstrom, *Review of Taylor, Nuremberg and Vietnam: An American Tragedy* (1970), New York Review of Books, June 3, 1971, p. 8.

[4]Taylor, *supra* note 3, at pp. 172–73.

[5]American Banana Co. v. United Fruit Co., 213 U.S. 347, 356 (1909).

[6]Art. I, § 8, cl. (10).

[7]*Ex parte* Quirin, 317 U.S. 1 (1942); *In re* Yamashita, 327 U.S. 1 (1946).

[8]*See* 4 MOMMSEN, HISTORY OF ROME, Bk. V, ch. II (1875).

[9]*See* THUCYDIDES, THE PELOPONNESIAN WAR 193–205, 216–218 (Crawley transl. 1910).

[10]FROISSART, CHRONICLES 93 (Brereton transl. 1968).

[11]*Id.* at 106.

[12]II GIBBON, DECLINE AND FALL OF THE ROMAN EMPIRE 252 (Modern Library ed. 1932).

[13] *See* WINTHROP, at 773. Part II of Winthrop's work describes the law of war as it existed shortly before the Hague Conventions of 1907.

[14]The texts of all of them are contained in Department of the Army Pamphlet 27–1, *Treaties Governing Land Warfare* (1956).

[15]Art. 23*e.*

[16]Art. 25.

[17] *See, e.g.,* United States Department of the Army, Field Manual 27–10, *The Law of the Land Warfare* (1956), ¶ 40.

[18] *See generally* McDougal & Feliciano, *International Coercion and World Public Order: The General Principles of the Law of War,* 67 YALE L. J. 771, 826–29 (1958).

[19]Article 28 of the Geneva Convention on the Protection of Civilian Persons says that "The presence of a protected person may not be used to render certain points or areas immune from military operations."

[20]Aerial photographs, two of which were published in the New York Times, show that the bombing of Hanoi in December, 1972, was directed at military targets. Heavy damage was done to the main railway station and yards and the Bac Mai military airfield. The civilian areas which were hit, including the Bac Mai hospital, were all in close proximity to the military targets. *See* New York Times, May 2, 1973, p. 2. The propaganda of North Vietnam and its supporters naturally mentioned only the damage to the hospital and civilian homes; the damage to military targets was shown neither to Swedish television crews nor to such friendly pilgrims as Ramsey Clark and the Reverend William Sloane Coffin, Jr.

[21]Article 70 of General Order No. 100, Instructions for the Government of Armies of the United States In the Field, dated April 24, 1863 ("Lieber's Code"), provided that "The use of poison in any manner, be it to poison wells, or food, or arms, is wholly excluded from modern warfare. He that uses it puts himself out of the pale of the law and usages of war." Poison gas was not used in warfare until Germany introduced it in 1915, but the possibility of its use was probably known in 1907. The poisoning of wells, and the smearing of poison on spears, arrows, and bullets, had often been resorted to by primitive and more or less civilized warriors,

and the British in the eighteenth century were accused of giving blankets which had been used by smallpox victims to potentially hostile Indians.

[22]Ratification has been delayed by dispute as to whether the Protocol prohibits, or should prohibit, the use of chemical herbicides and non-lethal riot-control agents, such as tear gas, which can plausibly be argued to be more humane than bullets. *See generally* Moore, *Ratification of the Geneva Protocol on Gas and Bacteriological Warfare: A Legal and Political Analysis*, 58 VA. L. REV. 419 (1972).

[23]*Id.* at 468–70.

[24]Judges, 15: 4–5.

[25]*See* I VASILIEV, HISTORY OF THE BYZANTINE EMPIRE 214 (2d ed. 1958).

[26]*See* Note, *The Geneva Convention and the Treatment of Prisoners of War in Vietnam*, 80 HARV. L. REV. 851 (1967).

[27]*In re* Yamashita, 327 U.S. 1 (1946).

[28]If, in a civil war, the insurgents govern a substantial territory and put in the field organized and disciplined forces which obey the law of war, they acquire "belligerent rights" and are entitled to the full protection of the customary law of war. *See* Field Manual 27–10, *supra* note 17, ¶ 11. The United States takes the position that the treaties also represent the customary law. *Id.*, ¶ 6. A classic example of an insurrection sufficiently formidable to entitle the rebels to belligerent rights is the American Civil War. *See* The Prize Cases, 67 U.S. 635, 666–68 (1863).

[29]This provision is contained in Article 3 of each of the Geneva Conventions of 1949.

[30]Mohamed Ali v. Public Prosecutor, 3 ALL ENGLAND 488 (1968).

[31]Boudin, *War Crimes and Vietnam: The Mote in Whose Eye?* 84 HARV. L. REV. 1940, 1942 (1971). He cites an article by Professor Noam Chomsky in the New York Review of Books, an editorial in The New Yorker's "Talk of the Town," and other authorities of similar objectivity and legal weight.

[32]*See* 57 A.B.A.J. 797 (1971).

[33]*See* Bishop, *The Origin and Nature of the Rights of the Western Allies in Berlin,* in WEST BERLIN: THE LEGAL CONTEXT (Stanger ed.), at 23 (1966).

[34]*See* Gerson, *Trustee-Occupant: The Legal Status of Israel's Presence*

in the West Bank, 14 HARV. INT. L. J. 1 (1973). Israel, which neither recognizes Jordanian sovereignty over the West Bank nor claims such sovereignty for itself, denies that the Convention is legally applicable. The status of the other conquered territories (except for East Jerusalem, which has in effect been annexed) is nearly as ambiguous.

35 *E.g.,* Fahy, *Legal Problems of German Occupation,* 47 MICH. L. REV. 11 (1948); VON GLAHN, THE OCCUPATION OF ENEMY TERRITORY 283 (1957).

36 *E.g.,* Laun, *The Legal Status of Germany,* 45 AM. J. INT. LAW 267 (1951).

37 *See generally* DAVIDSON, THE NUREMBERG FALLACY: WARS AND WAR CRIMES SINCE WORLD WAR II (1973).

38 *See* Taylor, *supra* note 3, Ch. 3.

39 *See* Davidson, *supra* note 37, at 2–3.

40 *See* Paust, *My Lai and Vietnam: Norms, Myths and Leader Responsibility,* 57 MIL. L. REV. 99, 126–27 (1972).

41 It is curious to note that nowhere in the 590 pages of CRIMES OF WAR (1971), edited by Professors Falk, Gabriel Kolko, and Robert Jay Lifton, is there any reference to Hué or Duc Duc.

42 FALK, *The Circle of Responsibility,* in CRIMES OF WAR, *supra* note 41, at 231.

43 2 American Society of International Law, The Vietnam War and International Law 240 (Falk ed. 1969).

44 Chomsky, *The Rule of Force in International Affairs,* 80 YALE L. J. 1456, 1465 (1971).

45 *E.g.,* United States Department of the Army, Field Manual 27–10, ¶ 507.

46 Paust, *supra* note 40, at 118.

47 Field Manual 27–10, ¶ 501.

48 Toth v. Quarles, 350 U.S. 11 (1955). *See supra,* Ch. 3.

49 *Ex parte* Quirin, 317 U.S. 1 (1942). *See supra,* Ch. 5.

50 *E.g.,* Keenan, 18 U.S.C.M.A. 108 (1969).

Conclusion

*T*HE PRESENT SEEMS TO BE a good time to take a long and unemotional look at the military law of the United States and to consider what changes might really improve it. We have managed to extricate ourselves from a prolonged and unpleasant war, fought in novel and peculiarly difficult circumstances, and productive of domestic discord to an extent unparallelled since the Civil War. Considering the quantity and decibel-level of the diatribes against the military and all its works, including its penal system, which were chorused by the news media, large sections of the intellectual and pseudo-intellectual community, and other self-appointed opinion-makers, it is a tribute to our political institutions that most of the changes made by Congress and the courts in the midst of the Vietnam war were reasonable and just (although some of the Congressional and judicial rhetoric which accompanied them was neither).

Military justice, in particular, has changed greatly in the past decade. The curtailment of court-martial jurisdiction over crimes that do not affect military discipline; the creation of a relatively independent military judiciary; the slow but steady growth of the idea that soldiers have constitutional rights and the concurrent development by the federal courts of techniques, akin to those employed with state criminal law, for enforcing those rights; the reduction of command influence by giving soldiers a right to trial by military judges; the expansion of the accused's right to counsel; all these are major and, on the whole, beneficial changes. There is room for further reform before more change would present a substantial threat to military discipline and efficiency. I do not favor abolition of the separate system of military justice, nor even complete elimination of the military commander's role in it. But here are a few changes to which I think Congress might well give serious consideration.

1. I would expand the role of the independent military judiciary and, at least, in the United States and in time of peace, make it exclusive. I would favor the creation of permanent military courts, consisting of a single judge for the trial of such minor offenses as are now tried by special courts-martial and of three or five judges for the more serious offenses which are now tried by general courts. More civilians should be employed as military judges, at both the trial level and on

the Courts of Military Review. Commanders would retain their present discretion as to whether charges should be referred to such courts for trial or, in the case of petty offenses, punished nonjudicially under Article 15. The commander would also retain his present power to reduce, suspend, or commute punishments, but not his power to set aside a conviction or order a new trial. Although more difficult problems are raised in combat conditions and outside the United States, I see no obvious reasons why such courts could not function, at least as effectively as courts-martial of the present type, in those conditions too. Courts-martial did not sit in foxholes in any of our recent wars. Overall, it seems to me that such a system would relieve line officers of a burdensome and time-consuming task, retain the benefits of military expertise in the trial of military cases, and ensure adequate consideration of the needs of military discipline.

2. In all trials before such military tribunals the accused would be entitled to the services of a qualified lawyer as defense counsel. (As a practical matter, this is now the rule, but such doubt as remains might just as well be cleared up.) Such defense counsel should be responsible only to the Judge Advocates General, as military judges are now, and should include a substantial proportion of civilian employees. For reasons of administrative convenience, it might be advisable to organize prosecutors on a similar basis.

3. The Bad Conduct Discharge should be abolished, and only three-or five-judge military courts should be empowered to award Dishonorable Discharges. The

Bad Conduct Discharge is not really appreciably less severe a penalty than the Dishonorable, and it is hard to see what useful purpose it serves other than to preserve an ancient custom of the Navy.

4. The general articles should be repealed. Even if the Supreme Court holds them constitutional, I doubt the need for preserving them in their present form. Thus, there seems small reason to treat as criminal "conduct unbecoming an officer and a gentleman." Acts that show unfitness for command are either chargeable as crimes, punishable by punitive discharge, or grounds for administrative elimination from the service. The "disorders and neglects to the prejudice of good order and discipline" and "conduct of a nature to bring discredit upon the armed forces" clauses of Article 134 should be replaced by articles specifically proscribing the offenses, now spelled out in the Manual for Courts-Martial, which are actually charged under them. The "crimes and offenses not capital" clause should be recast as—what in fact it is —an assimilative crimes act, incorporating the United States Penal Code, and perhaps made also to cover violations of non-federal penal codes.

5. Military criminal jurisdiction over reservists not on active duty should be abolished. Such jurisdiction over retired regulars should be limited to power to dismiss or dishonorably discharge them from the service without, however, cutting off their entitlement to a pension.

6. Article 88, denouncing commissioned officers' use of contemptuous words against the President, the

Vice President, Congress, and so forth, ought to be repealed. It is probably unconstitutional under the First Amendment, and the very rarity of its invocation shows that it is not needed to preserve military discipline. Soldiers ought to have as much right as civilians to cuss out the Government, so long as they obey its lawful orders.

7. Decisions of the Court of Military Appeals should be made appealable to the Supreme Court, by petition for certiorari, in the same way as decisions of State Supreme Courts and the federal Courts of Appeal are.

Other improvements in military justice are certainly imaginable, but these seem to me to be both important and feasible. In other areas, it is harder to make constructive suggestions. The extent of the "war power" and of the power to use the armed forces in domestic emergencies are essentially constitutional questions which do not lend themselves to codification or to facile amendments of the Constitution. I prefer to leave these questions where they are now and to trust to the integrity and good sense of the courts. But I think Congress could make one useful improvement in American enforcement of the international law of war. If I am wrong in believing (see Chapter 7) that courts-martial and military commissions can constitutionally try honorably discharged servicemen (or, for that matter, other civilians) for war crimes, then Congress should fulfill the United States' treaty obligation to enact whatever legislation is needed to make "grave breaches" of the Geneva Conventions triable in its own courts by giving the federal courts jurisdiction to try such breaches, no matter where committed.

We may have all-volunteer armed forces for quite a while to come, as we have had them for most of our history. (And then again, we may not.) But there will be a couple of million or more people in the Army, Navy, and Air Force of the United States for as far as anyone can see into the future, and there will be occasions for their use, abroad and at home. I see no convincing sign that the Millennium is at hand. Now is a good time to think about the problems of the future.

Index

INDEX / 311

ABOUT THE AUTHOR

Joseph W. Bishop, Jr. was born in New York in 1915 and was educated at Dartmouth College and the Harvard Law School. His interest in military law began when Judge Robert P. Patterson, whose law clerk he was, became Under Secretary of War in 1940, and took Mr. Bishop to Washington with him. That interest continued when he was drafted into the Army and later was commissioned in the Judge Advocate General's Corps. Mr. Bishop served in the European Theater from March 1944 to June 1946 and got some first-hand acquaintance with war crime by serving as legal advisor to a Board of Inquiry appointed by General Eisenhower to investigate the murder of British and Canadian prisoners of war by members of a German SS Division. In 1952 and 1953 he was Deputy General Counsel and Acting General Counsel of the Army, fought in the opening skirmishes of the Army-McCarthy war, and had the honor of being denounced by the Senator.

Mr. Bishop has also been in private practice with a large Wall Street law firm and, since 1957, has been a professor of law at Yale. He is a frequent contributor to *Esquire, Harper's, The New York Times Magazine,* and *Commentary,* as well as to legal periodicals. His book on law, "Obiter Dicta" was published in 1971.

Mr. Bishop lives with his wife and son in Connecticut.